Lernkrimi Englisch

LONDON CRIME TIME

Im Schatten des Towers

Tod eines Dandys

Diebstahl im Morgengrauen

Compact Verlag

Bisher sind in dieser Reihe erschienen:
- Sammelband Lernkrimi Englisch, Spanisch: B1/B2

In der Reihe Compact Lernkrimi sind erschienen:
- Englisch, Französisch, Italienisch, Spanisch: B1, B2
- Englisch GB/US, Business English: B1, B2
- Deutsch: B1

In der Reihe Compact Lernkrimi Kurzkrimis sind erschienen:
- Englisch, Französisch, Italienisch, Spanisch, Deutsch: A2

In der Reihe Compact Lernkrimi History sind erschienen:
- Englisch: B1, B2, Italienisch: B1

In der Reihe Compact Lernthriller sind erschienen:
- Englisch: B1, B2, Spanisch: B1

In der Reihe Compact Lernstory Mystery sind erschienen:
- Englisch: B1, B2

In der Reihe Compact Lernkrimi Hörbuch sind erschienen:
- Englisch: B1, B2, Business English: B2
- Französisch, Italienisch, Spanisch: B1

In der Reihe Compact Lernkrimi Audio-Learning sind erschienen:
- Englisch: A2, B1, Französisch, Spanisch: B1

In der Reihe Compact Lernkrimi Sprachkurs sind erschienen:
- Englisch, Spanisch: A1/A2

Lernziele:
- Grundwortschatz, Grammatik (A2, B1)
- Aufbauwortschatz, Konversation (B2)

In der Reihe Compact Schüler-Lernkrimi sind erschienen:
- Englisch, Französisch, Spanisch, Latein, Deutsch, Mathematik, Physik, Chemie

Weitere Titel sind in Vorbereitung.

Chefredaktion: Dr. Angela Sendlinger
Redaktion: Patrizia Ginocchio
Fachredaktion: Alison Frankland, Robert Laversuch, Angela Billington
Produktion: Wolfram Friedrich
Titelillustration und Stadtplan: Karl Knospe
Typographischer Entwurf: Maria Seidel
Umschlaggestaltung: Carsten Abelbeck

ISBN 978-3-8174-7787-6
7277874

Besuchen Sie uns im Internet: www.compactverlag.de, www.lernkrimi.de

Vorwort

Mit dem neuen, spannenden Compact Lernkrimi-Sammelband können Sie Ihre Englischkenntnisse auf schnelle und einfache Weise vertiefen, auffrischen und überprüfen.
Inspector Hudson ermittelt in drei fesselnden Fällen und erleichtert das Sprachtraining mit Action und Humor.
Jeder Krimi wird durch abwechslungsreiche und kurzweilige Übungen ergänzt, die das Lernen unterhaltsam und spannend machen.
Prüfen Sie Ihr Englisch in Lückentexten, Zuordnungs- und Übersetzungsaufgaben, in Buchstabenspielen und Kreuzworträtseln!
Dieses umfassende Sprachtraining zum englischen Grund- und Aufbauwortschatz sowie zur englischen Grammatik bietet die ideale Trainingsmöglichkeit für zwischendurch.
Schreiben Sie die Lösungen einfach ins Buch!
Die richtigen Antworten sind in einem eigenen Lösungsteil am Ende des Buches zu finden.
Das ausführliche Glossar im Anhang erleichtert das Verständnis der Krimis. Es umfasst die schwierigsten Wörter, die im Text kursiv markiert sind.

Und nun kann die Spannung beginnen ...

Viel Spaß und Erfolg!

Lernkrimi Englisch Sammelband

Inhalt

Lernkrimi Englisch

Grammatik

In the Shadow of the Tower

Barry Hamilton

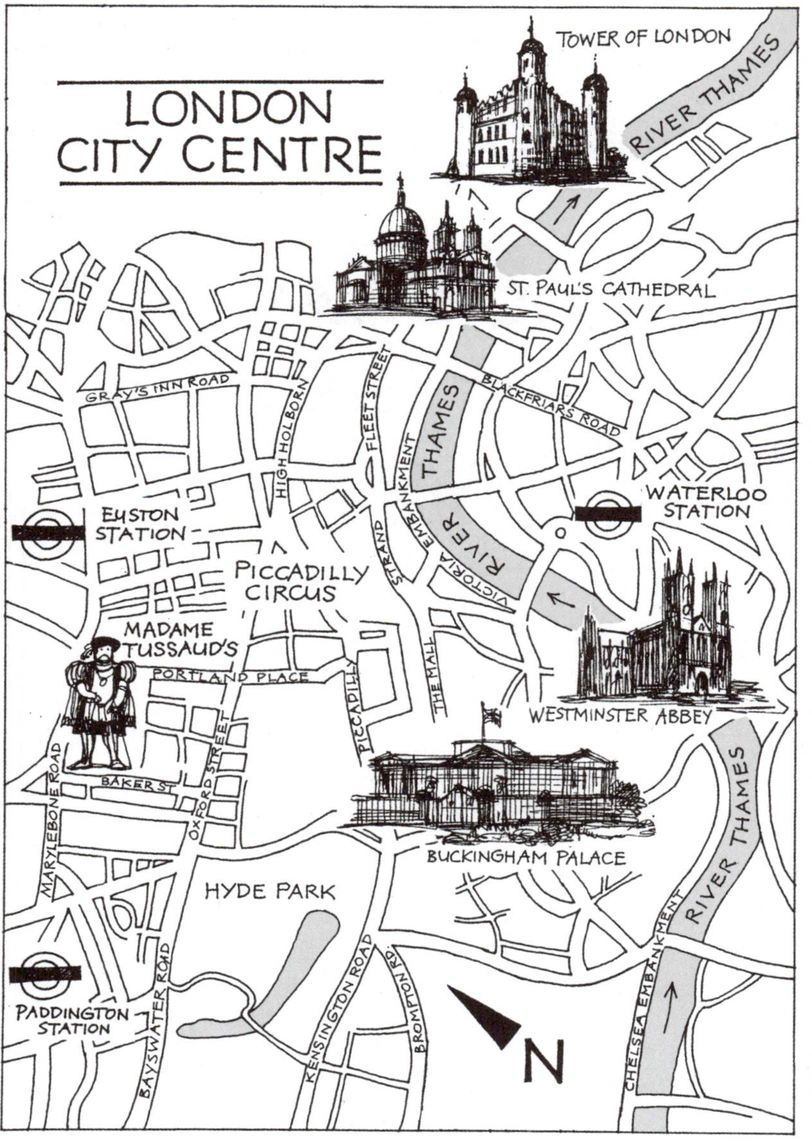
LONDON
CITY CENTRE
TOWER OF LONDON
RIVER THAMES
ST. PAUL'S CATHEDRAL
GRAY'S INN ROAD
HIGH HOLBORN
FLEET STREET
THAMES
BLACKFRIARS ROAD
EMBANKMENT
WATERLOO
STATION
EUSTON
STATION
STRAND
RIVER
VICTORIA
PICCADILLY
CIRCUS
MADAME
TUSSAUD'S
PORTLAND PLACE
PICCADILLY
THE MALL
WESTMINSTER ABBEY
MARYLEBONE ROAD
BAKER ST
OXFORD STREET
BUCKINGHAM PALACE
RIVER THAMES
HYDE PARK
CHELSEA EMBANKMENT
PADDINGTON
STATION
BAYSWATER ROAD
KENSINGTON ROAD
BROMPTON RD.
N

Inhalt

Story

James Hudson arbeitet als Inspector bei der legendären Polizeibehörde Scotland Yard. Er ist einer der fähigsten Männer und wird immer dann zu Rate gezogen, wenn seine Kollegen mal wieder vor einem Rätsel stehen. Seine resolute und krimibegeisterte Haushälterin Miss Paddington unterstützt ihn stets mit liebevoller Fürsorge.

Aus dem Tower of London wird der berühmte Diamant „Kohinoor" gestohlen, der Teil der Kronjuwelen ist. Ganz England ist entsetzt. Sir Reginald beauftragt Inspector Hudson mit den Ermittlungen in diesem brisanten Fall, die ihn quer durch London zu vielen Sehenswürdigkeiten führen.
Steckt vielleicht der Wächter Marc Drum, der seit dem Einbruch spurlos verschwunden ist, hinter dem Überfall? Und was führt der mysteriöse indische Prinz im Schilde, der so viel über die Geschichte des Diamanten weiß?

Chapter 1: The Ceremony of the Keys

At exactly 21:53, the Chief *Yeoman Warder* emerged from the Byward Tower – an outer tower guarding the entrance of the fortress also known as the Tower of London. He was wearing a long red coat and a large round black hat called a Tudor *bonnet*. Mr and Mrs Moore watched with great excitement as the *Beefeater appeared*. They were from York in Northern England and were visiting London for the first time. It had been really difficult for them to get tickets for the ceremony. They had booked three months in advance, and were very pleased to be participating in such an *ancient* tradition.

"Oh, isn't this exciting!" said Mrs Moore to her husband, with a big smile on her face.

Mr Moore nodded, agreeing fully with his wife. In one hand the Chief *Yeoman Warder* was carrying a shining *lantern*, in the other the *Queen's Keys*. He solemnly marched along Water Lane towards *Traitor's Gate*. *Armed foot guards* awaited him there. He *handed* the *lantern* to one of the guards and together they moved on towards the outer gate.

"Did you know that this ceremony has been repeated every night for almost 700 years?"

Mrs Moore looked at her husband in *astonishment*.

"Really!" she exclaimed. "That's amazing!"

"Yes, it was only ever interrupted once during the Second World War."

Mr Moore pointed up to the sky. Mrs Moore looked at her husband with irritation. She looked up to the sky, following his finger.

"*Air raid*!" he said *conspiratorially*.

"Oh!" said Mrs Moore, *relieved*. "I thought you were going to tell me another one of your alien stories."

Mr Moore shook his head and turned his attention back towards the ceremony. So did his wife. They watched enthusiastically as the guards walked right past them, their steps echoing off the narrow *cobbled* path. As they advanced towards the outer gate, all of the guards and *sentries* saluted the *Queen's Keys*.
"It's a shame you aren't allowed to film or take pictures, isn't it?" said Mr Moore, a note of disappointment in his voice. He looked *longingly* at his camera, which was switched off.
"You could get some really good shots, I tell you."
Mrs Moore *shrugged*, more or less unconcerned by her husband's disappointment. She did not take her eyes off the ceremony.
"There's nothing better than the real thing, that's what I always say," she said.

Übung 1: Wie heißt das Simple Past der folgenden unregelmäßigen Verben?

! ÜBUNG 1

1. be ______	6. come ______
2. get ______	7. do ______
3. go ______	8. eat ______
4. hear ______	9. let ______
5. fall ______	10. say ______

In the meantime, the Chief *Yeoman Warder* had locked the outer gate. He and his escort turned around again. They were *heading back* in the direction they had come from. Mr Moore took his London tourist guide out of his bag and started *flicking through* the pages. Eventually, he found the page he was looking for. Mr

Moore started running his finger along it. Then his finger stopped. "Ah, do you know what happens now?"
Mrs Moore *tutted.*
"No, but I'm about to find out, am I not?" she said a little annoyed.
Mr Moore *sighed* and put his book back into his bag. The Chief *Yeoman Warder* marched towards the great *oak* gates. They were located at the Middle Tower. He locked them too.
"Now he just needs to lock the gates at the Byward Tower!" exclaimed Mr Moore excitedly.
Mrs Moore gave her husband an *aggravated* look.
"Could you just hold your breath for five minutes, please, Kevin?"

ÜBUNG 2 !

Übung 2: Lesen Sie weiter und setzen Sie die Begriffe in Klammern richtig ein!
(direction, escort, answer, guard, think, along, archway)

Mr Moore *sulked.* The Chief Warder now returned (1.) ______________ Water Lane. He marched towards *Traitor's Gate.* In the shadows of the Bloody Tower (2.) ______________, a *sentry* awaited him. Mr Moore's face suddenly lit up again. He was about to say something when his wife said, "Don't even (3.) ______________ of it!"
Mr Moore closed his mouth. As soon as the (4.) ______________ saw the three men *approach* him, he removed his machine gun from his shoulder. The guard pointed it in their (5.) ______________. He *barked,* "*Halt*, who comes there?"

The Chief *Yeoman Warder* and his (6.) ______________ came to a *stately halt*. "The Keys!" replied the Chief *Yeoman Warder.*

"Whose keys?" asked the guard.

"Queen Elizabeth's Keys," is the (7.) ______________ they received.

"Pass Queen Elizabeth's Keys", answered the *sentry*, "and all's well!"

The men were just passing the guard through the so-called Bloody Tower *Archway* when suddenly there was a small explosion. Mr and Mrs Moore and all the other tourists around them jumped. Some murmured and others let out a cry of surprise. The guards also ducked and *took to their guns*. Mr Moore took his tourist guide back out of his bag and nervously started *flicking through* the pages.
"I can't remember reading anything about this!" he remarked.
Then, all of a sudden, there was another explosion. This one was louder and more powerful than the last one. Some people started screaming and shouting. Mr and Mrs Moore *crouched* down.
"What's going on?" Mrs Moore asked her husband *anxiously*.
"I have no idea."
"Lost for an explanation for a change!" said Mrs Moore sarcastic-ally.
Mr Moore had no time to defend himself because white smoke had started to *spread* all around them. Mr and Mrs Moore's eyes began to water and they both began to cough.
"Tear gas!" exclaimed Mr Moore. "We've got to get out of here fast!"
Suddenly, there was a third explosion. This one was even more

powerful than the first two together. Everybody started running, screaming and shouting. Mr Moore took his wife by the hand.

"The exit must be over this way somewhere."

By now there was a great *commotion*. People were beginning to panic. They were running all over the place. Every now and again, people *bumped into* Mr and Mrs Moore. Mr Moore decided to turn on his camera.

"What on earth are you doing?" cried Mrs Moore.

"Someone has got to film this," said Mr Moore, *fumbling* with the power *switch*. This was not easy, because he was holding his wife's hand at the same time. He eventually managed to switch it on and held the camera up to his eye.

Through it he could see that some guards were standing at the side of the *cobbled* lane. They were pointing in the direction of the exit.

"Don't panic, now!" one of them said as he waved them past. "Just keep moving. The exit is near."

Another group of guards came rushing past them, their *rifles* pointing out in front of them. Suddenly Mrs Moore stumbled and lost her *grip* on her husband's hand.

"Arghhhh!" she cried out and fell to the ground.

Mr Moore stopped *instantly*. He had to get his wife up fast. There were people behind them already pushing forward. If he did not get his wife up in time, she might be trampled to death. Mr Moore put his camera down and helped his wife to her feet. He was just in time because at that moment, a group of nervously *babbling* Japanese tourists ran by.

"That was close!" breathed Mr Moore heavily.

Mrs Moore smiled gratefully at her husband. They were in a slight state of shock and so just stood still for a moment. The swarm of Japanese tourists seemed to go on forever. One of them stopped and gestured to the Moore's to move on. He was speaking very fast. Then he just shook his head and ran on. Mr and Mrs Moore pulled themselves together again quickly. They had just started to run again, when Mr Moore came to an abrupt *halt*.

"My camera!" he shouted, pointing back in the direction they had come from. "I need to get my camera back!"

"Forget your camera, Kevin! We need to get out of here fast!" Mrs Moore shouted.

She was *tugging* at his hand, signalling him to move on.

"No, it was very expensive and it's just over there on the ground, I can see it. You run on and I'll catch up with you."

"Oh, well then!" Mrs Moore agreed *reluctantly*. "You can be so *stubborn* at times, but I'm coming with you."

Übung 3: Übersetzen Sie und enträtseln Sie das Lösungswort!

ÜBUNG 3 !

1. Auto ☐ _ _
2. bewaffnet _ _ _ ☐ _
3. Wache _ _ _ ☐ _
4. Laterne _ _ _ _ ☐ _ _
5. Geld ☐ _ _ _ _
6. schießen _ _ ☐ _ _
7. enttäuscht _ _ _ _ _ _ _ _ ☐ _ _ _
8. glücklich _ _ _ _ ☐

Lösung: _ _ _ _ _ _ _ _

Mr and Mrs Moore hurried towards the camera. The smoke was beginning to clear.

"Ah, here it is," said Mr Moore.

Just as he was *bending down* to get it, a man ran past and *accidentally* kicked it.
"Sorry about that, *mate*!" he shouted as he ran on.
The camera shot along the *cobbled* lane.
"Oh, no!" exclaimed Mr Moore and started running in the direction in which it had been kicked.
"Just leave it, Kevin. Let's just get out of here!"
Mr Moore ignored his wife and kept on walking. Suddenly, huge amounts of smoke started to *spread* around him and a figure dressed all in black *bumped into* him. Mr Moore jumped in fright and looked up in surprise at the person in front of him. He was completely dressed in black. Even his face was *covered – apart from* the sparkling dark eyes staring at him. Mr Moore felt uncomfortable.
"I'm sorry, I was just…"
"Kevin? Kevin, where are you?" Mrs Moore's voice sounded through the clearing smoke. The person in black gave Mr Moore a *piercing* look and disappeared into the smoke. Mr Moore could not believe his eyes as the strange person ran off elegantly, like a *cat of prey*. He was *dumbfounded*. Mrs Moore *appeared*.
"I was worried – I couldn't see you anymore. Where did all that smoke come from? At least it's not tear gas this time," said Mrs Moore, trying in vain to wave the smoke away.
"Did you see that?"
"See what?"
"That mysterious person dressed in black."
"No, I didn't! I think you're beginning to see things," replied Mrs Moore. She *bent down* and picked up the camera.
"No, really…Maybe the *SAS* has arrived."
"*SAS*, Ninja Turtles, whatever. Let's get out of here!"
Mrs Moore gave her husband his camera and they started hurrying

back. Mr Moore *inspected* his camera on the way. It seemed to be okay. He started to film again. Mr and Mrs Moore were getting close to the entrance gates.

Übung 4: Finden Sie das passende Gegenteil und setzen Sie die richtige Ziffer ein!

ÜBUNG 4

1. hurry	☐ uncover
2. shout	☐ calm
3. cover	☐ push
4. nervous	☐ enemy
5. strong	☐ slow down
6. keep	☐ ask
7. pull	☐ weak
8. light	☐ whisper
9. friend	☐ give
10. reply	☐ heavy

"There's Byward Tower!"
Mr Moore pointed at the top of a brown stone building *sticking out* of the smoke. He moved his camera up to take in the picture. All of a sudden, Mr and Mrs Moore could hear someone shouting:
"Help me, help me! The Keys, someone's taken the *Queen's Keys*!"
The smoke was beginning to clear away again. Mr and Mrs Moore moved in the direction of the voice. They found the Chief *Yeoman Warder* leaning against the wall, holding his *bleeding* head. Mr Moore did not stop filming. Mrs Moore ran over to the man.
"Are you all right?" she asked.
"I'm okay, I'm okay!" he *gasped*. "Someone hit me on the head and took the *Queen's Keys*."

Out of nowhere, guards arrived and helped the Chief Warder to his feet.
"Sir, Madam, please move on!" one of them ordered *harshly*.
Mr Moore was still filming.
"He ran in that direction!" said the Chief Warder and pointed at Byward Tower.
"Okay, you four *secure* Byward Tower. I'll escort Mr Drum and these two to the exit. Mr Drum really needs a doctor. I'll be back in a second."
"Yes, sir!" the men shouted. They started running towards Byward Tower.
The guard who stayed behind said to Mr and Mrs Moore:
"Now, follow me!"
He noticed Mr Moore was still filming.
"And could you please turn that damn thing off!" he *barked*.
Mr Moore *was startled*.
"Yes, of course…Sorry!" he said, a little *intimidated*.

ÜBUNG 5 !

Übung 5: Welche Adjektive werden gesucht?
(good, clever, helpful, strange, funny, exhausted)

1. The guard was very ______________.

2. The Chief Warder was ______________.

3. Mr Moore is a very ______________ filmmaker.

4. The thief was a ______________ person.

5. Mrs Moore was not amused; she did not think it was very ______________.

6. The Tower was not in a ________________ condition after the robbery.

The Chief Warder was a little *unsteady* on his feet. The guard put his arm around his shoulders to support him and they all *proceeded* towards the exit. The Chief Warden was still holding his head. Blood was *trickling* over his eyebrow, making it difficult for him to see out of his right eye. Mrs Moore noticed this and took a *handkerchief* out of her bag.
"Here you are, love. Looks quite *nasty*, that wound of yours."
Mrs Moore *dabbed* it gently and then gave him another *handkerchief* to press against his *bleeding* forehead. Not long after that they reached the Tower's entrance. They crossed the bridge over the *moat*. In the distance, police cars and a couple of ambulances were arriving. There were *flashing* lights everywhere. Two *paramedics* came running towards them. The guard *handed* the Chief Warder over to them.
"Take care of this *chap*, he is one of our best men!" said the guard.
The *paramedics* took him and started helping him walk towards the ambulance for treatment. They eventually got there.
"Are you both okay?" they asked Mr and Mrs Moore kindly.
"Everything is fine," replied Mr Moore.
Suddenly Mr Moore's knees *gave way* and he would have fallen to the ground if the *paramedic* had not caught him in time. Mrs Moore *started* with fright.
"Kevin!" she exclaimed *anxiously*.
"Was a bit much, eh? All that *commotion* and stuff!" said the *paramedic*, who had caught him, in a sympathetic tone.
"I'm fine, perfectly fine!" Mr Moore protested, *whilst* the *paramedic* helped him to sit down at the back of the ambulance.

However, Mr Moore did look quite pale and so did Mrs Moore.
"Just sit here and wait, we'll be back soon with a hot cup of tea," said one of them.
"Well, that wasn't quite the show we expected," Mrs Moore said after the two men had left.
Her voice was *shaky*, but Mrs Moore had a weak smile across her face.
Mr and Mrs Moore looked towards the Tower of London. Smoke was still *floating* up into the dark, cloudless sky.
"I certainly hope Buckingham Palace is a bit safer than that place," *sighed* Mrs Moore.

Chapter 2: The Jewel House Rock

Inspector Hudson was looking forward to reading the new novel he had just bought at his favourite bookstore. The book was about a man who had emigrated to New Zealand in the late 19th century.

ÜBUNG 6 !

Übung 6: Lesen Sie weiter und unterstreichen Sie im folgenden Absatz alle sechs regelmäßigen Verben im Simple Past!

Inspector Hudson sat on the edge of his bed in his blue and white *striped* pyjamas. He removed his *slippers* and placed them *neatly* to the side, and then he swung his feet onto the bed and *covered* himself up with the blankets. The inspector *propped up* his pillow, took his book from the bedside table and began to read. He had not been reading long when Miss Paddington knocked on his door. Inspector Hudson *frowned*; he did not like being disturbed while reading a good book.

"What is it, Miss Paddington? I'm already in bed – reading!"
"Sorry to disturb you, Mr Hudson, but Sir Reginald is on the phone for you."
"Sir Reginald?"
"Yes!"
Inspector Hudson looked at the clock. It was just after 11 p.m. He *sighed*.
"Thank you, Miss Paddington, tell him I'll be with him in a minute."
"Will do!" she replied.
Inspector Hudson threw back the covers.
"This can't be good news," he *mumbled* to himself.
Inspector Hudson came down the stairs fully dressed, walked over to the telephone in the hall and picked up the receiver.
"Sir Reginald?"
"Inspector Hudson; at last! We have a national emergency," said Sir Reginald, who sounded extremely worried.
"Why? What's happened?" asked an alarmed Inspector Hudson.
Miss Paddington was standing nearby. She was *pretending* to dust the hall *mantelpiece*, but was actually moving a little closer.
"There has been a robbery at the Tower of London."
"A robbery? You mean to say the Crown Jewels have been stolen?"
Miss Paddington dropped her *duster* and moved right up to Inspector Hudson.
"Not quite. As far as we can tell, only the Kohinoor diamond has been stolen."
"The Kohinoor diamond," said Inspector Hudson thoughtfully. "That's one of the largest diamonds in the world!"
Miss Paddington *was all ears* now. She was trying to get as close to the receiver as she could. She wanted to hear what Sir Reginald was saying, but she *pretended* to dust a vase.

"It's strange, though, that they only took the diamond," said Inspector Hudson, while he tried to move away from Miss Paddington. She was so busy trying to find out exactly what was going on that she did not notice Inspector Hudson move away from her.
"Let us discuss the details when you get here, Inspector, shall we say in half an hour?"
"I'll be there as fast as I can," replied Inspector Hudson.
"Good, see you soon."
"Yes! Goodbye!"
Inspector Hudson put down the phone.
"What's happened?" *inquired* Miss Paddington excitedly.
"I'm not fully *in the picture*; however, someone *appears* to have stolen the Kohinoor diamond from the Tower of London."
"Oh, dear!" exclaimed Miss Paddington, putting her hand to her mouth. "That is *dreadful*. Has anybody been *hurt?*"
"I don't know. I'll soon find that out too."
Inspector Hudson put on his coat and hurried towards the door.
"Mr Hudson!" Miss Paddington shouted. "You still have your *slippers* on."
Inspector Hudson looked down at his feet.
"Oh, so I have," he laughed.
Miss Paddington hurried over with his shoes; he put them on and rushed back to the door.
"*Keep me posted*," shouted Miss Paddington to the inspector as he was closing the door behind him.

ÜBUNG 7 !

Übung 7: Beantworten Sie folgende Fragen im Simple Past!

1. What did Inspector Hudson look forward to?

....

2. What did Inspector Hudson wear while he sat on his bed?

---

3. What did the thieves steal?

---

4. What did Miss Paddington try to do while Inspector Hudson talked to Sir Reginald?

---

5. What did Inspector Hudson forget to put on?

Inspector Hudson walked *swiftly* towards the Tower of London. He passed ambulances and police cars – their lights shooting red and blue rays into the dark London sky. The inspector walked past people with blankets around their shoulders, drinking hot tea. Some of them were talking to the police; others were having *minor* wounds treated. Sir Reginald was standing near the entrance of the Tower. He was talking to a group of police officers. He looked up and saw Inspector Hudson *approaching*. Sir Reginald excused himself and hurried in the inspector's direction. They met and shook hands.

Übung 8: Welches Wort ist das „schwarze Schaf"? Unterstreichen Sie das nicht in die Reihe passende Wort!

ÜBUNG 8 !

1. anybody, somebody, nobody, someone
2. I, you, his, they
3. looked, frowned, sat, disturbed

4. dark, dim, bright, gloomy
5. say, think, speak, talk
6. far, near, close, next to
7. wound, blood, scar, cut
8. paramedic, doctor, ambulance, nurse
9. shoes, slippers, boots, socks
10. immediately, later, instantly, directly

"Inspector Hudson, thank you for coming so quickly," he said *firmly*. "It's probably best we *proceed* to the crime scene *straight away*."

The two men started walking towards the Tower.

"What exactly happened?" asked Inspector Hudson.

"We are not quite sure. All we know for certain is what I have already mentioned. Someone broke into the Jewel House and stole the Kohinoor diamond. It all happened during the *Ceremony of the Keys*. The thieves used smoke bombs and tear gas to create a *diversion* – the whole place was in an *uproar*."

"Thieves?" *inquired* Inspector Hudson. "Do you know for sure it was more than one person?"

"We are not sure. However, do you really believe someone could have *pulled* this *off* by himself?"

"Stranger things have happened," said Inspector Hudson with a philosophical undertone.

"Did anybody see them?"

"Well, yes and no," replied Sir Reginald. "Our main *witness* has *disappeared into thin air*. The Chief *Yeoman Warder*, Marc Drum, was knocked *unconscious* and the *Queen's Keys* were stolen from him. The thieves used them to *make* their *way* into the Jewel House."

"Disappeared? When was he last seen?"

"He was being treated outside the Tower *premises*. After his head was bandaged, he *vanished*."

"That's very strange," said Inspector Hudson thoughtfully.

"Do we know what he saw?"

"All we know just now is that he was knocked *unconscious* and then the *Queen's Keys* were taken from him."

"But why would he disappear?"

"Nobody knows. The *paramedics* think it could be post-traumatic shock or something like that. I have men out there looking for him."

"You don't think he could…?" asked Inspector Hudson carefully.

"Certainly not, Inspector! Mr Drum is a very *honourable* man – he has *bravery* awards and has achieved everything a man of honour can accomplish."

Inspector Hudson *shrugged*, "It was just a thought. And anyway, what does that mean, 'Man of Honour' – a very rare *species* if you ask me."

Sir Reginald was just going to say something back when Inspector Hudson *wisely* changed the subject.

"Are there any other *witnesses*?" he asked.

"Yes, a Mr and Mrs Moore from York. Mr Moore says he *collided* with one of the thieves."

"Did he see who it was?"

"No, he only saw the *intruder's* eyes. *Apart from* that, the thief was dressed in black – from head to toe. We have asked him to come round to the station tomorrow. He was a bit *shaken*, so we sent him and his wife home. They are staying at a hotel on Piccadilly Circus."

By this time the two policemen had reached the Jewel House, which is located inside the Tower in the so-called Waterloo *Barracks*. They entered.

ÜBUNG 9

*Übung 9: Vervollständigen Sie die Sätze, wenn nötig, mit den Artikeln **a**, **an** oder **the**!*

1. Inspector Hudson travelled by __________ car.
2. __________ Kohinoor diamond was stolen.
3. The guards made __________ big mistake.
4. The robbery happened half __________ hour ago.
5. Inspector Hudson got back out of __________ bed.
6. Mr Moore collided with one of __________ thieves.
7. If caught, the thieves will have to go to __________ prison.
8. The Jewel House is inside __________ Tower.

"This is so much bigger than I remember it," said an impressed Inspector Hudson.
The whole ground floor of the Waterloo *Barracks* was taken up by the Crown Jewels. They were shining and *sparkling* in their *see-through* glass boxes – resting peacefully on French *velvet*.
"The Jewel House was newly constructed between 1991 and 1994," said Sir Reginald. "The display area is three times the size of the old Jewel House – the room *is capable of* handling up to 2,500 visitors an hour." Sir Reginald nodded intently at Inspector Hudson.
"That is very *impressive*," said Inspector Hudson, who was almost *spellbound* by the *riches* around him – something that did not happen very often to Inspector Hudson.
Sir Reginald saw this and smiled. Inspector Hudson noticed this and felt a little embarrassed. He cleared his throat:
"But they could have invested a little more in security!" exclaimed the inspector. He tried to sound *matter-of-factly*.

"There is nothing wrong with being impressed, Inspector. I mean, you are standing in front of one of the most exclusive collections of jewels in the world."

Inspector Hudson just *grunted*.

"Where was the Kohinoor diamond kept?" he asked, changing the subject.

"Over there!"

Sir Reginald pointed to the other end of the room, where a group of policemen were busy *securing evidence*. The policemen walked towards the glass case which used to contain the Kohinoor diamond. As Sir Reginald led the way to the case, Inspector Hudson could not help admiring the Crown Jewels they passed on their way. He saw the *Sceptre* with the Cross – its diamond shining in the light, almost blinding him. He also admired the three *swords*: The *Sword* of *Spiritual Justice*, the *Sword* of *Temporal Justice*, and the *Sword* of *Mercy*. The *latter* has a *blunt* point because it is a symbolically broken *sword*. Sir Reginald turned around slightly and again saw the *astounded* look on Inspector Hudson's face. He smiled triumphantly.

"The legend says that the *Sword* of *Mercy's* tip was broken off by an angel to prevent a *wrongful* killing."

"Oh really!" replied Inspector Hudson, trying hard not to show too much interest.

Sir Reginald and Inspector Hudson eventually reached the empty case where the Kohinoor diamond had been kept. They could clearly see where a circle had been cut out – large enough for a hand and the diamond to fit through.

"Clean cut," remarked Inspector Hudson. "The thieves seem to have been well *equipped*."

"Yes, it's not easy to open one of these cases. The jewels are protected by two inch-thick *shatter-proof* glass."

Inspector Hudson nodded thoughtfully.
"The thieves must have used a special kind of machinery, possibly even a diamond to open the case. They were obviously very well organized and very competent – it's certainly not *philistines* we are *dealing with*."
"No, that's for sure," agreed Sir Reginald.
"And the fact that almost nobody saw them; so many people and only two *witnesses*."
"There was a lot of smoke and tourists were running around *frantically* – it was chaos, total chaos."
"It's strange that none of the guards saw anything. Did they not *secure* the Jewel House *straight away*?" asked Inspector Hudson *incredulously*.
"Well, the thing was that most of the guards ran towards Byward Tower."
"But that's more or less in the opposite direction from the Jewel House," stated Inspector Hudson. "Why did they do that?"
"Marc Drum, the Chief *Yeoman Warder*, told them the thief who *struck* him *down* had run in that direction."
"Did he now?" asked Inspector Hudson *suspiciously*.
"It was probably *due* to the *blow* on the head. I mean the man was quite obviously disorientated," Sir Reginald fired back.
"Yes, maybe," Inspector Hudson said, more to himself.
Inspector Hudson looked *pensively* around the room. He looked up at the cameras staring down on them.
"Do we have anything on film?" he asked.
Sir Reginald *shrugged*.
"I have not found that out yet."
"Where is the control room where the soldiers monitor the Jewel House?"
"It's also in the *barracks*."

Übung 10: Übersetzen Sie die folgenden Sätze!

ÜBUNG 10 !

1. Das ist sehr beeindruckend.

2. Sie gingen auf die Vitrine zu.

3. Inspector Hudson bewunderte die Juwelen.

4. Sir Reginald lächelte triumphierend.

5. Es gab fast keine Zeugen.

6. Inspector Hudson sah sich nachdenklich im Zimmer um.

7. Sir Reginald zuckte mit den Schultern.

Inspector Hudson turned around to the policemen who were *securing* the crime scene. One of them was busily scanning the broken case with an ultraviolet light.
"Sergeant Wood, have your men checked the film material yet?" asked Inspector Hudson.
Sergeant Wood looked up at the Inspector. He did not stop what he was doing.
"Yes, I'm afraid we have nothing," he said with a sigh. Sergeant

Wood *carried on* with his work. "One of the thieves managed to get into the control room and take out the cassettes."
"But where were the guards?" asked an *astonished* Sir Reginald.
"They were all running towards Byward Tower," answered Sergeant Wood dryly. "The two that stayed behind were *stunned* by electroshock guns."
"And none of them saw the thief or thieves either?" asked Inspector Hudson, a little frustrated.
"*Nope*!" Sergeant Wood looked up from his work. A guard had just entered the room. The three of them looked in his direction.
"You can ask Mr Gunn. He was one of the guards who were *stunned*."

ÜBUNG 11 !

Übung 11: Setzen Sie die richtigen Fragepronomen ein!
(who, whose, which (2x), why, where, what)

1. __________ does the Kohinoor diamond originally come from?
2. In __________ part of the Tower was the diamond stolen?
3. __________ happened to the Chief Yeoman Warder?
4. __________ was one of the stunned guards?
5. __________ sword is that?
6. __________ room did the thief manage to get into?
7. __________ did they steal only one diamond?

Inspector Hudson and Sir Reginald walked towards the guard. He was still wearing his traditional *Beefeater* uniform called the blue undress uniform – it was dark blue in colour and *emblazoned* with red *trimmings*. His face was rather pale and he was not wearing his Tudor *bonnet*. The policemen introduced themselves to the *Beefeater*. He returned their greeting tiredly.

"It's a very sad day for us *Yeoman Warders*, a *nightmare* come true," said Mr Gunn, *gloomily* shaking his head.

Sir Reginald and Inspector Hudson looked at him *sympathetically*.

"Sergeant Wood told us you were attacked?"

"Yes, we had no chance. The thief came out of nowhere…Like in some Batman film…I didn't even have time to turn round. Before I knew it I felt this terrible pain *rack* my body – that's the last thing I remember," said Mr Gunn *dully*.

"And your colleague?" asked Inspector Hudson.

"Nothing, he dropped to the ground before I did…It was terrible…I never thought…We totally *failed*…"

Mr Gunn's voice broke.

"Now, now!" said Sir Reginald clapping the man on the back. "You did the best you could."

Mr Gunn smiled *wearily*.

"Whatever you say; I guess the other men and I will have to live with this failure somehow. I hope to God you get them. That would at least be a small comfort."

"We'll do our best," replied Inspector Hudson.

"I hope you do better than us," said Mr Gunn and with this he left the room, his shoulders and head hanging low.

"Poor soul," said Sir Reginald *compassionately* as he watched the *Beefeater* leave.

"I should get back to the police station. For all I know, the Queen herself could be waiting in my office to find out what exactly has happened," he said worriedly.

"This whole affair is going to be all over the newspapers tomorrow! We need some answers, we need some answers fast!"

"I'll do my best, Sir," Inspector Hudson assured him. "Let me *accompany* you back outside. I could do with some fresh air."

ÜBUNG 12 !

Übung 12: Lesen Sie weiter und ordnen Sie die Buchstaben in Klammern zu einem sinnvollen Wort!

The two policemen (1. xetied) ______________ the Jewel House. Sir Reginald and Inspector Hudson (2. dlkeaw) ______________ over to the *moat* bridge. Inspector Hudson took a deep breath and *inhaled* the fresh night air.

"I wonder why they just stole the Kohinoor (3. nomadid) ______________; I mean they could have taken the lot? What is so (4. icaleps) ______________ about it?"

Sir Reginald (5. shggedur) ______________ slightly and said thoughtfully: "No idea!"

At that moment a red car suddenly (6. eepsedd) ______________ around the corner and came to a sudden *halt*. The two policemen looked over to the road to see what was going on. Sir Reginald smiled. Inspector Hudson did not look (7. pldeeas) ______________.

"However, maybe Miss Elliot can help you on that one, Inspector Hudson," said Sir Reginald with a tone of amusement in his voice as he watched Elvira Elliot – a young and attractive insurance *investigator* – walk quickly but elegantly towards them – her long red hair flying through the air like the trail of a *blazing* comet.

Chapter 3: An Absent Husband

The next day, Inspector Hudson and Elvira Elliot decided to visit the wife of the missing *Beefeater*, Marc Drum. The Drums lived in the *outskirts* of London, in Barnet.
Elvira Elliot was driving her fire-red sports car round a bend at speed, Inspector Hudson was holding on to the *dashboard*. He was trying very hard not to fall into Miss Elliot's lap.
The road straightened up.
Inspector Hudson relaxed.
Elvira turned to face him and smiled.
"It's strange that Marc Drum is still missing, isn't it?" she said conversationally.
"Yes, very strange, *suspiciously* strange," he replied.
Elvira Elliot was still looking at the inspector. He nodded in the direction of the road.
"Maybe you should keep an eye on the road," he said worriedly.
Miss Elliot turned her attention back to the road and asked:
"You're not frightened, are you, Inspector?" She smiled *pensively*.
"No, I'm not frightened; just cautious," Inspector Hudson answered calmly.
They shot round another bend. The inspector grasped the *dashboard* again.
"That's us nearly there, not far to go now," Miss Elliot grinned.
"What do you know about the Kohinoor diamond?" the inspector asked, looking at Miss Elliot.

ÜBUNG 13 !

Übung 13: Fügen Sie die richtige Präposition ein!
(onto, in, under, on (2x), over, to)

1. The sword lay ____________ a silk cushion.
2. Elvira Elliot walked ____________ to them.
3. Inspector Hudson and Miss Elliot were ____________ her red sports car.
4. The red sports car was ____________ the road.
5. As she drove round the bend, the inspector was close ______ her.
6. Elvira Elliot drove ____________ a bridge.
7. Inspector Hudson nearly fell ____________ Miss Elliot's lap.

Elvira Elliot turned and faced him again. Inspector Hudson pointed in the direction of the road. Miss Elliot faced the road again. "It's the oldest diamond known to *mankind*…"
"Approximately five thousand years old," interrupted Inspector Hudson.
"Oh, I'm impressed. I see you've done your homework. Anyway, it's one of the largest diamonds in the world and the legend says that whoever carries it in their crown shall rule the world."
"Does it? It's amazing how many legends and secrets are attached to all these jewels."
"Yes, it's a diamond which has never been bought or sold, but it has *changed hands* many times. The diamond has left a trail of *greed*, power, murder, *misfortune* and unhappiness behind it."
"Oh, dear, then the thief is in big trouble!" Inspector Hudson said ironically.
"Yes, he is *indeed* – especially after we get him," she laughed.

"How much is the diamond worth?" the inspector asked.
"That's very difficult to say. It has 105 carats, which is rather a lot. Plus you have the, how shall I put it, sentimental value. I guess it goes into millions."
Inspector Hudson *whistled*.

Übung 14: Welches Wort hat die stärkere Bedeutung? Kreuzen Sie an!

1.	☐ trouble	☐ danger
2.	☐ miserable	☐ unhappy
3.	☐ difficult	☐ thorny
4.	☐ alert	☐ cautious
5.	☐ much	☐ loads
6.	☐ argue	☐ disagree
7.	☐ greed	☐ excess

"So it wouldn't make much sense to cut the diamond into pieces?"
"Not really."
"But is that not stupid? I mean, it won't be easy to sell because of its fame."
"Yes and no. Countries such as Pakistan and India have often *claimed* to be the *rightful* owners of the diamond."
"That means you just need the right connections."
"Yes, you need to know the right people. But as you know, this is all speculation."
"I guess you're right there, for all we know the thief might just want to put the diamond on his living room *mantelpiece*."
Miss Elliot and Inspector Hudson laughed.
"There is one other thing that's annoying me," the inspector said.

"And what might that be?"
"Why was the Kohinoor diamond stolen? There were much more *valuable treasures* in the Jewel House. The 'Great Star of Africa', for example – it has 530 carats."
Elvira Elliot *shrugged*. "As I pointed out, the Kohinoor diamond has a special *reputation*."
Inspector Hudson nodded. "We should keep that in mind. It is a very good point, Miss Elliot."
Elvira Elliot smiled.
"Oh, here we are!" exclaimed Elvira Elliot, suddenly hitting the brakes.
The car came to an abrupt *halt*. Inspector Hudson flew forward.
"Sorry about that!" she apologized. "But we nearly drove past Mr and Mrs Drum's house."
Inspector Hudson just looked at her *disapprovingly* and got out of the car.

ÜBUNG 15 !

Übung 15: Geben Sie die verneinte Form in ihrer Kurzform an!

1. he is — he isn't
2. they are — ____________
3. we will — ____________
4. she did — ____________
5. it can — ____________
6. she would — ____________
7. we have — ____________
8. they should — ____________

The *investigators* walked towards the house and rang the bell. A young woman in her early thirties opened the door. She looked pale and worried. Inspector Hudson and Miss Elliot introduced themselves. Mrs Drum let them in and led them to her living room.

"Please take a seat," Mrs Drum said nervously.

Miss Elliot and the inspector sat down.

"Can I offer you a cup of tea?" Mrs Drum asked.

Inspector Hudson and Miss Elliot *declined*.

Mrs Drum sat down on the armchair opposite them.

"Have you heard anything?" she *inquired anxiously*.

"No, I'm afraid not. Your husband has *disappeared into thin air*," the inspector replied.

Mrs Drum played around *uneasily* with her hands. Then she put a hand to her eyes and started to cry.

"It's all so *dreadful*. I'm so worried about him. And these journalists...", Mrs Drum pointed at her phone which she had taken off the hook, "...they have not stopped calling all morning," she *sobbed*.

"I *suspect* your husband has not *been in touch* with you either?" Miss Elliot asked cautiously.

Mrs Drum shook her head. She took a *handkerchief* out of her pocket and blew her nose.

"Do you also believe he has something to do with the robbery?" she asked sadly.

"We can't say for sure, but to be honest, Mrs Drum, he is one of our main *suspects* at the moment," replied Inspector Hudson.

Mrs Drum started to cry again. She could not stop. Elvira Elliot went over to her and tried to calm her down. She *stroked* her back gently.

"Now, now Mrs Drum, there might be a harmless explanation for his disappearance."

"Yes, it might be shock. My men are out there looking for him," the inspector said.
Mrs Drum started to calm down. She blew her nose again.
"I understand your worry", Inspector Hudson *carried on,* "but I need you to answer some questions."
Mrs Drum nodded.
"What would you like to know, Inspector?"
"When was the last time you saw your husband?" Inspector Hudson asked.
"Yesterday evening around five o'clock before he went to the Tower."
"Did he act strangely in any way?"
"No, everything was the same as usual."
"Did he seem nervous or *distracted*?"
"No, not really," Mrs Drum thought for a short moment. "But come to think of it, he received a phone call just before he left. After that he did seem somewhat nervous."

ÜBUNG 16 !

Übung 16: Lesen Sie weiter und unterstreichen Sie jeweils die richtige Variante!

"Do you know who (1.) named/called?"
"No!"
"(2.) Him/He didn't say anything about the phone call?" Inspector Hudson *inquired*.
"I'm afraid not, Inspector. Perhaps (3.) me/I am overestimating its relevance – maybe he just lost a bet."
"A bet?" the inspector asked (4.) interestedly/interested.
"Yes, that does happen sometimes."
"Did your husband bet a lot?"

"No, not really. He just puts the *odd* one on now and again."
"So you had (5.) no/know money problems or anything?"
"What are you trying to (6.) tell/say, Inspector? Do you think my husband stole the Kohinoor diamond to pay off his *gambling debts*?" Mrs Drum asked annoyed.
"(7.) Came/Calm down Mrs Drum," said Miss Elliot. "Inspector Hudson is only (8.) doing/making his job."

"Yes, I'm sorry. I guess I'm a little *worked up*."
Inspector Hudson took a deep breath and *carried on*.
"*Apart from* the incident yesterday evening, Mrs Drum, is there anything else you can think of?"
Mrs Drum had another good think.
"Well, to be honest there was. During the last few months he often came home late and the *secretive* phone call last night was not the first."
"Why didn't you say so in the first place?" Elvira Elliot asked pointedly.
"I was a little embarrassed to talk about it." Mrs Drum ran her fingers through her hair nervously.
"Why is that?" *inquired* the inspector.
"Well you see…How shall I put it…I believe my husband is having an affair."
"What makes you think that?" Inspector Hudson asked.
Mrs Drum looked at Elvira Elliot. Her face looked sad.
"Just one of these female intuition things, if you know what I mean."
Elvira Elliot nodded understandingly.
"I see, so you have no proof?"
"No, Inspector, I have no proof. Nor can I prove my husband is innocent – but I do feel he is."

ÜBUNG 17

Übung 17: Welche Synonyme gehören zusammen? Setzen Sie die richtige Ziffer ein!

1. ask	☐ advance
2. innocent	☐ heave
3. exclaim	☐ comprehend
4. close	☐ inquire
5. accomplice	☐ violent
6. pull	☐ shout
7. understand	☐ blameless
8. force	☐ shut
9. proceed	☐ assistant
10. rough	☐ might

Mrs Drum started to cry again. Elvira Elliot comforted her.

Suddenly a bright *flash* came from outside the living room window.

"What on earth was that?" exclaimed Miss Elliot, who was nearly blinded by the light.

Inspector Hudson ran to the window. He saw a man with a camera and a film crew.

"Journalists!" he exclaimed.

Elvira Elliot went to the window too. She looked out.

"It certainly is!" she remarked. A cameraman pointed the camera in her direction.

Inspector Hudson closed the *blinds*.

"I'll see to them!" he *snarled*.

Inspector Hudson opened the front door.

"Okay, you lot. Make a move!"

A presenter recognized the inspector *straight away* and moved towards him. He was followed by a camera. He stuck his micro-

phone right in James Hudson's face.
"So what have you found out, Inspector? Have you caught the *Beefeater* Marc Drum yet?"
"I said, clear off! This is *trespassing*!" Inspector Hudson said *harshly*.
The reporter did not move.
"Did he *pull off* the robbery on his own or did he have *accomplices*?"
"No comment!" answered the inspector. And with that he started to push the cameraman and the reporter back. He put his hand over the lens of the camera.
"What are you doing?" cried the news reporter. "You can't do this!"
"Oh, yes I can!" Inspector Hudson answered as he forced them back onto the pavement outside the Drums' *property*.
"Now you can stand here all you want, but I don't want to see you anywhere near that window. Do you understand? Or I'll have you all arrested."
The man with the photo camera took a picture of the *enraged* inspector, who was already walking back to the front door. He went inside, locked it and then walked back into the living room.
"That was a bit rough, wasn't it?" Elvira Elliot remarked.
Inspector Hudson *shrugged* unconcernedly.
"Is that all you can do, Inspector? Can you not ban them from my street?"
"I'm afraid not, Mrs Drum. As much as I'd like to, that's all I can do for now."
Mrs Drum was very *upset* and *distressed*.
"What a scandal. The whole affair is going to be splattered all over tomorrow's newspapers and poor Marc is just *fodder* for their *sensation-craving* readers. And…"
Inspector Hudson cleared his throat. Mrs Drum stopped talking.

"If you don't mind, Miss Elliot and I would like to have a look around your house – and especially search your husband's *belongings* for any *clues*. Would you mind?"
"Not at all. The sooner you prove his innocence the better. If you follow me, I'll show you his little office. That's where he spends most of his free time."

ÜBUNG 18 !

*Übung 18: Setzen Sie **many** oder **much** richtig ein!*

1. Inspector Hudson didn't have __________ time to solve the case.
2. Mrs Drum could not tell them very __________ about her husband's motive.
3. Marc Drum had __________ friends.
4. There were not __________ reasons why Mr Drum could have disappeared.
5. The Beefeater spent __________ of his time in his office.
6. There are not __________ clues.

Mrs Drum took the *investigators* along the hall and led them into a small office. It had two full bookshelves and a desk with a *typewriter*.
"Does your husband not have a computer?" Miss Elliot asked.
"No!" answered Mrs Drum. "He is more of an old-fashioned type."
Mrs Drum left them to it.
"Well, what would you expect of a *Beefeater*," Elvira Elliot remarked. "He runs around with a large fork in his hand all day."
Inspector Hudson smiled.

"Let's get to work, see if we can find anything that might help us solve Drum's mysterious disappearance."

Übung 19: Verwandeln Sie das Adjektiv in ein Adverb!

1. gentle ______________________
2. thoughtful ______________________
3. uneasy ______________________
4. harmless ______________________
5. safe ______________________
6. rough ______________________
7. abrupt ______________________
8. mysterious ______________________

After searching for a while, Elvira Elliot found a card from the Savoy Hotel, a *renowned* London luxury hotel. She turned it over. On the back it had a time and date: "16.07. 8 p.m."
"Look at this," she said and *handed* the card to Inspector Hudson. "Strange, isn't it?"
"Yes, it is."
"Why would a man like Marc Drum have an appointment at that kind of luxury hotel?"
"Good question. Perhaps we should go there and find out. It could well be that somebody saw him there."
"Yes, good idea. Hotel receptions and *bellboys* are often the best informants."
Miss Elliot and Inspector Hudson left Mr Drum's office.

ÜBUNG 20 !

Übung 20: Sind die folgenden Aussagen richtig? Markieren Sie mit richtig ✔ oder falsch – !

1. Mrs Drum couldn't care less if her husband were dead or alive. ☐
2. Marc Drum has a very modern computer. ☐
3. Inspector Hudson and Miss Elliot look around the house. ☐
4. Marc Drum is old-fashioned. ☐
5. Elvira Elliot found a fax from the Savoy Hotel. ☐
6. The Savoy Hotel is very expensive. ☐
7. The inspector and Miss Elliot plan to go to the Savoy. ☐

Miss Elliot and Inspector Hudson arrived at the Savoy Hotel. It is located in a very famous street in London called "Strand". The Strand, as the street is also referred to, starts at Trafalgar Square and runs east to the *boundary* of the City of London, where it becomes Fleet Street. Elvira Elliot stopped her car right in front of the entrance. A *bellboy* walked *swiftly* towards the car. He was no older than seventeen.

"Did we need the *grand entrance*?" Inspector Hudson asked, irritated. "We could have just parked on the street!"

Elvira Elliot was fixing her hair in the *rear-view mirror*.

"Why shouldn't we take a little luxury when we can get it?" she smiled.

The *bellboy* opened Inspector Hudson's door.

"Good day, sir!" he said.

Inspector Hudson did not really like this special attention. He *sighed* and got out of the car.

"Well, yes, a good day to you too, young man," the inspector said, slightly unsure of himself.

The *bellboy* thought this reaction a little strange and walked around

to the other side of the car. He opened the door and let Miss Elliot out. She slid elegantly out of the car.
"Good day, Madam!"
"Good day!"
Elvira Elliot *handed* him the keys and smiled. The *bellboy* took them from her, got in the car and drove it away.
"I hope you get it back!" remarked Inspector Hudson. "For all we know he's planning on having a *joyride* through London."
Miss Elliot laughed. They walked into the hotel.

Übung 21: Ergänzen Sie die fehlenden Verbformen!

	Infinitive	Simple Past	Past Participle
1.	arrive	______	______
2.	______	______	run
3.	______	hid	______
4.	make	______	______
5.	______	______	kept
6.	______	shone	______
7.	think	______	______
8.	______	______	worn

The reception area was *vast*. The hotel first opened in 1889 and still had a unique *Victorian* touch. Although very exquisite, the Savoy had a warm and friendly atmosphere. Inspector Hudson and Miss Elliot *made* their *way* to the reception. The inspector took out his

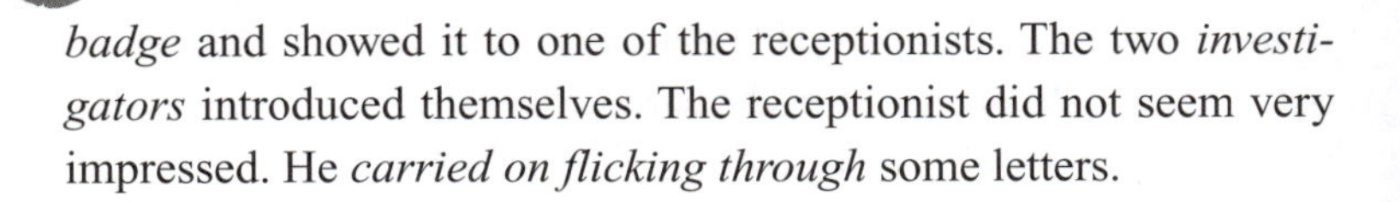

badge and showed it to one of the receptionists. The two *investigators* introduced themselves. The receptionist did not seem very impressed. He *carried on flicking through* some letters.

ÜBUNG 22 !

Übung 22: Welche Wörter gehören zusammen? Bilden Sie zusammengesetzte Begriffe!

1. boy	☐	hotel
2. joy	☐	police
3. lobby	☐	bell
4. badge	☐	old
5. book	☐	type
6. fashioned	☐	ride
7. writer	☐	shelf

"How may I help you?"
Elvira Elliot lay down a photograph of Marc Drum.
"Have you ever seen this man?" she asked.
The receptionist *glanced* at it.
"I've never seen him," he replied.
The receptionist *carried on* sorting the letters. Miss Elliot and Inspector Hudson looked at each other. Elvira Elliot just shook her head. They also asked the other receptionists; however, nobody recognized Marc Drum. The *investigators* walked away from the reception.
"That was not very successful, was it?" Inspector Hudson said dryly. "They've all got their noses too high in the air here if you ask me."
Elvira Elliot *shrugged* and said excitedly, "I like the Savoy!"
The insurance *investigator* looked around, her eyes *sparkling* with

joy. Inspector Hudson *frowned* and shook his head.
"Do you come here often?" he asked *mockingly*.
"No, but I would if I could afford it!"

Chapter 4: The Stunning Prince

Elvira Elliot and the inspector were just about to leave the hotel when a little blond woman came hurrying up behind them. She was wearing the same uniform as the other receptionists. The young woman looked to the left and then to the right. It was as if she wanted to check she was not being watched.

Übung 23: Das englische Wort hat verschiedene Übersetzungsmöglichkeiten. Welche?

ÜBUNG 23

1. watch ____________ ____________
2. uniform ____________ ____________
3. ring ____________ ____________
4. hand ____________ ____________
5. mine ____________ ____________
6. muse ____________ ____________

"Can I see that photograph again, please?" she asked.
Inspector Hudson showed it to her.
"Have you seen this man here?" Inspector Hudson *inquired*.
The woman looked at the photograph; she bit on her lip.
"Yes, I think so."

"When?" the inspector wanted to know.
"It must have been about a week ago. He was sitting in the tea room talking to an Indian gentleman."
"Do you know who this Indian gentleman was?" the inspector asked with great interest.
"Yes, his name is Prince Vikram."
"Is he…"
The woman interrupted Inspector Hudson.
"That's all I know. I must get back to work."
The receptionist walked away *swiftly*.
"Now isn't that interesting? Marc Drum meeting up with an Indian prince," Miss Elliot stated.
"Yes, it is rather strange. Why should a wealthy Indian prince meet up with an English working-class *Beefeater*?"
In that moment the *bellboy* walked by. It was the same one who had parked Elvira's car.

ÜBUNG 24 !

Übung 24: Setzen Sie die passenden Synonyme ein!
(eagerly, point, waved, generous, approached, inquired, usual)

Miss Elliot *caught* his *eye* and (1. gestured) ____________________ him over. He smiled and (2. moved towards) ________________ her. She smiled *flirtatiously* at him.

"Do you *by any chance* know who Prince Vikram is?" she (3. asked) ____________________.

"Everybody knows Prince Vikram! He's a very (4. charitable) ____________________ man."

Then he *bent* over and whispered into Miss Elliot's ear, "Like most people who come in here."

The *bellboy* nodded *conspiratorially*. Then he moved back and said in his (5. normal) ______________ voice, "So what do you want to know?"

Miss Elliot got the (6. message) ______________ and took out her purse. She held it in her hand.

"Do you happen to know where the prince is just now?" she asked.

The *bellboy* looked (7. enthusiastically) ______________ at the purse.

"Well, he's not at the hotel at the moment, but I *overheard* a conversation earlier on."
"Regarding what?" the inspector asked.
"Prince Vikram was planning a tour of London today. His first destination was St. Paul's Cathedral."
"When did he leave?" Miss Elliot asked.
The *bellboy* looked at his watch.
"About half an hour ago."
"What does he actually look like, this prince?" Inspector Hudson asked.
"You can't really miss him; he wears a white turban with a large shiny *scarlet gem* stuck on the front."
Elvira Elliot *handed* the *bellboy* ten pounds.
"Thank you for your assistance!" she said.
The *bellboy* just looked at the money as if to say: Is that all?
Miss Elliot *sighed* and shook her head.

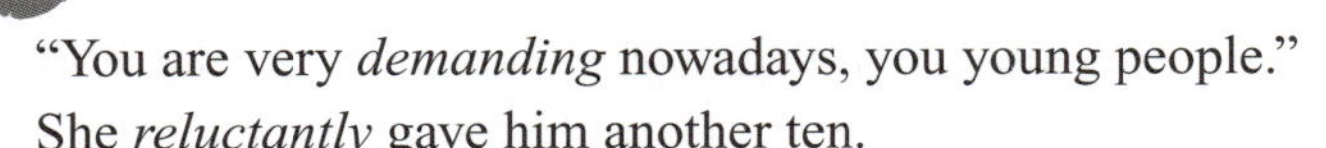

"You are very *demanding* nowadays, you young people."
She *reluctantly* gave him another ten.
"Thank you, Madam!" he smiled.
"Don't Madam me, just get my car!" Miss Elliot exclaimed.
Inspector Hudson could not help laughing – *affectionately* amused by Elvira Elliot's sudden *objection* to *snobbishness*.

ÜBUNG 25 !

Übung 25: Wie lauten die Sätze? Achten Sie auf die Wortstellung!

1. always fast Miss drives Elliot

2. she saw suddenly the bellboy

3. the Inspector Hudson into Elvira Elliot walked and just hotel

4. just already Prince Vikram left had

5. first Inspector Hudson asked the should probably have bellboy

Elvira Elliot was *speeding* along Fleet Street.
"It's not far to St. Paul's Cathedral. The cathedral is on Ludgate Hill; and at some point Fleet Street in fact becomes Ludgate Hill. We should be there *in no time*," Miss Elliot said.
"Yes, if we actually get there alive!" *mumbled* Inspector Hudson.
Shortly after Miss Elliot's race down Fleet Street, they arrived at St.

Paul's Cathedral. Elvira Elliot parked the car and the *investigators* walked quickly towards the cathedral.

Übung 26: Lesen Sie weiter und unterstreichen Sie die fünf inhaltlich nicht dazugehörenden Sätze!

They entered the cathedral, which lies to the east of the so-called Great West Door. They walked outside. Being one of London's most visited sites, it was quite busy. Some people were *strolling* up the *nave* – the main *approach* leading to the high altar. They were admiring the cathedral's architecture, which was constructed in late Renaissance style. It was a very modern building. The visitors were obviously *spellbound* by the Cathedral's *seemingly eternal* vastness. Some of them were seated along the *aisles* praying or just *marvelling at* the spectacular *dome*. It was inspired by St. Peter's Basilica in Rome and rose up to 108 metres. It was a very cheap copy. Inspector Hudson and Elvira Elliot walked up the *nave*. They could see land in the distance. The *pillars* on both sides, like colossal fingers reaching out to heaven, held the gigantic roof in place. The whole *interior* of St. Paul's Cathedral was mainly greyish-white in colour. It was like a rainbow. It reflected *beams* of pure white light – *illuminating* the darkest corners of the Cathedral.

"Can you see him anywhere?" Miss Elliot asked and *inspected* the *aisles* on the left side of the *nave*.
Inspector Hudson, who was *inspecting* the *aisles* on the right, answered, "No, I'm afraid not. Maybe it is best if we split up," he suggested.
"Good idea!" replied Miss Elliot. "I'll check out the Stone Gallery and you can check out the Golden Gallery."

"Golden Gallery?" the inspector asked confused.
"Yes, it's one of the external galleries which runs over there."
Miss Elvira pointed towards the outer *boundaries* of the Cathedral.
"Ah, that's what they call that area," remarked Inspector Hudson.
"Let's meet in the Whispering Gallery in fifteen minutes," Miss Elliot *carried on*.
"Okay, I know where that is. I'll see you then." The two *investigators* parted.

ÜBUNG 27 !

Übung 27: Setzen Sie die richtigen Pronomen ein!
(him, mine (2x), his, me, your, them)

1. Excuse __________!
2. He told __________ that they had the wrong guy.
3. To __________ disappointment he had arrested the wrong man.
4. "The turban does not belong to me, it isn't __________."
5. The inspector recognized the man. He had seen __________ before.
6. "That was __________ idea to talk to him, not __________!"

After fifteen minutes they met at the top of the Whispering Gallery which runs around the *interior* of the *dome*. It gets its name from the special construction of the *dome*. A whisper against the wall at any point is *audible* to a listener with their ear held to a point on exactly the opposite side. Whispering voices were echoing off the walls. It sounded like the ghostly echoes of long-lost souls.
"Any luck?" the inspector asked.

"I'm afraid not; and you?"
Inspector Hudson shook his head.
"So what do we do now?" Miss Elliot *inquired*.
James Hudson caught a *glimpse* of the cathedral *caretaker*, who was wearing a grey overall and *inspecting* a *pillar*.
"Let's ask that gentleman if he saw our prince," suggested the inspector.
"Why not!" remarked Miss Elliot.

Übung 28: Übersetzen Sie die Sätze im Konditional!

1. Inspector Hudson würde niemals Miss Elliot sein Auto fahren lassen.

   Inspector Hudson would never let Miss Elliot drive his car.

2. Elvira Elliot würde nie zugeben, dass sie zu schnell Auto fährt.

   ....

3. Inspector Hudson würde niemals alleine die „Flüstergalerie" finden.

   ....

4. Prince Vikram würde niemals ohne Turban aus dem Haus gehen.

   ....

5. Sir Reginald würde sehr gerne den Dieb schnappen.

   ....

6. Miss Elliot würde immer mit dem Inspektor zusammenarbeiten.

____

The *investigators* introduced themselves to the *caretaker* and asked about the prince.
"You could not miss him," said the *caretaker*. "He walked in here with a *bunch of people*. There were about ten or fifteen of them. Their limousines were parked right outside the door – caused quite a *commotion*."
"Did you *by any chance* hear where their next destination was?"
"I could not tell you for sure, but the Indian fellow with the flashy *gem* was really *keen on* seeing Westminster Abbey."
"I see," the inspector said. "Well, thank you very much!"
"Any time!" the *caretaker* replied.
Miss Elliot and Inspector Hudson said goodbye and walked towards the entrance.

ÜBUNG 29

Übung 29: Was ist gemeint? Finden Sie den passenden Begriff!

1. a very large church ______________
2. a long object which supports a building ______________
3. Leonardo Da Vinci's epoch ______________
4. the passage between benches ______________
5. the holy table in a church ______________
6. the central part of a church ______________
7. a person who looks after a building ______________

Elvira Elliot and Inspector Hudson arrived at Westminster Abbey.
"No limousines!" the inspector remarked, disappointed.
"Let's have a look anyway, you never know. Perhaps they just parked somewhere else. As you know, there are no *public parking facilities* available at the Abbey."
"Yeah, tell me about it. I used to work around the corner from here. I always took the underground Circle Line to 'Westminster' and walked."
They got out of the car. Since the car was parked illegally, Inspector Hudson leant back in and placed his police *badge* on the *dashboard*.
"That will save us from being *towed* away," the inspector said.

Übung 30: Lesen Sie weiter und setzen Sie die Verben in Klammern in die richtige Zeitform!

ÜBUNG 30 !

Just as they were walking towards the church, Inspector Hudson's mobile (1. ring) ______________. He (2. answer) ______________ it.

"Hello?"

"Hello, this (3. be) ________________ Sir Reginald!"

"Hello, Sir!"

"How is the investigation coming along? Have you (4. find) ________________ Marc Drum yet?"

"I'm afraid not, anything on your side?"

"No, nothing! My men (5. check) ________________ hospitals, hotels, bus and train stations, and the airport – the man

(6. seem) ____________________ to have disappeared off the planet."

"Well, we're onto something. Mr Drum *appears* to have been

(7. see) ____________________ some kind of Indian prince."

"A prince? That is strange. Why should he be (8. meet)

____________________ an Indian prince?"

"That's just what we (9. try) ____________________ to find out.

When I (10. know) ____________________ more, I'll let you know."

"Sergeant Wood told me to tell you that Mr and Mrs Moore are coming to the station later."
"Mr and Mrs Moore?"
"Yes, you know, the couple who saw one of the thieves."
"Oh, yes of course. You must excuse my forgetfulness – too much sightseeing I guess."
"Too much what?"
"Doesn't matter! I remember they had some kind of *footage covering* the robbery. Please tell Sergeant Wood to remind them to bring their camera."
"Did nobody *secure* that important *evidence* last night?"
Inspector Hudson realized *straight away* that he should not have mentioned the camera to his *superior*.
"No, Sir, I'm afraid not. Don't know what went wrong," said Inspector Hudson *matter-of-factly*.
"Well, that's not very…"
Inspector Hudson interrupted Sir Reginald.
"What did you say, Sir. I think the line is going..." he *pretended*.
"I said that's not…"
"Sir, Sir? You're gone!" Inspector Hudson pressed the red button

on his mobile and cut off the call. He *winked* at Miss Elliot, who was smiling.
"Was that your boss?" she asked.
"Yes, it was. These damn mobiles; they're so *unreliable* sometimes," he smiled.

Übung 31: Setzen Sie das passende Reflexivpronomen ein!

ÜBUNG 31

1. Miss Elliot had to force herself into liking Madame Tussaud's.
2. Inspector Hudson did not travel to Westminster Abbey by ______________.
3. Inspector Hudson and Elvira Elliot laughed at ______________.
4. Elvira Elliot asked Inspector Hudson, "Will you find the Whispering Gallery by ______________?"
5. Inspector Hudson said to Sir Reginald, "We are doing all the investigating by ______________."
6. Miss Elliot's car is great, but it cannot drive by ______________.

Elvira Elliot and Inspector Hudson *proceeded* towards the church doors. However, when Elvira Elliot tried to open them, they did not move.
"What a *waste of time*, it's closed!" Miss Elliot exclaimed.
Inspector Hudson looked at his watch.
"It's nearly four o'clock."
Miss Elliot looked at a notice that read: "OPEN MO, TUE, THUR, FRI 09:30-15:45; WED 09:30-18:00; SAT 09:30-13:45."

"What shall we do now?" Miss Elliot *sighed*.
"It's probably best we drive back to the Savoy and wait until Prince Vikram gets back."
They returned to the car.
Elvira Elliot and Inspector Hudson were driving up Brompton Road – a street located in the London district called City of Westminster. The street was *renowned for* its expensive shops, such as Harrods. It started from Knightsbridge *tube* station and ran south west through an extremely wealthy *residential area*. As well as the top shops, there are also five-star hotels and many top restaurants to be found on Brompton Road.

ÜBUNG 32 !

Übung 32: Lesen Sie weiter und unterstreichen Sie die Übersetzungen der Substantive in Klammern!
(1. Bremsen, 2. Reifen, 3. Herzanfall, 4. Leute, 5. Laden, 6. Blick, 7. Edelstein)

Just as the red car was shooting past Harrods, Elvira Elliot all of a sudden hit the brakes. The car's tyres *squealed* and Inspector Hudson nearly had a heart attack.
"What on earth are you doing – trying to kill us?" he said angrily.
"No, trying to help us!" was her answer.
Miss Elliot put the car into *reverse* and *approached* Harrods. Cars were *tooting* and people shouting at them. Elvira Elliot did not seem to care. She came to a *halt* in front of Harrods and pointed behind them. Inspector Hudson turned around and saw three big limousines parked in front of the store.
"I think I just saw Prince Vikram walk in. I caught a *glimpse* of a white turban and something *flashed* in the light. I *assume* that was his *scarlet gem*," Elvira Elliot said.

"Well, I didn't see anything. On the other hand I'm not surprised, *due* to the speed you were going."

Inspector Hudson and Elvira Elliot entered Harrods, an *upmarket* and exclusive department store.
"We'll need to hurry and find the prince before we lose him again. This place is enormous. I read in some women's magazine that the store has over 92,000 *square metres* of selling space."
Inspector Hudson was impressed.
"I didn't know women's magazines could be so informative," he remarked.
The *investigators* eventually found Prince Vikram in the great Food Hall, which is world-famous for the *abundance* and quality of its *merchandise*. Everything looked so fresh and inviting: the large grapefruits looked like miniature suns *beaming* red and orange. Bright red juicy tomatoes stood right next to fresh *crisp* salads. Unusual fruits, rich green vegetables and fresh herbs filled the air with exotic and appetizing *scents*.

Übung 33: Welche Wörter gehören zusammen?

1. Brompton Road	☐ shop
2. City of Westminster	☐ toot
3. tyres	☐ residential
4. horn	☐ car
5. metre	☐ borough
6. Harrods	☐ square
7. area	☐ street
8. Savoy	☐ Tower of London
9. Crown Jewels	☐ hotel

Elvira Elliot and Inspector Hudson *approached* Prince Vikram. Before they could get near him, however, they were surrounded by tall, muscular men in dark suits.
"What do you want?" one of them *barked*.
Inspector Hudson showed them his police *badge*.
"We'd like to talk to Prince Vikram regarding a very important matter."
"What matter?" another bodyguard asked.
"I can only talk about it to him personally."
"Well then, you don't talk to him at all."
Inspector Hudson *smirked*.
"Do you rehearse this?" he asked *mockingly*.
"Why don't you just *beat it*, *copper*?"
"I'd watch my mouth if I were you!" Inspector Hudson replied.
People were starting to stare. Some of them pointed, others whispered to each other.

ÜBUNG 34 !

Übung 34: Lesen Sie weiter und unterstreichen Sie im Text die Synonyme der Wörter in Klammern!
(1. shining 2. speak 3. issue 4. elegantly 5. undisclosed 6. to escort)

Suddenly the prince seemed to notice what was going on and came over to see what all the *commotion* was about. He was a very handsome man with dark sparkling eyes which even *outshone* the *scarlet gem* on his white turban.
"Now, now gentlemen," he said to his bodyguards in perfect English. "What is all the *fuss* about?"
"This policeman here says he would like to talk to you."
"Does he now," the prince remarked.
"Yes, he does!" Inspector Hudson said.
"In what matter, may I ask?"

"It has something to with the investigations into the robbery of the Kohinoor diamond," Inspector Hudson said very quietly. "My name is Inspector James Hudson from the London police and this is a colleague of mine, Miss Elvira Elliot."
The prince *bowed gracefully.*
"Well, you obviously *appear* to know who I am. I read about the robbery in the newspaper – it is a great loss, I must say."
"Maybe we can talk somewhere private," Inspector Hudson suggested.
"Yes, of course. If you would like to *accompany* me to my car – nobody will disturb us there."

Elvira Elliot and Inspector Hudson sat in the back of Prince Vikram's limousine. It had very comfortable seats and was *equipped* with a mini bar and a television in the back. Prince Vikram sat opposite them – a distance of at least two metres between them. He smiled warmly at Miss Elliot and looked deep into her eyes. Then he turned his attention towards the inspector.
"Now how can I *be of assistance*?" he asked.
"Do you know a man called Marc Drum?" Elvira Elliot asked.
"Yes, we met a couple of times – has something happened to him?" the prince *inquired*, full of concern.
"We're not quite sure about that, he has disappeared. Nobody has seen him since the robbery in the Tower of London."
"I see," said the prince, understanding immediately that Marc Drum was obviously a main *suspect*.
"So what was your relationship with this man, Prince Vikram?" Inspector Hudson asked.
"That is a simple question to answer: I'm planning to make a documentary about the 'long journey' of the Kohinoor. Over the centuries, the diamond has travelled around almost the whole world."

Übung 35: Wie heißt das Wort auf Englisch?

1. rückwärts fahren ________________
2. endlich ________________
3. Polizeimarke ________________
4. geschlossen ________________
5. unzuverlässig ________________
6. Öffnungszeiten ________________
7. eintreten ________________
8. sich verbeugen ________________
9. Verdächtiger ________________

The prince smiled warmly at Miss Elliot. She smiled back a little *self-consciously*.
"And what did this have to do with Marc Drum?" the inspector asked in a *firm* tone, trying to put a stop to the *flirtatious* atmosphere developing between the prince and his colleague.
„I interviewed him about the '*Ceremony of the Keys*' and his work in the Tower. I was also looking for a real *Beefeater* to take on a short part in my film."
"That's all?"
"Yes, that's all there was to it."
"When was the last time you saw Mr Drum?" Elvira Elliot asked in a kind, warm voice, which was very unlike her normal style.
"I think it must have been two or three days ago. I would have to look in my diary to be sure."
"We believe you, Prince Vikram. There's no need for that," smiled Elvira Elliot.

Übung 36: Steigern Sie die folgenden Adjektive!

ÜBUNG 36 !

1. long longer longest
2. deep ______ ______
3. nice ______ ______
4. helpful ______ ______
5. narrow ______ ______
6. exhausted ______ ______
7. bad ______ ______
8. comfortable ______ ______

Inspector Hudson tried to keep his *outrage* to himself.
"Well, that will be all for now," he said.
"I was glad I could *be of assistance*."
Prince Vikram got out his card and *handed* it to Miss Elliot.
"You can call me anytime", Prince Vikram paused and looked intensely at Elvira Elliot, "if you have any further questions."
They all got out of the limousine and said goodbye. Prince Vikram returned to Harrods, the *investigators headed for* their car.

*Übung 37: Setzen Sie die Wörter **since, for, ago** in die Sätze richtig ein!*

ÜBUNG 37 !

1. Miss Elvira spotted the prince five minutes ______.
2. Prince Vikram has been staying in the Savoy ______ Monday.

3. Months ____________, Inspector Hudson dealt with a similar case.

4. Marc Drum has been missing ____________ two days.

5. Inspector Hudson has not been on holiday ____________ August.

6. Mrs Drum has been married to Mr Drum ____________ years.

7. Prince Vikram has not seen Marc Drum ____________ two days.

"Well, that wasn't very professional, was it?" the inspector said, with irritation.
"Do you think so, Inspector?" Miss Elliot *mocked* him. "You're not jealous, are you?"
"Certainly not!" he exclaimed.
Inspector Hudson held out his hand, *palm* upwards. Elvira Elliot looked at him in surprise.
"What?"
"Give me the car keys!" he said *firmly*. I've had enough of your *roller-coaster* driving techniques for one day!"
Elvira Elliot *tutted* and placed the car keys into his *palm*.
"Fine!" she said, *aggravated*. "But get us to the police station before tomorrow morning, please!"

ÜBUNG 38 !

Übung 38: Haben die Wörter dieselbe Bedeutung? Markieren Sie: richtig ✔ oder falsch – !

1. hand/give	☐	2. Miss/Ms	☐
3. outrage/anger	☐	4. relieved/glad	☐
5. help/betray	☐	6. assistance/helper	☐

Chapter 5: Smoke and Shadows

Mr and Mrs Moore were staying at a two-star hotel on Piccadilly Circus. They walked down the stairs and out onto the street.
"So what's the best way to get to Scotland Yard?" Mrs Moore asked her husband.
Mr Moore took an underground map out of his bag and studied it.

Übung 39: Lesen Sie weiter und unterstreichen Sie die englische Übersetzung der Wörter in Klammern!
(1. Verbindung, 2. stolz, 3. klingt, 4. Haltestellen, 5. zögerte, 6. Indizien, 7. aufklären)

"Let me see... Ah, here we are. We have to get on the Piccadilly Line here at Piccadilly Circus and get off at South Kensington, where there's a connection to the Circle Line. From there it's only two more stops to Victoria Street, where Scotland Yard is located."
"Well, that sounds simple enough," said Mrs Moore. "Did you remember the camera?"
"Of course, dear!" answered Mr Moore, *patting* his camera bag.
"Good! The police seem to think there could be very important *clues* on the *footage*. Who knows – we might help them solve the crime," said Mrs Moore proudly.
"Just as well I filmed then, eh?" Mr Moore said excitedly.

Mrs Moore hesitated and looked at her husband.
"Yes, maybe it was," she answered sceptically.
Mrs Moore looked at her watch.
"Oh, we'd better hurry along, I told Inspector Hudson we'd be there at six p.m. I don't want to keep him waiting."

Mr and Mrs Moore walked towards the underground.
Mr and Mrs Moore were standing in the underground station waiting for the train to arrive.
"I really wonder what Scotland Yard is like. I've only ever seen it on TV," Mrs Moore said.
Mr Moore got out his tourist guide of London and *flicked through* the pages.
"It says here that Scotland Yard is the *headquarters* of the Metropolitan Police Service, responsible for policing Greater London. It occupies a 20-storey office block."
"Why, that's huge, isn't it?" Mrs Moore said, impressed. "I wonder what the view is like from the top."

! ÜBUNG 40

Übung 40: Ersetzen Sie das unterstrichene Wort durch das Gegenteil!

1. They were walking in the underground station. ______
2. Inspector Hudson has often met Prince Vikram. ______
3. Scotland Yard's office building is huge. ______
4. Mrs Moore was very excited about going to Scotland Yard. ______
5. Mr Moore hates filming. ______
6. The Moores walked away from the underground. ______
7. Scotland Yard is easy to find. ______

A dark figure was *making* its *way* towards the area where Mr and Mrs Moore were standing. They were so busy talking that they did

not see the person *approach*. The dark figure managed to get right up to the Moores. The person *grabbed* the camera bag which Mr Moore was carrying over his shoulder.
"Hey!" Mr Moore shouted and turned around.
He nearly *jumped out of his skin* when he saw the masked person.
The dark figure *tugged* at the bag. Mr Moore would not let it go.
"Get off, you *scoundrel*!" he cried.
However, the mysterious person was stronger; he pulled the bag off Mr Moore's shoulder and ran. Mr and Mrs Moore chased the thief, who was already disappearing into the crowd.
"Stop him! Stop him!" Mr Moore cried.

Übung 41: Wie lauten die Imperative auf Englisch? Übersetzen Sie!

ÜBUNG 41 !

1. Geh! ____________________
2. Haltet sie! ____________________
3. Sag ihm das nicht! ____________________
4. Hör auf damit! ____________________
5. Lass mich in Ruhe! ____________________
6. Bleib hier! ____________________

The Moores got to the underground steps that led towards ground level. They were out of breath. The thief was far ahead. There was no chance of them catching him now. Just as he was climbing the last step, something fell out of his pocket – the thief did not notice and disappeared onto Piccadilly Circus.
"I think I have seen that person before – those *piercing* dark brown

eyes…Yes, it was the same person in black I saw at the Tower of London." Mr Moore *shuddered* and held on to the *railing*, *puffing* and *panting*.
"Well, that's the film *footage* gone!" *sighed* Mrs Moore, who was also breathing very heavily.
Mr Moore smiled and started to *fumble* around in his coat pocket.
"What are you smiling about? I don't think it's very funny!" Mrs Moore exclaimed.
Mr Moore took a cassette out of his pocket and waved it *slyly*.
"The cassette isn't in the camera. It's here."
Mrs Moore smiled back.
"Well done, Kevin, well done!" she *praised* him.
Mrs Moore started walking up the stairs.
"Where are you going?" Mr Moore asked.
"I'm going to get that knife the thief dropped. If that was the thief from the Tower, then that knife he dropped is *vital evidence*."
Mrs Moore *made* her *way* towards the knife lying at the top of the stairs.

! ÜBUNG 42

Übung 42: Beantworten Sie die Fragen zum Text!

1. Where were Mr and Mrs Moore staying?

____

2. Was the underground near the hotel?

____

3. Why do the police think Mr and Mrs Moore can help them?

____

4. Was the thief in the underground the same thief who stole the Kohinoor diamond?

---

5. What fell out of the thief's pocket?

---

6. Did the thief manage to steal the tape?

---

7. Which underground lines did the Moores take?

It was 6:40 p.m. by the time Mr and Mrs Moore reached Scotland Yard. They were taken immediately to Inspector Hudson's office, where he and Miss Elliot were waiting for them impatiently. Mr and Mrs Moore told him exactly what had happened.

"And you believe it to be the same person you saw during the robbery at the Tower?"

"Yes, definitely! I'll never forget those dark brown eyes."

"What height would you say the person was?"

"I'd say around 1.75m," Mr Moore answered.

"Anything else you noticed about the person – anything *distinctive*?"

"Not really," Mrs Moore replied. "Although the person was very slim…and built more like a woman than a man."

"Interesting!" Inspector Hudson remarked. "And that's all?"

"Yes, that's all we can really say about the thief."

"Well, if it was the same person, then he was obviously trying to get the tape," the inspector said.

ÜBUNG 43 !

Übung 43: Welcher Satz enthält die richtige Zeitform? Kreuzen Sie an!

1. Mr und Mrs Moore gingen die Treppe herunter.
   a) ☐ Mr and Mrs Moore walk down the stairs.
   b) ☐ Mr and Mrs Moore walked down the stairs.
   c) ☐ Mr and Mrs Moore had walked down the stairs.

2. Sie waren außer Atem.
   a) ☐ They were out of breath.
   b) ☐ They were going out of breath.
   c) ☐ They will be going out of breath.

3. Mr and Mrs Moore spazierten gerade zur U-Bahn.
   a) ☐ Mr and Mrs Moore walked to the underground.
   b) ☐ Mr and Mrs Moore walk to the underground.
   c) ☐ Mr and Mrs Moore were walking to the underground.

4. Inspector Hudson hat schon viele Fälle gelöst.
   a) ☐ Inspector Hudson solved many cases.
   b) ☐ Inspector Hudson has solved many cases.
   c) ☐ Inspector Hudson solves many cases.

5. Früher hat Mr Moore mehr fotografiert.
   a) ☐ Mr Moore used to take more pictures.
   b) ☐ Mr Moore was taking pictures earlier than usual.
   c) ☐ Mr Moore takes pictures early.

"I wonder how he knew about the *footage* and where to find Mr and Mrs Moore?" Elvira Elliot asked. "Only Marc Drum knew that Mr Moore was filming the *commotion* at the Tower."

"Has Mr Drum still not turned up?" Mrs Moore asked. "We read in the morning newspaper that he had *vanished*."
"No, I'm afraid not. He's still missing."
"Do you think he is in on the robbery?" Mr Moore *inquired*.
"Sorry, I can't answer your question – police internal information, if you know what I mean."
"Oh, of course, I understand completely," Mr Moore said.
"Well, thank you for bringing round the film material and answering our questions. You've been very helpful; we'll *be in touch*," Inspector Hudson said.
Mr and Mrs Moore shook hands with the inspector and Miss Elliot. Just as they were walking out of the door, Mrs Moore turned around.
"Oh, I nearly forgot!" she exclaimed. "The knife!"
Mrs Moore opened her handbag and took the folding knife out. Its silver handle *sparkled* in the office light.
"A knife?" the inspector asked.
"Yes, the thief dropped it as he escaped from the train."
Mrs Moore gave it to Inspector Hudson. He took a *handkerchief* out of his pocket and *took hold of* the knife. He looked at it in amazement and opened up the *blade*. The inspector *scrutinized* it.
"Very interesting, very interesting *indeed*," he remarked.
"It's beautiful, isn't it?" Mrs Moore said.
"Yes, it shows great *craftsmanship*."
Inspector Hudson *handed* it in the *handkerchief* to Miss Elliot. She looked at it – turning it around in her hand.
"What do you think?" the inspector asked.
"I'm not quite sure. Knives are not my speciality; however, it wasn't cheap, that's for sure. I'll have to do some research."
"Yes, and we'll have to check it for fingerprints as well," the inspector added, still looking at the knife.

Then he looked at Mr and Mrs Moore. He was very pleased with them.

"Thanks for your cooperation! You don't happen to be looking for a job with the London police," the inspector joked.

Mr and Mrs Moore shook their heads, smiling.

"No, thank you!" they *declined*. "I think we've had enough crime action to last us a lifetime."

Mr and Mrs Moore said goodbye and left the office.

ÜBUNG 44 !

Übung 44: Lesen Sie weiter und tragen Sie die Vergangenheitsform der angegebenen Verben ein!

Elvira Elliot (1. pick) ______________ up the knife again.

"Looks like something that could belong to an Indian prince," she remarked.

"What are you getting at?" (2. ask) ______________ the inspector, *puzzled*.

"I don't know, just a theory: Dark brown eyes, around 1.75m, *narrow-shouldered* and slim, and this extraordinary knife."

"We shouldn't *jump to conclusions* now, Miss Elliot. And anyway, I (3. think) ______________ he was your new best friend?"

Elvira Elliot (4. laugh) ______________.

"I (5. know) ______________ you were jealous, Inspector!" Elvira Elliot (6. tease) ______________ him.

Inspector Hudson (7. try) ________________ to ignore her remark. He picked up the tape, (8. walk) ________________ over to his video recorder and (9. *insert*) ________________ the tape. The recorder (10. *swallow*) ________________ it. The inspector (11. pull) ________________ his fingers back quickly as if he had just fed a dangerous animal.

"And just because I thought him to be stunningly attractive does not mean I believe he is as good a man as he looks."
"Well, you could have fooled me," the inspector *mumbled*.
"What?"
"I said: What motive do you think he has?"
"Oh, I thought that's what you said," Elvira Elliot *mocked* Inspector Hudson.
The inspector just *grunted*. He was desperately trying to find the video channel on the television.
"Are you all right there?" Elvira Elliot *inquired*.
"Yes, I'm perfectly fine!" Inspector Hudson answered, sounding irritated, while he nervously *fumbled* about with the *remote control*.
Elvira Elliot *sighed*.
"Anyway, as I told you this morning, India has *claimed* to be the *rightful* owner of the Kohinoor diamond more than once," she explained.
"Yes, I guess that could be a motive. It would also explain why only the Kohinoor was stolen and nothing else. Last but not least, he did meet up with our main *suspect,* Marc Drum. However, I'm not quite sure if we're on the right track there – after all, he is friendly with the Royal Family."
"Maybe you're right. Let's put Prince Vikram to one side for now and see what the video has to offer."

Übung 45: Welches Wort ist das „schwarze Schaf“?

1. suspect, disregard, guess, assume
2. last, second, first, three
3. motive, aim, why, reason
4. worse, worst, terrible, bad
5. perfectly, carefully, sadly, good
6. day, morning, afternoon, evening
7. track, search, hunt, path

Inspector Hudson started the tape. At first, all they could see and hear was smoke and people shouting and screaming. The camera work was also very *shaky*.

"That looks *terrifying*," Miss Elliot commented on the *footage*.

"It sure does!" the inspector said.

He *fast-forwarded* the tape until he got to the bit where they could hear the *Beefeater* shouting for help. They could hear his voice, but he could not be seen. There was still a lot of smoke around and the camera was constantly shaking. You could also hear Mr and Mrs Moore's voices commenting on what was happening. They *made* their *way* towards the *Beefeater*. The smoke had cleared a little and Inspector Hudson and Elvira Elliot saw Marc Drum sitting against the wall. He was holding his *bleeding* head.

"It certainly looks like a real wound to me," Elvira Elliot said. Suddenly Mr Moore moved the camera down.

"What is he doing!" exclaimed Miss Elliot. "It was just starting to get interesting!"

"He's probably trying to help Marc Drum to his feet," answered the inspector. "But I think I'll *rewind* it back to the bit where he was *approaching* Marc Drum and put the *recording* into slow motion – maybe we missed something."

"I was looking very carefully. I don't think there was anything to see," Miss Elliot said.
"Just wait and see. This is the latest technology. I can even zoom in on things like that."

Übung 46: Welche Gegenteile gehören zusammen? Ordnen Sie zu!

ÜBUNG 46 !

1. real	☐ let go
2. hold	☐ play
3. fast-forward	☐ hit
4. miss	☐ vague
5. clear	☐ rewind
6. whisper	☐ false
7. record	☐ scream

Miss Elvira folded her arms and watched the inspector sceptically. Inspector Hudson *rewound* the tape. He pressed the play button, but the tape kept on *rewinding*.
"Oh, this is such a stupid thing!" he complained.
Elvira Elliot rolled her eyes, but said nothing.
Inspector Hudson eventually managed to get the *recording* to where he wanted it and played the whole scene again in slow motion.
"All I can see is slow smoke!" *mocked* Miss Elliot.
Inspector Hudson ignored her. He was concentrating on what was happening on the screen. Suddenly, just faintly through the smoke, two shadows were visible.
"What's that?" Miss Elliot exclaimed.
One of the dark figures *appeared* to be a *Beefeater*. You could tell by the shape of the hat. He seemed to be gesturing.

ÜBUNG 47 !

Übung 47: Lesen Sie weiter und unterstreichen Sie alle sechs Adverbien im folgenden Abschnitt!

Inspector Hudson turned around and smiled triumphantly.
"Looks like our *Beefeater* had a lively conversation before he was hit on the head."
The *recording* went on. They could see the *Beefeater handing* something to the person dressed in black.
"Was that the *Queen's Keys*?" Elvira Elliot asked.
She moved up closer to the screen so she could see exactly what was going on.
"I'm quite sure it was the *Queen's Keys*," the inspector answered calmly.
With amazement, Elvira Elliot and Inspector Hudson watched the person in black hitting Marc Drum hard on the head. He fell to the ground. The black figure disappeared as if it had become *invisible*.
"Where did he go?" Miss Elliot exclaimed.
"No, idea!" *shrugged* the inspector. "But it might be the same person Mr Moore ran into earlier. Remember he said he was a fast mover – like an animal of prey."
"Wow!" said Elvira Elliot. "It's like in one of these crime movies!"
Inspector Hudson shook his head *disapprovingly*.
"Nothing we experience on a day-to-day basis has anything to do with crime movies!" he said, almost *reproachfully*.

Elvira Elliot *shrugged*.
"If you say so – I didn't know you *detested* crime fiction."
"I don't *detest* it; I just don't think it's very realistic. But let's turn our attention back to the *recording*. It certainly looks like Marc Drum is in on the robbery."
"Yes, there's no doubt about that. His whole *alleged* injury was a

set-up and he obviously *deliberately deceived* the other guards."
"That's right. And now we know for sure why he went missing – or perhaps I should say why he has *gone into hiding*."
"So that's one down, but who are his *accomplices*?"
"Good question. At least we know for sure that Marc Drum has something to do with the robbery; and he could never have *pulled* it *off* on his own."
"Yes, and one of his *accomplices* seems to have some kind of artistic skills. We're looking for someone who does gymnastics, climbing or specializes in some form of *martial arts*."
"And who obviously has a taste for extravagant knives," Miss Elliot added, pointing to the knife lying on the table.
Inspector Hudson nodded, agreeing fully with Miss Elliot.

Übung 48: Setzen Sie die richtige Zukunftsform ***will*** *oder* ***going to*** *in die Lücken ein!*

1. "Don't worry, we ________________ find the thieves soon!" Inspector Hudson said to Sir Reginald.
2. Miss Elliot and the inspector ________________ have the knife examined.
3. Inspector Hudson ________________ catch the thieves if it is the last thing he ever does.
4. Mrs Moore says she ________________ help find the thief.
5. The investigators ________________ look for an acrobat.
6. I have decided that I ________________ become a policeman.

"Let's have another look at the tape," suggested the inspector. "Maybe I can identify somebody in the crowd – a known criminal for example. It wouldn't surprise me if the robbers had somebody in amongst the tourists."
"Well, maybe you're right," *sighed* Miss Elliot. "I just hope my eyes aren't square by the end of the night."
Inspector Hudson *rewound* the tape and replayed it again.

ÜBUNG 49 !

Übung 49: Bilden Sie die Verlaufsform mit ***we are****!*

1. take ______________________
2. prefer ______________________
3. travel ______________________
4. lie ______________________
5. run ______________________
6. hum ______________________

Two hours later they were still analysing the tape. However, they did not see anything *suspicious*.
"Oh, not again!" Miss Elliot exclaimed as Inspector Hudson *rewound* the tape once more. "We've already watched it about ten times."
"Just once more and then we can finish for the night."
"If you must!" answered Elvira Elliot, a little annoyed.
The inspector was watching the tape *recording* again. Elvira Elliot was falling asleep. All of a sudden he let out a cry: "I've got something. At last! I knew there was something out there!"
Elvira Elliot *started* out of her *slumber* and moved up to the screen.

Übung 50: Lesen Sie weiter und setzen Sie für die Wörter in Klammern deren Gegenteil ein!

Inspector Hudson pointed at a middle-aged (1. hairy) ______________ man with a *moustache*. He was in amongst a crowd of people rushing (2. away from) ______________ the Tower exit.

"That's David Bucket!" he exclaimed.

"Who is David Bucket?" Miss Elliot (3. replied) ______________.

"He's a known criminal – has done a few bank robberies in his time. He just got out of jail not too (4. short) ______________ ago. I wonder what he is doing there."

"He's probably not there to enjoy the *Ceremony of the Keys*," Elvira Elliot remarked dryly.

"You can be (5. uncertain) ______________ about that. I think we should pay him a visit. I'll get one of my men to find out where he is (6. dying) ______________ and then we'll bring him in."

"If he has not disappeared like Marc Drum has," Miss Elliot said.

"Let's (7. to fear) ______________ not." Inspector Hudson looked at his watch. "It's (8. early) ______________. We should get some sleep."

Elvira Elliot stretched and *yawned*. "Yes, (9. bad) ______________ idea. It's been a very long day."

"It sure has been. My men will see to David Bucket. If they get him tonight, we can question him first thing in the morning."
The inspector and Miss Elliot left the office.

Chapter 6: Mingling with the Stars

The next day, Elvira Elliot and Inspector Hudson were sitting in the inspector's office at Scotland Yard again. The inspector was sitting in his chair and Miss Elliot was leaning against the wall. They were both drinking a steaming cup of tea when the office door opened. Sir Reginald walked in *briskly*. He was carrying newspapers under his arm.
"Good morning, Miss Elliot, good morning, Inspector!"
"Good morning!" they answered.
"What was all this about?"
Sir Reginald put the morning newspaper on the table. There was a huge picture of the inspector, showing him pushing a camera man away. It looked very violent. The *headline* was: "London Police Take Brutal Measures!" Inspector Hudson looked at the paper. He *shrugged* and took a sip of tea.
"I was just getting them off Mrs Drum's *premises* – they had no right to be there," the inspector said calmly.
"Well, it was also wrong of you to push them onto the street so violently," Sir Reginald said, a little angrily.
Inspector Hudson looked over at Elvira Elliot, who smiled *reassuringly* at him.
"They just wouldn't leave poor Mrs Drum alone," she *intervened*. "What Inspector Hudson did was fully justified."
Sir Reginald looked back and forth between the inspector and Miss Elliot. Despite his anger he had to smile.

"You two seem to be getting along fine these days," he said, with a slight hint of sarcasm in his voice.
Sir Reginald opened up another newspaper. The *headline* read: "Scotland Yard still fishing in the dark. Has the Kohinoor diamond gone forever?" He showed them another *headline*: "What's next – Buckingham Palace?"

Übung 51: Lesen Sie weiter und unterstreichen Sie das im Kontext passende Wort!

"As you can see, the (1.) *pressure*/television is on. You know I hate bad (2.) people/publicity and as you can imagine, my phone has not stopped (3.) ringing/knocking all morning: The *Home Secretary*, the Queen's private (4.) secretary/guard – to name but two! So tell me, Inspector, how is the (5.) invasion/investigation coming along?"
"I'm glad you *got round to* that, Sir," the inspector said, (6.) *relieved*/released.
"First of all, we have (7.) *evidence*/confirmation that Marc Drum has something to do with the robbery."
"Marc Drum – the Chief *Yeoman Warder*?" Sir Reginald asked in (8.) disbelieve/disbelief.

"Yes, I'm afraid so!"
"Oh dear, of all things…" Sir Reginald was lost for words. "This country is going downhill faster than I thought! No room for honour and integrity anymore, eh?" he *carried on* in a very disappointed, almost sad tone. "Why would he do such a thing – a man of his position?"
"We don't know yet. He might have money problems we *are*

unaware of; he might have been forced into doing it. At the moment we have no answers to that question," answered Inspector Hudson.
"Do you have any answers at all?" asked Sir Reginald impatiently.
The Inspector took a deep breath. He was trying to control his anger.
"Yes, in fact we do! We know Drum had probably at least two *accomplices*. We have already identified one of the *suspects*. His name is David Bucket. My men have found out that he works as a *caretaker* at Madame Tussaud's. We're going to take him in for questioning as soon as he shows up at work."
"And the second *accomplice*?"
"We don't know the identity of the second person. However, we have a vague description of him. We also believe him to be an expert in gymnastics or acrobatics."
"I see," Sir Reginald said thoughtfully.
At that moment someone knocked on the door. Sergeant Wood entered. He greeted everyone and turned his attention towards the inspector.
"I've just been contacted by our man observing Madame Tussaud's. David Bucket has arrived."
"Very good, Sergeant!" Inspector Hudson said and *grabbed* his coat. "Let's go and arrest him!"
Elvira Elliot, Sergeant Wood and the inspector said goodbye to Sir Reginald. He wished them luck.

ÜBUNG 52 !

*Übung 52: Vervollständigen Sie die Sätze mit **ago**, **during**, oder **last**!*

1. Sir Reginald walked into Inspector Hudson's office ________ his tea break.

2. ______________ week's newspaper was full of bad news.

3. It was a while ______________ since Reginald had been so angry.

4. Elvira Elliot lost her purse ______________ Wednesday.

5. He was much happier two weeks ______________.

6. The suspect was very nervous ______________ the interview.

Inspector Hudson, Elvira Elliot, Sergeant Wood and three uniformed policemen stood on the pavement at the opposite side of the road from Madame Tussaud's – a very famous wax figure museum in London. It was originally founded by the wax *sculptress* Marie Tussaud in 1835. At that time, the wax museum had been located in Baker Street. Today, Madam Tussaud's is located on Marylebone Road in London. Walking along the street one can hardly miss the museum because of its *distinctive* green *dome*-shaped roof.

Übung 53: Setzen Sie, wenn nötig, das passende Relativpronomen ein!

ÜBUNG 53 !

1. Inspector Hudson, __________ works for Scotland Yard, told his men exactly what to do.

2. David Bucket works at Madame Tussaud's, __________ is on Marylebone Road.

3. The investigators don't know __________ the second thief is.

4. The day __________ the robbery occurred, David Bucket was at the Tower.

5. Marie Tussaud was the woman __________ founded Madame Tussaud's.
6. Elvira Elliot, __________ hair is red, likes the Savoy.

"When does the museum open?" Inspector Hudson asked Sergeant Wood.
"It opens at 9:30 a.m."
The inspector looked at his watch.
"That means we have half an hour to bring David Bucket in, before the museum opens. We don't want to cause any publicity whatsoever. And we should create as little of a *fuss* as possible," Inspector Hudson instructed his men. They nodded approvingly. With this, the policemen and Miss Elliot started to walk across the road, *heading* straight towards the entrance of Madame Tussaud's.
The woman behind the ticket counter did not even look up when Inspector Hudson stood in front of her.
"We don't open until half past nine!" she said.

ÜBUNG 54 !

Übung 54: Schreiben Sie die Uhrzeit aus!

1. 06:30 *half past six*
2. 10:10 __________
3. 03:15 __________
4. 08:35 __________
5. 12:45 __________
6. 07:55 __________
7. 05:05 __________

Inspector Hudson placed his *badge* on the counter. The woman looked up. She *started* when she saw the large group of policemen standing in front of her. She looked nervously at Inspector Hudson and then at his *badge*.
"Is there anything wrong?" she asked, looking up *anxiously* again.
"Nothing to be alarmed about," the inspector answered. "Where can we find Mr David Bucket?"
"David?" she asked in *astonishment*. "He should be doing his rounds, checking the wax figures – seeing if everything is in place. If you just walk in that direction, you will find him."
Inspector Hudson thanked the woman. He and his men *headed for* the wax figure show rooms. They walked past celebrities, politicians, well-known actors and musicians, and famous cooks such as Jamie Oliver.
Elvira Elliot looked around in amazement.
"They look so real!" she said to Inspector Hudson, looking at a wax figure of Johnny Depp. He was dressed up as a pirate.

Übung 55: Unterstreichen und verbessern Sie im folgenden Textabschnitt die sechs falsch geschriebenen Wörter!

ÜBUNG 55 !

"You can say that again!" remarcked Sergeant Wood, who was eyeing up a life-like image of Britney Spears in a very short skirt.
"Keep your eyes out for David Bucket!" the inspector *admonished* his collegue.
Inspector Hudson suddenly stoped his men. He put his finger to his lips signalling everybody to be quite. In the distance they could here somebody *whistling*. It was the tune of the song "New York, New York" by Frank Sinatra.
"That could be our man," Inspector Hudson wispered.

1. ______________________

2. ______________________

3. ______________________

4. ______________________

5. ______________________

6. ______________________

"Or it's old Frankie boy come to life!" *smirked* one of the police-men quietly.

One of his colleagues in uniform laughed as well. Inspector Hud-son gave them a *disapproving* look.

They fell silent *straight away*.

"No time for jokes just now, men," he whispered. "Let's move in on Bucket, but carefully."

Elvira Elliot and the group of policemen *sneaked up* on the person, following the sound of the *whistling*. Eventually they could see a man in the distance. He was *inspecting* the wax figures.

"That's David Bucket," said the inspector in a low voice. They all tried to hide behind wax figures so that the *suspect* could not see them.

Inspector Hudson was hiding behind Winston Churchill. Elvira Elliot chose the Dalai Lama, who was smiling peacefully at *nothing in particular*.

David Bucket was standing in front of a wax figure of the Queen. He smiled at it.

"Care to dance?" he said to the Queen and *bowed*.

The policemen looked at each other. They were very amused.

"Not in the mood for talking today, eh?" David Bucket *carried on*. "Are you sad about the Kohinoor diamond?"

David Bucket *bent* over to the Queen's ear.

"Don't worry, I'm sure it's in a safe place," he whispered and walked on, *whistling* the Frank Sinatra tune.

Übung 56: Ergänzen Sie die Sätze mit dem passenden Question Tag!

ÜBUNG 56 !

1. Inspector Hudson would never buy a sports car, *would he*?
2. Elvira Elliot would always help Inspector Hudson, ______________?
3. Madame Tussaud was a very hard-working lady, ______________?
4. The Dalai Lama is a very peaceful man, ______________?
5. Britney Spears has great legs, ______________?
6. Johnny Depp can really act, ______________?
7. David Bucket stole the diamond, ______________?
8. They will catch the suspect, ______________?

The policemen and Elvira Elliot came out from their *hiding places* and moved on. David Bucket stopped at the Robbie Williams wax figure. He was holding two women in his arms. They were both kissing him on the *cheek*.

"Well, *it's all right for some*!" said David Bucket to the *motionless* figure.

Übung 57: Setzen Sie die folgenden Wörter in die Lücken!
(dashing, heading, sneak, bumped, opposite, crashed, near)

ÜBUNG 57 !

Inspector Hudson signalled to his men that it was time to arrest David Bucket. He indicated to the three uniformed policemen to (1.) ______________ over to the (2.) ______________ side, so that

David Bucket was surrounded by them. All of a sudden one of them *accidentally* knocked over one of the Spice Girls. The figure (3.) ________________ to the ground. David Bucket looked up and saw the policemen. He started to run. The policemen ran after him. "Stop! Police!" they shouted.

Sergeant Wood, Elvira Elliot and Inspector Hudson followed them. They were all running through Madame Tussaud's – *dodging* famous people, (4.) ________________ around stunning celebrities. Sergeant Wood (5.) ________________ right into Prince Charles, he fell over. He stopped and lifted him up.

"Sorry about that!" he said as he quickly *brushed* the dust *off* of the wax figure's dinner jacket.

The sergeant ran on. (6.) ________________ the entrance they were eventually catching up with David Bucket, who ran out onto the street. The policemen and Elvira Elliot were close behind him. He was running down Marylebone Street. He *appeared* to be (7.) ________________ for the underground station closest to Madame Tussaud's – Baker Street.

"We need to reach him before he gets into the underground!" Inspector Hudson shouted.

He was extremely out of breath. Sergeant Wood and the three uni-

formed policemen *speeded* up. The sergeant was only two metres away from David Bucket now. He jumped and *grabbed* the *suspect's* jumper. They both fell to the ground. David Bucket tried to fight Sergeant Wood off. The three other men hurried to his assistance. *In no time* David Bucket was in *handcuffs* and pulled back up on his feet. Inspector Hudson and Elvira Elliot arrived.
"What do you want? I didn't do anything!" *barked* David Bucket.
"Really?" Inspector Hudson said *sardonically*. "How about stealing the Kohinoor diamond? Is that nothing?"
"That's not true!" panicked David Bucket.
"Well, we'll take you in for questioning anyway, Mr Bucket."
Two policemen took David Bucket to the police car and sat him in the backseat.

Übung 58: Setzen Sie die passende Verbform ein!

David Bucket was (1. sit) ____________ in the *interrogation* room. Elvira Elliot and Inspector Hudson could (2. see) ____________ him from the other side. They were behind a glass mirror.
"Do you think he'll talk?" Elvira Elliot (3. ask) ____________.
"I think so – eventually," Inspector Hudson answered. "But Sergeant Wood will probably have to bluff."
Sergeant Wood (4. enter) ____________ the *interrogation* room.
"So are you (5. go) ____________ to tell me what exactly you were doing at the *Ceremony of the Keys*?" he asked the *suspect*.
"As I said, I wanted to see the show."

"You're still trying to tell me you were there for fun? Come on, Bucket!" the sergeant (6. exclaim) ____________________. "Do you really think I (7. believe) ____________________ you've turned into a culture lover overnight?"

"Why not?"

"Because you don't even know where Buckingham Palace is!"

"Yes, I do!" (8. insist) ________________ David Bucket.

"Where is it then?"
David Bucket thought hard for a moment.
"I can't remember at the moment," he *stammered*. "But if you let me think for a minute…"
Sergeant Wood banged his fist angrily on the table.
"We don't have time for thinking!" he said impatiently. "We want the truth."
David Bucket looked *upset*.

ÜBUNG 59 !

Übung 59: Welche Substantive werden immer groß geschrieben? Kreuzen Sie an!

1. thursday ☐
2. world war II ☐
3. prince ☐
4. doctor ☐
5. tower bridge ☐
6. december ☐
7. inspector ☐

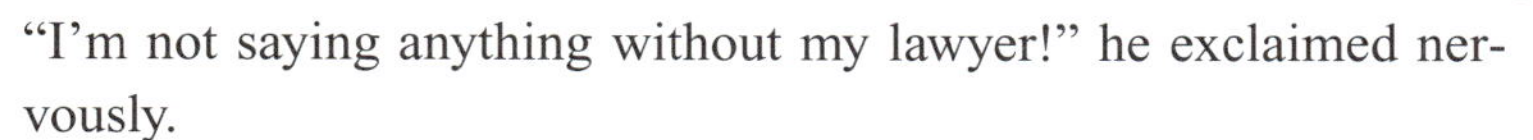

"I'm not saying anything without my lawyer!" he exclaimed nervously.

"Lawyer?" laughed Sergeant Wood. "How are you going to explain to your lawyer that we actually have *footage* showing you holding the Kohinoor diamond?"

"What?" David Bucket asked *anxiously*.

"You heard what I said."

David Bucket looked *tensely* at his hands. He turned and faced the mirror. Then he looked back at the sergeant.

"You've really got me then," he said sadly.

"You can say that again, Bucket!"

David Bucket sat in silence.

"I want names. Who is in on this? Marc Drum? And who is the masked person?"

"I don't know!" *mumbled* David Bucket.

"What? Speak up, I can't hear you!"

"I said, I don't know!"

"What do you mean, you don't know?"

"I don't know if Marc Drum has anything to do with the robbery and I don't know who the masked person is."

"Well, you're a great help, aren't you?" the sergeant *mocked*. "Are you trying to tell me you're in on the robbery alone?"

"No, no – certainly not!" panicked David Bucket. "I had almost nothing to do with the whole thing!"

"You could have fooled me!"

"No, it's true. All I did was smuggle the diamond out of the Tower. The masked person gave it to me. But I have no idea who he is."

"Liar!"

"No, honest," David Bucket *stammered*. "That's all I did. All contact was done over the phone."

"What was the person's voice like?"

"I have no idea. It sounded very strange, almost mechanical."
"He probably used a *voice modifier*," Inspector Hudson said to Elvira Elliot. She nodded.

! ÜBUNG 60

Übung 60: Geben Sie die richtigen Formen von ***to do*** *mit* ***he*** *an!*

1. einfache Gegenwart ______________
2. Verlaufsform der Gegenwart ______________
3. Einfache Vergangenheit ______________
4. Verlaufsform der Vergangenheit ______________
5. Perfekt ______________
6. Verlaufsform des Perfekt ______________
7. Zukunft mit "going to" ______________
8. Zukunft mit "will" ______________

"So what did you do with the diamond? Did you take it home and hide it in your *closet*?"
"No, I hid it in a hole beside the altar in St. Paul's Cathedral."
Elvira Elliot and Inspector Hudson looked at each other.
"I hope you are not lying again?" Sergeant Wood asked *firmly*.
"It's true. There was a loose stone, I picked it up and underneath there was a hole. I put the diamond into it."
"How much did you get for your services, Bucket?"
"Enough!"
"How much, I asked?"
"10,000 pounds!"
Sergeant Wood *whistled*.

Übung 61: Setzen Sie, wenn notwendig, den passenden Artikel ein!

ÜBUNG 61

1. David Bucket hid the diamond in the hole beside ______ altar.
2. For his help he did not get ______ 1,000 pounds, but actually 10,000 pounds.
3. With the money he was going to buy himself ______ new house.
4. However, David Bucket felt so bad he went to ______ church.
5. After Sergeant Wood got ______ information, he whistled.
6. It took him over two hours to get ______ truth out of him.
7. The Kohinoor diamond is kept in ______ safe place.
8. David Bucket is certainly going to ______ prison.

"Now that's a lot of money!"
"Yes, it is. I really needed it…I know it was stupid," said David Bucket in a *remorseful* voice.
"Yes, it certainly was stupid. You can say that again."
Sergeant Wood left the room. On the other side of the mirror, Inspector Hudson's mobile phone rang. It was Inspector Reid from the Murder Investigation Team.
"I thought it might interest you to know that we've just fished a body out of the Thames," Inspector Reid said dryly.
"Who?"
"We're not quite sure, but he is wearing a *Beefeater's* outfit and I somehow don't think it's a *drunk* from last year's Halloween," she answered.
"Where exactly are you?" the inspector asked.
"Very close to the Tower Bridge. You can't miss us."

"Okay, I'll be over *straight away*!"
The inspector put his mobile back in his pocket.

ÜBUNG 62 !

Übung 62: Geben Sie die Pluralform an!

1. body ____________	6. day ____________
2. river ____________	7. woman driver ____________
3. wife ____________	8. knife ____________
4. bus ____________	9. box ____________
5. sheep ____________	10. policeman ____________

"Who was that?"
"Inspector Reid from the Murder Investigation Team."
"Oh, that can't be good news," Miss Elliot said worriedly.
"No, it isn't. They have just fished a dead man dressed in *Beefeater* clothes out of the Thames."
"Marc Drum?" Elvira Elliot asked *anxiously*.
"They don't know yet, but we should get down there *straight away* to clarify who it is."
They opened the door and nearly *bumped into* Sergeant Wood, who was holding a cup of coffee.

ÜBUNG 63 !

Übung 63: Setzen Sie das richtige Fragewort ein!

1. ____________ is Inspector Reid at the moment?
2. ____________ does she work for?

3. ____________ body did she find?

4. ____________ part of London is she in?

5. ____________ did she call Inspector Hudson?

6. ____________ is her job?

7. ____________ did they fish out of the Thames?

8. ____________ did David Bucket hide the diamond?

"Where are you off to in such a rush? Don't you think I did a great job?"
"Excellent!" smiled Elvira Elliot.
"But I thought we could talk about it," the sergeant insisted.
"Later, Sergeant, later!" said Inspector Hudson. "We're off to the Thames."
"The Thames?" he asked, a little *puzzled*.
"Yes, they just found a body."
"Oh! I see. Anybody we know?" the sergeant asked.
"Maybe, but we'll soon see."
Elvira Elliot and Inspector Hudson said goodbye.
"What shall I do with David Bucket?" Sergeant Wood shouted to his *superior*.
"Get him a lawyer. I'm more than sure he's going to need one!" Inspector Hudson answered.

Chapter 7: The Royal Suspect

Elvira Elliot and Inspector Hudson arrived at the crime scene on the banks of the River Thames near the Tower Bridge. Police lights were *flashing*, policemen and women were moving about. The two *investigators* had to fight their way through a group of *spectators* who were curious to see what was going on. The Tower Bridge was about 200 metres away from the place where the *drowned Beefeater* had been found. It was very close to the Tower of London. That's where it got its name.

ÜBUNG 64 !

Übung 64: Verbinden Sie die beiden Sätze, indem Sie einen zu einem Relativsatz umformulieren!

1. Inspector Hudson arrived at the crime scene. It was near the Thames.

   Inspector Hudson arrived at the crime scene which was near the Thames.

2. They fought their way through curious spectators. They were in the way.

   ____

3. The Tower was close to the bridge. The Tower could be seen in the distance.

   ____

4. It was not good news. The body was found near the Thames.

   ____

5. Inspector Reid was working in the distance. She could see them coming.

   ____

6. Sergeant Wood was holding a cup of coffee. They nearly bumped into him.

The Tower Bridge, with its two tall towers, has become a well-known symbol of London. It is often wrongly called London Bridge, which is in fact the next bridge upstream.

Inspector Hudson lifted the police barrier and let Miss Elliot pass through. He followed. In the background you could see policemen dressed in white overalls; some of them were scanning the area around the body for *clues*, others were examining the body.

Inspector Reid – a tall, short-haired woman – looked up and saw Inspector Hudson. She walked towards him. They greeted each other and the inspector introduced Elvira Elliot to her.

"So what have we got?" the inspector asked, as they walked towards the body.

"The body is male, between fifty and sixty. He was obviously a *Beefeater* – he is still wearing his costume. And he probably *drowned*, but we won't know for sure until the autopsy has been done."

Inspector Hudson looked at Miss Elliot.

"Sounds like the man we're looking for!" he said. "Does he have a wound at the head?"

"Let's take a look."

They had almost reached the body, which was *spread* out on the bank. Inspector Reid turned to Elvira Elliot.

"It's not a pleasant sight."

"It's okay," the insurance *investigator* answered bravely. "It's not my first!"

"Oh, I see," Inspector Reid said. "But be prepared," she added.

ÜBUNG 65 !

Übung 65: Lesen Sie weiter und unterstreichen Sie alle sieben Phrasal Verbs!

When they reached the body, Elvira Elliot nervously *stroked* her hair away from her face. Inspector Hudson looked at her *reassuringly*. She smiled back at him.
"This is him," Inspector Reid said.
Inspector Hudson looked down at the body.
"Yes, that's Marc Drum," he said without *flinching*.
"He's been in the water for a while, that's why he's a bit *swollen* up," Inspector Reid said.
Elvira Elliot looked away.
"Are you okay?" Inspector Hudson asked. "You look a little pale."
"I'm fine," Elvira Elliot replied, pulling herself together again.
"Was he murdered?" Inspector Hudson asked Mrs Reid.
"Yes, it looks very much like it. His hands and legs were tied together. He was also weighed down by a few heavy stones."

"So do you think he was *drowned* somewhere near here?" the inspector asked.
"Yes, he could not get far with those weights holding him down."
Inspector Hudson looked in the direction of the Tower Bridge.
"How long do you think he has been dead?" he asked thoughtfully.
"I'd say around two, maybe three days," Inspector Reid answered.
"He could have been killed the same night as the robbery," Miss Elliot said.
"That was just what I was thinking," the inspector replied.
He turned towards Inspector Reid.
"I think we've seen enough for just now, we'll leave you to it," Inspector Hudson said to her.
Inspector Reid nodded.

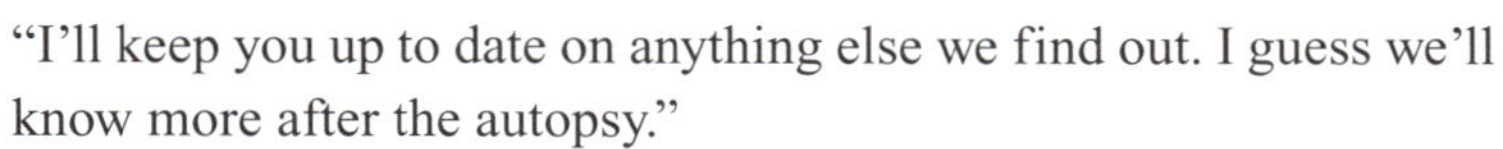

"I'll keep you up to date on anything else we find out. I guess we'll know more after the autopsy."
Inspector Reid said goodbye and turned her attention back to her work. Elvira Elliot and Inspector Hudson walked away from the body.

Übung 66: Lesen Sie weiter und setzen Sie die richtige Präposition ein!

ÜBUNG 66 !

"Do you think he was murdered (1.) ________ his *accomplice*?" Miss Elliot asked.

"Could well be!"

"But why?"

"I don't know yet. But it sure doesn't look like he was murdered (2.) ________ sudden rage or something like that."

"Yes, it looks planned. Just look (3.) ________ the ropes and the heavy stones – looks very much like the murderer was prepared," Miss Elliot added.

"Maybe Marc Drum was used (4.) ________ the beginning. He was the best person to have (5.) ________ the team if you wanted to get to the Crown Jewels. He knew all the *safety regulations*, just everything."

"They must have offered him a great *reward* (6.) ________ his help. Otherwise I cannot understand why he did it."

"Yes, it is strange because only the most loyal get a job like he had," the inspector said thoughtfully. "I really do wonder what made him do it. He obviously met his murderer soon (7.) ________ the robbery – their meeting point was probably somewhere very close (8.) ________ the Tower."

"Where do we go from here?" Elvira Elliot asked.
"I guess first of all we have to tell Mrs Drum."
"Oh, dear! The poor woman will be *devastated*!" Elvira Elliot *sighed*.
Inspector Hudson nodded. They walked towards the car in silence.

The inspector was just about to ring Mrs Drum's doorbell when the door opened. A tall man in his mid thirties nearly *bumped into* him.
"Oh, I'm sorry!" he exclaimed.
Mrs Drum *popped* her head out.
"Inspector Hudson!" she said, sounding surprised.
"Yes, hello!" he said *grimly*.
Inspector Hudson looked at the man.
"Don't I know you from somewhere?"
The man stretched out his hand.
"Yes, Inspector, I work at the Tower. I'm a guard. We met the night of the robbery."
"Ah, yes, exactly!"
The two men shook hands.
"Mr Gunn, wasn't it?" the inspector *inquired*.
"Yes, that's me! How are things getting along, Edith and I are worried sick. Have you heard anything about Marc? You don't really believe he has anything to do with the robbery, do you?" Craig

Gunn was smiling politely at the inspector.
"My colleague and I would like to talk to Mrs Drum privately, if you don't mind," Inspector Hudson said.
"Oh, yes, of course!" Craig Gunn replied, a little *taken aback*.
He *glanced* at Edith Drum. She nodded as if to say it was okay.
Craig Gunn said goodbye and left.

Übung 67: Übersetzen Sie und enträtseln Sie das Lösungswort!

ÜBUNG 67

1. nervös _ _ _ _ _ _ ☐
2. Mörder _ ☐ _ _ _ _ _ _
3. Kollegen _ _ _ _ _ _ _ _ _ ☐
4. Zuschauer _ ☐ _ _ _ _ _ _ _
5. zögern _ ☐ _ _ _ _ _ _
6. Komplize _ _ ☐ _ _ _ _ _ _ _
7. strecken _ ☐ _ _ _ _ _

Lösung: _ _ _ _ _ _ _

"Come in!" Mrs Drum said to the *investigators*.
Elvira Elliot and Inspector Hudson entered the house.
"Are you and Mr Gunn close?" the inspector asked.
"We get along very well, yes, if that's what you mean," Mrs Drum answered. "He and my husband are good friends."
"Are they? You never mentioned that," Inspector Hudson said.
"Well, you never asked," Mrs Drum replied.
Mrs Drum led them into the living room.
"Please sit down," she said.
Elvira Elliot and Inspector Hudson did not move. They looked sad and serious. The inspector did not like the task before him.

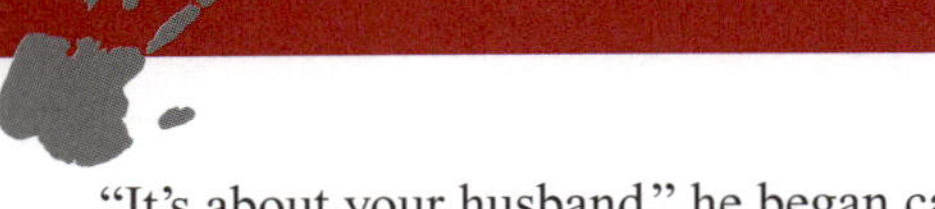

"It's about your husband," he began carefully.
"Marc? Have you heard anything? Is he okay?"
"I'm very sorry to tell you this...but your husband is dead," Inspector Hudson said.
Edith Drum looked at the *investigators* as if she was checking to see whether this was all a big joke.
"You're serious!"
Elvira Elliot and Inspector Hudson nodded sadly. Mrs Drum put her hand to her mouth.
"Oh, my God! Oh, my God!" she kept on repeating.

! ÜBUNG 68

Übung 68: Welche Sätze sind fehlerfrei? Markieren Sie mit richtig ✔ oder falsch – !

1. Mrs Drum popped her head away. ☐
2. It was the brutalest murder the inspector had ever seen. ☐
3. Yesterday the investigators will visit Mrs Drum. ☐
4. Tomorrow Inspector Reid is going to take a break. ☐
5. Mrs Drum wants the thief to go to prison. ☐
6. "You have found him, hasn't you?" Mrs Drum asked. ☐
7. Marc Drum had been missing since three days. ☐

Mrs Drum fell to the floor and started to *cry* her *heart out*. Miss Elliot tried to help her to her feet, but she refused to move. Edith Drum started to scream and beat her fists against the floor.
"Maybe you should call an ambulance," Miss Elliot said to the inspector. "I think she'll *crack up* if she doesn't get any *tranquillizers*."
Inspector Hudson took out his mobile phone and called an ambulance. Elvira Elliot tried to calm Mrs Drum down, but nothing

helped. It did not take long for the ambulance to arrive. By this time, Edith Drum was lying *motionless* on the floor. She *appeared* to have *fainted*. The *paramedics* rushed in and took her into the ambulance. Elvira Elliot and Inspector Hudson watched it *speed* away.

Übung 69: Present Simple oder Present Progressive? Unterstreichen Sie die richtige Variante!

ÜBUNG 69 !

1. Inspector Hudson is calling/calls an ambulance at the moment.
2. Miss Elvira always drives/is driving too fast.
3. Elvira Elliot believes/is believing Mrs Drum is going to crack up.
4. Mrs Drum has/is having a nervous breakdown.
5. Calming her down does not help/is not helping.
6. Craig Gunn says/is saying goodbye and leaves/is leaving.

"Poor soul, she must have loved her husband very much!" Miss Elvira said sadly.
"Yes," Inspector Hudson *sighed*. "We'll have to talk to her about her husband later, when she's feeling a little better."
"I guess it's time for another tourist tour!" Miss Elliot said in a more cheerful tone.
Inspector Hudson gave her a *puzzled* look. Then all of a sudden he understood what she meant.
"Of course, St. Paul's Cathedral!" the inspector exclaimed. "Where David Bucket *allegedly* placed the Kohinoor."
"Exactly!"
"I'm already *eager* to see if his story is true."
They walked towards the car.

A little later, Elvira Elliot and Inspector Hudson entered the cathedral. As it was close to closing time, it was not as busy as on their last visit. This made the cathedral seem even larger – like the inside of some gigantic ship. The *investigators* walked up the *nave* straight towards the altar. They climbed up the stone steps and started walking around the altar.

ÜBUNG 70 !

Übung 70: Welche Synonyme gehören zusammen?

1. cathedral	☐ within
2. ship	☐ huge
3. large	☐ comprehend
4. enter	☐ boat
5. understand	☐ go into
6. investigation	☐ enquiry
7. inside	☐ church

"David Bucket said there was a loose stone here somewhere, right?" Miss Elliot asked.

"That's what he told us, anyway," the inspector said, *whilst* testing the stone floor with his foot.

"Hey, you two! What are you doing up there?" someone suddenly shouted – his voice echoing off the cold, white walls.

Inspector Hudson and Elvira Elliot looked up. A man was hurrying towards them. It was the *caretaker*; they recognized him from the last visit.

"What are you up to?" he asked them *suspiciously.*

Inspector Hudson showed him his police *badge*.

"Remember us? We were here yesterday. You told us about the Indian prince and his *companions.*"

"Ah, yes, I remember now," the *caretaker* said, calming down. "But what in heaven's name are you looking for at the altar?"
"We are looking for a loose stone with a hole underneath," Miss Elliot answered.
"A loose stone?" the *caretaker* asked, *astonished.*
"Yes! Ah, here we are!" The inspector exclaimed. He *bent down* and removed a loose stone.

Übung 71: Wandeln Sie die Sätze ins Present Perfect um!

! ÜBUNG 71

1. Inspector Hudson solved many crimes.

....

2. The caretaker saw different kinds of tourists.

....

3. Prince Vikram was near St. Paul's Cathedral.

....

4. Inspector Hudson caught many criminals.

....

5. Elvira Elliot worked a lot with Inspector Hudson.

....

6. They are looking for a loose stone.

....

The *caretaker* and Miss Elvira watched him excitedly.
"Well, I'll be damned!" the *caretaker* commented.

Then he suddenly looked up at the cross *remorsefully*.
"Sorry!" he apologized.
Elvira Elliot and the inspector were *crouching* down, examining the hole.
"It's empty, I'm afraid," said a disappointed Inspector Hudson. "Either nothing was put here, or it has been removed."
"What's gone?" the *caretaker* asked.
"*Nothing in particular*," the inspector answered.
By now the *caretaker* seemed very confused.
Inspector Hudson carefully put the loose stone back into position and stood up.

ÜBUNG 72 !

Übung 72: Setzen Sie die richtige Präposition ein!
(away, up (2x), into, down (2x), from, at)

1. crouch	______	5. hide	______
2. mix	______	6. calm	______
3. run	______	7. stare	______
4. stand	______	8. bump	______

"Did you *by any chance* see anybody else here looking about?" the inspector asked.
The *caretaker* thought hard for a moment.
"Yes, there was! I mean a lot of people are interested in the altar, but that man from India…"
"Prince Vikram?" Miss Elliot questioned.
"Yes, exactly! Anyway the man from India was particularly interested in the altar. I remember he looked at it for ages. He also asked my permission to go up close to it."

"And you allowed him?" the inspector asked.
"Yes, he was such a gentleman and so polite. One could never say no to a man like that."
"Really," said Inspector Hudson, looking over to his colleague *teasingly.* "Is that so?"
"Did you see him try to move the stones?" Elvira Elliot asked.
"No, no! He just walked around the altar a few times."
"When was that?" asked Inspector Hudson.
"Last night, just before closing time."

*Übung 73: Ergänzen Sie die Sätze mit **any** oder **some**!*

1. Miss Elliot and the inspector were at the cathedral to collect __________ evidence.
2. There were not __________ diamonds in the hole.
3. Prince Vikram was not alone; he had __________ people with him.
4. The caretaker does not have __________ idea what the prince was doing at the altar.
5. "Did Price Vikram walk around the altar at __________ point?" Miss Elliot asked.
6. __________ of the Crown Jewels had gone missing.
7. Inspector Hudson is tired. He would love to have __________ holidays.

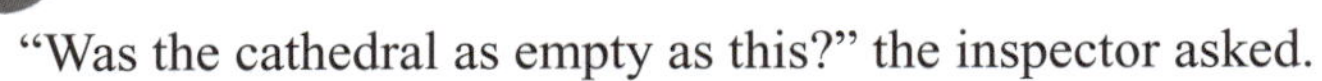

"Was the cathedral as empty as this?" the inspector asked.
"Yes, more or less."
"Was the prince alone?"
"No, he had a very large and muscular *companion*."
"Probably one of his bodyguards," Miss Elliot said to Inspector Hudson.
He nodded, agreeing with what she said.
"Were you with the prince all of the time?" the inspector asked.
"No, not all the time. His *companion* had to go to the toilet, so I showed him where to go."
"And during that time Prince Vikram was alone?"
"Yes!"
The two *investigators* looked at each other, *acknowledging* they might be on to something.
They thanked the *caretaker* for his assistance and walked towards the cathedral's exit.

! ÜBUNG 74

Übung 74: Lesen Sie weiter und ordnen Sie die Buchstaben in Klammern zu einem sinnvollen Wort!

"Maybe I was (1. thgri) ______________ after all," Miss Elliot said excitedly. "Maybe the prince is our thief!"

"I don't know, Miss Elliot. It does seem *far-fetched*. (2. hapsrep) ______________ he is just interested in altars."

"Well, he obviously likes them so (3. chum) ______________ that he has been to St. Paul's Cathedral two days in a (4. owr) ______________," she replied *suspiciously*.

The inspector opened his mouth to say (5. gomesihtn) ____________.

"Let me finish," Miss Elvira *admonished* him.

Inspector Hudson (6. grughdes) ____________.

"The diamond originally comes from (7. andiI) ____________ and did not fall into British hands until the end of the nineteenth century. Perhaps the (8. creinp) ____________ wants to take it back to where he believes it belongs? He does come from the same part of India where the (9. omandid) ____________ got into British possession – I checked that out!"

Inspector Hudson still looked sceptical. They walked out of the church into the evening air. The inspector stopped and looked straight at Elvira Elliot.
"Okay, let's say he does have a motive and he stole the diamond. First question is: Did the prince pay Marc Drum and David Bucket to help him steal the diamond? Second question is: Did he kill Marc Drum after the robbery? If he did, he wasn't very careful, was he?"
"Why?"
"Because Prince Vikram made no secret of meeting Marc Drum. They met in the hotel lobby. Everybody saw them together."
"I guess you're right. Perhaps he feels very secure that nothing can happen to him. Or maybe Marc Drum wanted more money or something, got too greedy – he wasn't planning it in the beginning, but then had no other choice," Miss Elliot argued.
Inspector Hudson thought for a moment.

ÜBUNG 75 !

Übung 75: Welche Gegenteile gehören zusammen?

1. admonish	☐ moderation
2. greed	☐ full
3. be silent	☐ push
4. assist	☐ speak
5. always	☐ fight
6. pull	☐ praise
7. empty	☐ never

"Then why did he just kill Drum? He might as well have *got rid of* David Bucket while he was at it!" he said.

"Yes, but unlike David Bucket, Marc Drum knew his identity, because they had quite *evidently* met."

The inspector walked on. He was thinking hard about something. Elvira Elliot hurried along to catch up with him.

Inspector Hudson *sighed*.

"All right, maybe you have a point. And *apart from* that, we have no other *lead*. Let's go to the Savoy and question Prince Vikram – ask him what he was doing wandering around the altar shortly before closing time."

Elvira Elliot seemed very pleased. Inspector Hudson looked at her *suspiciously*.

"You're not making all of this seem plausible just so you can have another glance at pretty Prince Vikram?" he asked ironically.

"No, not at all," Miss Elliot answered. "It isn't always good to combine business and pleasure," she joked.

Inspector Hudson could not help but laugh.

"If Sir Reginald finds out we're after one of the Queen's friends, he's going to be *furious*!" the inspector exclaimed.

"Well, you can tell him it was my idea."

"I most certainly will," he answered. "That is, if you are wrong!" They both laughed and went towards the car.

Übung 76: Setzen Sie das passende Adjektiv ein!
(ancient, low, frightened, busy, helpful, difficult, wide)

ÜBUNG 76 !

1. A case that is hard to solve is ______________.

2. A motorway with many lanes is ______________.

3. A person who works very hard is ______________.

4. A person who screams is ______________.

5. A tower which is not very high is ______________.

6. People who help you find a thief are ______________.

7. A very old tree is ______________.

Chapter 8: Party Time

Elvira Elliot and Inspector Hudson walked into the lobby of the Savoy Hotel. Close by, near the bar, someone was playing the piano. The pleasant tune travelled throughout the lobby, *soothing* stressed-out businessmen and providing a pleasant welcome to new guests. The two *investigators* looked around to see if *by any chance* Prince Vikram happened to be in the hotel lobby, but he was nowhere to be seen. Inspector Hudson *shrugged* and looked over to the reception.
"No point in asking at the reception – looks like the same *bunch* that were working last time," the inspector said.

"Yes, they weren't very helpful the last time," Miss Elliot replied.
"I guess we'll just have to wait in the lobby and hope he turns up soon."
"We could leave a message that he has to report to Scotland Yard."
"Then he might get alarmed and leave the country before we have a chance to question him."
"I guess you're right," Miss Elliot said.
A waiter walked past them with a tray full of large exotic cocktails.
"Mmmm, do you fancy one of those?" Miss Elliot asked.
Inspector Hudson smiled.
"I think I'll go for some mineral water just now," he replied.
The inspector and Elvira Elliot were sitting at the bar. Inspector Hudson was drinking a mineral water. Elvira Elliot had a large alcoholic cocktail full of fruit. The bar was quite busy. Elegant women – their *precious* jewels *sparkling* in the light – were sitting beside men in hand-tailored suits. People were talking quietly. A man whispered something into a woman's ear. She laughed. The piano player was playing in the background.
"It's a bit like something out of a lifestyle magazine, isn't it?" said Elvira Elliot, as she sipped red juice through a straw.
"I don't know. I've never read a lifestyle magazine," Inspector Hudson answered.
Elvira Hudson laughed.
"What do you like to read in your free time?"
Inspector Hudson was about to answer when he saw Prince Vikram walk towards the reception followed by two of his bodyguards. They were carrying cases.
"Look, there's Prince Vikram!" he exclaimed.
The two *investigators* watched Prince Vikram take out his credit card.
"It looks as if he's checking out," Inspector Hudson said.

"Do you think he is *heading back* to India?"
"No idea!"
Prince Vikram took his credit card back and walked towards the exit.
"Let's follow him!" said the inspector. "Let's see if they are *heading* to the airport."

Übung 77: Ergänzen Sie die If-Sätze mit ***will, would*** *oder* ***would have****!*

! ÜBUNG 77

1. If Inspector Hudson catches the prince, he ____________ solve the case.
2. If Inspector Hudson found the diamond, he ____________ solve the case.
3. If Inspector Hudson had caught the prince, he ____________ solved the case.
4. Things ____________ get easier if Inspector Hudson is on the right track.
5. It ____________ get easier if Inspector Hudson can get a good night's sleep.
6. If the thief escaped, Inspector Hudson ____________ be very angry.

Elvira Elliot and Inspector Hudson hid *neatly* behind a *bellboy* carrying cases and waited for them to pass. Then they walked care-

fully after them. They saw the prince and his *companions* get into a limousine. Miss Elliot and the inspector hurried towards the red sports car. They both got into the car and it shot off. They soon caught up with the limousine.
"They don't seem to be *heading for* the airport," Elvira Elliot said, as she *squealed* round a corner.
"No, they don't!" answered Inspector Hudson, a little nervously. "They seem to be *heading for* the South Bank."
"What could he be doing down there?" Elvira Elliot asked.
"Don't know, there are a number of important cultural buildings and institutions down that way." Inspector Hudson looked at his watch. "But everything will be more or less closed at this time," he continued.

ÜBUNG 78 !

Übung 78: Unterstreichen Sie das bekannte Sprichwort im folgenden Textabschnitt und übersetzen Sie es!

Elvira Elliot shot through a red light to keep up with the limousine. Inspector Hudson closed his eyes. A car *approaching* from the other side of the crossing just missed them. The driver *tooted*. Inspector Hudson opened his eyes again.
"Well, that was close!"
"A miss is as good as a mile!" Miss Elvira said dryly and put her car into fifth gear.
"Yes, so they say!" the inspector replied *uneasily*.
By this time they had reached the London Borough of Lambeth, belonging to inner London.
"He's *heading* straight *for* the Jubilee Gardens," Inspector Hudson remarked.

In the distance they could see the London Eye – a huge modern version of Vienna's Prater wheel, which dominates the river skyline opposite the Parliament. It is the largest *observation wheel* in the world and stands 134 meters high on the western end of the Jubilee Gardens. Its lights *flashed* wildly, as if asking everyone to come and have a ride.

"Have you ever been up there?" Elvira Elliot asked the inspector.

"No, but I've heard you get the best view of London from there."

"Did you know that if you wish, you can book a whole *capsule*? Some people actually party all night in it," Elvira Elliot said.

"Sounds like fun," Inspector Hudson remarked ironically.

The London Eye was getting closer and closer.

"It seems to me that he is *heading* straight *for* that wheel," the inspector said in *astonishment*.

Übung 79: Lesen Sie weiter und vervollständigen Sie die Sätze mit dem passenden Wort!
(headed, gigantic, dressed, after, group, carrying, warmly)

ÜBUNG 79 !

Not long (1.) ______________ this, the prince's limousine stopped very close to the entrance. Then the three men (2.) ______________ for the London Eye. They were (3.) ______________ the cases. Inspector Hudson and Miss Elliot followed them. They watched the prince meet up with a (4.) ______________ of people who had obviously been waiting for him to arrive. They greeted the prince (5.) ______________ and happily. Everybody was (6.)

_______________ very well, and looked very *sophisticated*. In the background stood the massive wheel, which was turning steadily in the sky like a (7.) _______________ UFO preparing to take off.

"It's amazing, isn't it?" Elvira Elliot said, her voice filled with wonder.
"Yes, it is", Inspector Hudson replied, "and it looks like Prince Vikram is boarding."
"Let's talk to him before he goes up in the air," the inspector said. "God knows when he'll be back down."
Miss Elliot and Inspector Hudson hurried along to catch up with the prince and his *companions*. They were all just climbing into the *capsule*, which looked like a miniature *spaceship*, when Inspector Hudson tapped the prince on the back.

ÜBUNG 80 !

Übung 80: Lesen Sie weiter und unterstreichen Sie im Text die gegenteiligen Begriffe der Wörter in Klammern!
(1. small, 2. coldly, 3. ugly, 4. free-time, 5. downwards, 6. closed, 7. loudly)

Prince Vikram turned round.
"Inspector Hudson!" he said in great surprise. "What a *coincidence* to meet you here," Prince Vikram smiled warmly.
"Well, yes it is. We have a few questions, actually."
"Then why don't you and your beautiful colleague come for a ride?" Prince Vikram asked.
"Well, I don't know…" said the inspector.
"Oh, come on – mix business and pleasure."

Inspector Hudson looked at Elvira Elliot. She looked at him as if to say: Oh, why not!
"All right then!" Inspector Hudson said, and they all climbed *aboard*.
Soon after that, the egg-shaped *capsule* started to move upwards slowly. In the middle of the *capsule* was a built-in table. One of the bodyguards laid a case on top and opened it. The case was full of Champagne. Everybody cheered.
Inspector Hudson leant over to Elvira Elliot and said quietly to her, "So that's what he's got in the cases, drinks for his party."
"I know, and I thought he was off to India with the Kohinoor in one of the cases."

Champagne corks *popped* and loud disco music began to play out of a ghetto blaster. Prince Vikram came over to Miss Elliot and Inspector Hudson. He offered each of them a glass of Champagne. They *regretfully declined*, telling the prince they were still *on duty*.
"Still *on duty*, are you?" Prince Vikram asked with an ironical, sceptical undertone. "That means you probably have some more questions about the missing *Beefeater*?"
"I'm afraid he's no longer missing," said the inspector.
"Good, then he has probably *confirmed* that we met to talk about my film."
"No, I'm afraid not. Marc Drum is dead," Inspector Hudson replied.
"Dead!" the prince exclaimed. "Why, that's *awful*!"
"Yes, he *drowned* in the Thames!"
"Oh, dear!"
The prince hesitated for a minute. He was thinking about something and was looking out at the city below him.

ÜBUNG 81 !

Übung 81: Ordnen Sie die Wörter auf der rechten Seite den Begriffen auf der linken zu!

1. decline	a) ☐ sink, go under, soak
2. probable	b) ☐ pause, delay, falter
3. glance	c) ☐ give, present, propose
4. hesitate	d) ☐ glimpse, peek, look
5. offer	e) ☐ likely, apparent, possible
6. pleasure	f) ☐ terrible, bad, dreadful
7. drown	g) ☐ delight, joy, bliss
8. awful	h) ☐ refuse, reject, turn down

"Wait a minute; you don't think I have anything to do with his death, do you?"
Inspector Hudson did not say anything at first.
"That is *ridiculous*!" Prince Vikram exclaimed.
"Where were you on the night of the Tower robbery?" asked the inspector.
"*That's none of your business*!" said the prince, who was starting to get very annoyed. His whole gentlemanly style was beginning to *fade*.
"And what were you doing at the altar in St. Paul's Cathedral? Were you looking for anything in particular?" asked Elvira Elliot.
Prince Vikram downed his Champagne.
"I'll tell you something", he said, "your *accusations* are *ridiculous*. If you have any further questions, contact my lawyer. Also I ask you to leave my *capsule* as soon as we've gone round once – and now if you would excuse me!"
Prince Vikram turned away from them and moved towards a group of friends. The prince started laughing and talking as if the conversation with the police had never taken place.

*Übung 82: Vervollständigen Sie die Sätze mit **anywhere, nobody, anybody, nothing** oder **anything**!*

1. Prince Vikram says he has ________________ to do with the robbery.
2. He believes the investigators do not have ________________ that could prove his guilt.
3. The prince was not ________________ near the Tower at the time of the theft.
4. His bodyguards normally did not let ________________ near him.
5. The capsule was absolutely full. You couldn't say there was ________________ in it.
6. Inspector Hudson did not say ________________.
7. The prince acts as if ________________ has happened.

"Well, that didn't go very well," remarked the inspector. "And we have no *evidence*, just some wild speculations."

"But he did react rather *harshly*, don't you think?" said Elvira Elliot.

"Yes, he did. And now we're stuck up here with this *bunch*!" the inspector complained.

"We might as well enjoy the view," Miss Elvira said, trying to *cheer* the inspector *up*.

"We might as well," the inspector *sighed*. "Our whole theory stands or falls on whether he has an alibi or not."

ÜBUNG 83 !

Übung 83: Bilden Sie Sätze mit dem Komparativ!

1. Prince Vikram/Inspector Hudson (rich)

   Prince Vikram is richer than Inspector Hudson.

2. tower/bridge (high)

   ....

3. London Eye/Prater Wheel (big)

   ....

4. Savoy/two-star hotel (expensive)

   ....

5. Westminster Abbey/Madame Tussaud's (old)

   ....

6. unknown thief/David Bucket (bad)

   ....

7. Elvira Elliot/Inspector Hudson (drive fast)

   ....

The inspector looked over at the prince.
"I mean, look at him. He's about 1.75m, *narrow-shouldered* and has dark brown eyes. For all we know it could be him, but it could also be someone else entirely. Can you think of anybody else who looks like that?"
"No, not at the moment," Elvira Elliot answered.
"Neither can I," said Inspector Hudson thoughtfully.

*Übung 84: Geben Sie die richtigen Formen von **to hit** mit **we** an!*

1. Einfache Gegenwart: ____________
2. Verlaufsform der Gegenwart: ____________
3. Einfache Vergangenheit: ____________
4. Verlaufsform der Vergangenheit: ____________
5. Perfekt: ____________
6. Verlaufsform mit Perfekt: ____________
7. Zukunft mit "going to" ____________
8. Zukunft mit "will" ____________

All of a sudden his mobile phone rang.
"Sergeant Wood?" the inspector said.
"Good evening, sir!" he answered
"What's up? Any news on that knife I gave you?"
"Yes, that's why I'm calling."
"And?"
"Well, as you *assumed,* it is a very *precious*, rare knife – it was made by a Japanese knife craftsman called Arishima Yoshimi about 60 years ago. Only three of these knives exist: One belongs to an American millionaire, one to a Japanese businessman and the last one belonged to a British major. The old man died a couple of years ago and the knife has been missing since."
"What was his name?"
"Brian Smith."
"I see. So Prince Vikram is definitely not the owner."
"I'm afraid not!"

"Were there any fingerprints on the knife?"
"No, just Mr and Mrs Moore's."
"Thought so!" Inspector Hudson *sighed*. "Well, thanks for calling."
"Goodbye!"
"Yes, goodbye!"

! ÜBUNG 85

Übung 85: Welche Wörter gehören zusammen?

1. afraid	☐ to
2. drive	☐ shouldered
3. finger	☐ man
4. belong	☐ up
5. true	☐ fast
6. gentle	☐ duty
7. fed	☐ of
8. narrow	☐ prints
9. on	☐ story

The inspector put his mobile back into his pocket. He looked over at Prince Vikram, who was flirting with a pretty English girl.
"It's not his knife anyway," he said, nodding in the prince's direction.
"I can see our theory is falling apart more and more," Miss Elliot *sighed*.
"Looks like it."
"Who did the knives belong to?"
"Two guys who don't live *remotely* anywhere near Britain."
"And the third?"
"Belonged to some British major called Brian Smith."
"I see. We should check him out then."

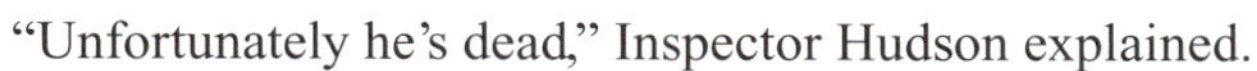

"Unfortunately he's dead," Inspector Hudson explained.
"Oh, and the knife?"
"Well, it's obviously the knife we have."

Übung 86: Lesen Sie weiter und unterstreichen Sie die richtige Variante!

ÜBUNG 86 !

The wheel was slowing (1.) down/up. The *capsule* came to a *halt*. Prince Vikram signalled to one of his men that the two *investigators* had to leave. Elvira Elliot and Inspector Hudson could not wait to get (2.) out/away of the smoky, noisy *capsule*. They went towards the door, climbed out and (3.) stopped/started walking in the direction of the car.
"I'll have my men find out whether Brian Smith has any relatives – maybe a *Beefeater*."
"How did you come to that (4.) seclusion/conclusion?" Miss Elliot asked, *puzzled*.
"Perhaps we've been on the (5.) wrong/rong track all along. Perhaps more than one *Beefeater* was in on the robbery."
"But what does that have to do with Brian Smith?"
"Just a logical (6.) sought/thought: Brian Smith was a soldier. Soldiers' sons often become soldiers (7.) to/too, and you have to be a soldier to become a *Beefeater*."
"Oh, I see," said Miss Elliot, (8.) impressed/*depressed*. "It would seem (9.) causable/plausible if more than one was in on it – after all, it was a big coup and (10.) nothing/nobody was caught."
Inspector Hudson nodded.

"If one of the *Beefeaters* or guards is our masked robber, we need to find out which ones fit our limited description of the masked

robber. We should also check out who was not *on duty* that night. However, we'll still have to verify Prince Vikram's alibi as soon as his lawyer gets it to us – I still don't think we should leave him off the hook. His behaviour certainly has been somewhat *suspicious*," the inspector said.
"And tomorrow I think we should pay Mrs Drum another visit," Elvira Elliot added.
"Yes, good idea, she should be out of hospital. But for now I need a good night's sleep."
"Same here!" Miss Elliot *yawned*. They got into the car and drove away.

Chapter 9: Trapped

The next morning, Inspector Hudson was sitting in his office reading a book. He was waiting for Elvira Elliot to arrive so that they could drive out together to Mrs Drum's house.
Suddenly, Sir Reginald burst in and threw the morning newspaper onto the inspector's desk.
"Here. Look at this! I hate repeating myself, Inspector Hudson, but this whole investigation is getting out of hand," Sir Reginald said angrily.
The inspector calmly put his book down and looked at the newspaper *headline*. It read: "Is Indian Prince the Diamond Thief?" Below was a large picture of Prince Vikram.
"Can you explain this to me?" Sir Reginald asked crossly.
"No, not really," Inspector Hudson answered.
"Not really?" Sir Reginald exclaimed. "So tell me: how in heaven's name did this information *leak* to the papers? It's a scandal – I'll have the Queen herself on the phone next!"

Übung 87: Setzen Sie die Sätze ins Passiv!

1. Inspector Hudson caused the scandal.

   The scandal was caused by Inspector Hudson.

2. The thieves killed Marc Drum.

   ....

3. The inspector understands Sir Reginald's point.

   ....

4. Sir Reginald slammed the newspaper on the desk.

   ....

5. The journalist wrote a scandalous article.

   ....

6. The inspector put his mobile into his pocket.

   ....

Inspector Hudson *sighed* and explained to his *superior* the reasons why he and Miss Elliot had questioned Prince Vikram. After he had finished, Sir Reginald was no more amused than he had been to start with.

"I know there is hardly any *evidence* except that he met Marc Drum once and *scrutinized* the altar at St. Paul's Cathedral. However, it was just one *clue* we had to follow – police routine. But how the story got to the newspapers, I don't know," Inspector Hudson said.

"Well, I am going to call Prince Vikram and apologize to him personally. The poor man must be *devastated*. Do you know what news like this can do to a man's *reputation*?"

ÜBUNG 88 !

Übung 88: Enträtseln Sie die folgenden Definitionen!

1. a sharp, pointed object ______________ (ifekn)
2. a female monarch ______________ (enequ)
3. something which causes great outrage ______________ (anadlcs)
4. a noise of annoyance or relief ______________ (igsh)
5. to come to a stop ______________ (lath)
6. on top of a newspaper article ______________ (leinaedh)
7. to interview someone ______________ (euqnoits)
8. the London underground ______________ (ebtu)

"I'm sure he'll survive it", the inspector remarked *wearily*, "and I would like to state that he still is a *suspect*."
"And I would like to state that you leave the man alone!" Sir Reginald said *furiously*.
His face was red with anger. Without another word, he left the room. Just as Sir Reginald left, Miss Elliot arrived. He stormed past without saying hello to her.
"What was all that about?" she asked.
Inspector Hudson pointed at the newspaper.

ÜBUNG 89 !

Übung 89: Fügen Sie die Übersetzung der angegebenen Wörter ein!

"(1. kein Wunder) ______________________ he was angry. I would like to know how that reached the papers."

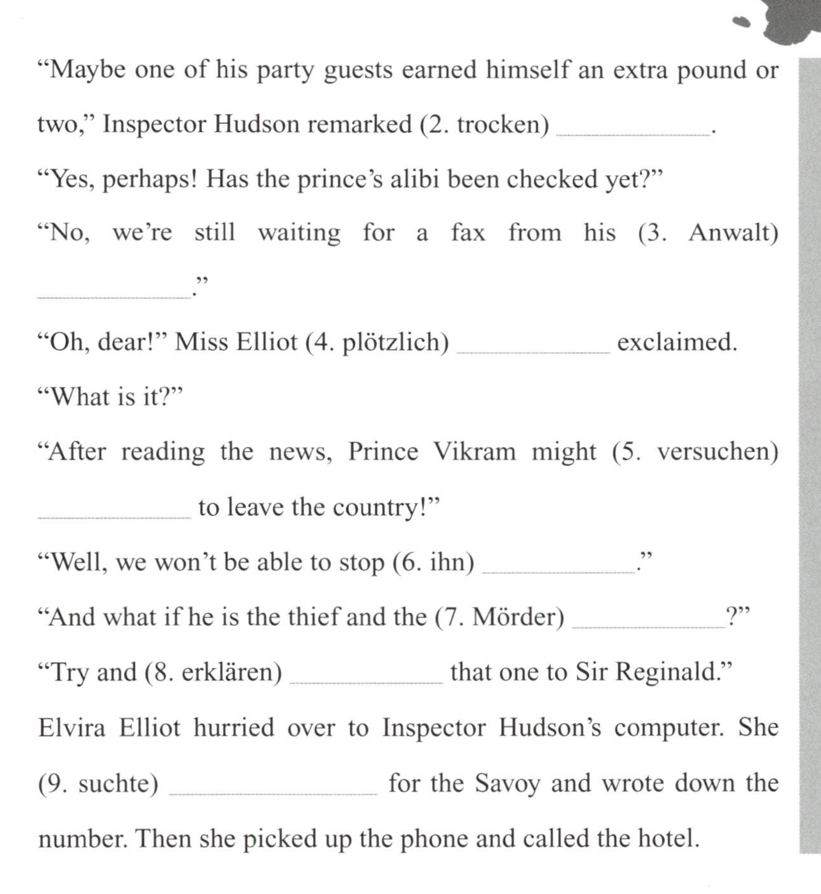

"Maybe one of his party guests earned himself an extra pound or two," Inspector Hudson remarked (2. trocken) __________.

"Yes, perhaps! Has the prince's alibi been checked yet?"

"No, we're still waiting for a fax from his (3. Anwalt) __________."

"Oh, dear!" Miss Elliot (4. plötzlich) __________ exclaimed.

"What is it?"

"After reading the news, Prince Vikram might (5. versuchen) __________ to leave the country!"

"Well, we won't be able to stop (6. ihn) __________."

"And what if he is the thief and the (7. Mörder) __________?"

"Try and (8. erklären) __________ that one to Sir Reginald."

Elvira Elliot hurried over to Inspector Hudson's computer. She (9. suchte) __________ for the Savoy and wrote down the number. Then she picked up the phone and called the hotel.

"The Savoy Hotel, how may I help you?"
"Yes, good day!" said Elvira Elliot in a *fake posh* voice. "My name is Lady Fellowes. Could you put me through to Prince Vikram, please?"
"Sorry Madam, but Prince Vikram has already checked out this morning."
"Oh, has he now. Is he still in the hotel?"
"I am afraid that is all I can tell you, Madam."

"Well, it is rather important. He left his wallet at my house yesterday evening and I have to return it to him."
"Okay Madam, no problem. You can send it to the hotel. He's sitting in the tearoom. As far as I *am aware*, his flight does not leave until the afternoon."
"Thank you very much. You have been a great help. Goodbye!"
"Goodbye!"

ÜBUNG 90

Übung 90: Wie heißt der Satz auf Deutsch? Kreuzen Sie die richtige Übersetzung an!

1. There is hardly any evidence.
   a) ☐ Es gibt schwerwiegende Beweise.
   b) ☐ Es gibt harte Beweise.
   c) ☐ Es gibt kaum Beweise.

2. Is there any news about the knife?
   a) ☐ Gibt es irgendwelche Neuigkeiten zum Messer?
   b) ☐ Gibt es keine Nachrichten zum Messer?
   c) ☐ Gibt es Neuheiten zum Messer?

3. They are pretty close to solving the case.
   a) ☐ Sie sind hübsch darin, den Fall zu lösen.
   b) ☐ Sie sind ziemlich nah dran, den Fall zu lösen.
   c) ☐ Sie sind ziemlich nah dran, den Fall abzuschließen.

4. Prince Vikram was at the hotel.
   a) ☐ Prince Vikram war im Hotel.
   b) ☐ Prince Vikram war am Hotel.
   c) ☐ Prince Vikram war auf dem Hotel.

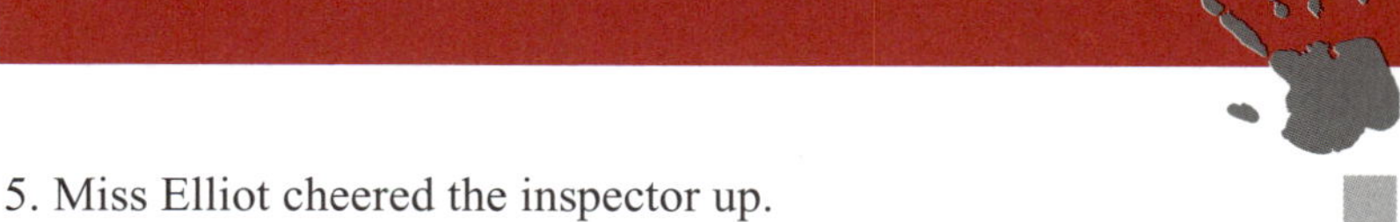

5. Miss Elliot cheered the inspector up.
   a) ☐ Miss Elliot jubelte den Inspektor an.
   b) ☐ Miss Elliot beklatschte den Inspektor.
   c) ☐ Miss Elliot munterte den Inspektor auf.

Elvira Elliot looked at Inspector Hudson and smiled.
"So what did you think of that?" she asked in her *fake posh* voice.
"I'm impressed!" the inspector replied.
"Prince Vikram is still at the hotel. We need to try and somehow *prevent* him *from* leaving the country until his innocence has been proven!"
"That sounds like a difficult one," Inspector Hudson said sceptically.
"I'll think of something – even if he just misses his plane today. That would give us at least a little more time. For all we know the Kohinoor diamond could be off to India today!"
"Okay, I see your point. You drive to the hotel and observe Prince Vikram. I'll go to Edith Drum and have another look around her *late* husband's office."
The two *investigators* hurried out of the office.

Übung 91: Unterstreichen Sie die Synonyme für die Ausdrücke in Klammern!
(1. wore, 2. memorial service, 3. upset, 4. miserably, 5. returned, 6. found, 7. walked by)

! ÜBUNG 91

Edith Drum opened the door and let the inspector in. She was dressed in a black jumper and trousers. She looked very sad as she led Inspector Hudson to Marc Drum's office.

"Well, I'll leave you to it, Inspector. I am just in the middle of organizing my *late* husband's *funeral*."
"I do have some questions I would like to ask you though."
Edith Drum *sighed*. She looked very *distressed*.
"Can't that wait?" she asked sadly.
Inspector Hudson hesitated and looked at her.
"Of course it can," he said. "We can talk later."
Edith Drum went back downstairs. Inspector Hudson started looking through Marc Drum's things. After searching for a while, Inspector Hudson came across some photographs. They showed Marc Drum and his wife climbing up a mountain. Inspector Hudson laid the photographs down and walked out of Marc Drum's office. He passed the bedroom and looked in.

The bed wasn't made and the window was open. On a shelf beside the bed he saw a number of *trophies* of various sizes, won in gymnastic *tournaments*.
"Climbing, gymnastics," the inspector *mumbled under* his *breath*.
Inspector Hudson walked down the stairs. He found Mrs Drum in the kitchen. She was smoking a cigarette.
"Are you doing okay?" he asked her.
"I get by," she answered, blowing out the smoke. He looked at her standing there in her black outfit. He noticed that she had narrow shoulders and was quite tall for a woman.
"Did you use to do gymnastics?" Inspector Hudson asked *casually*.
"Yes, a bit, when I was younger. Why?"
"Just wondering," the inspector asked. "And climbing?"
"That was more Marc's passion, but I did go along with him occasionally."
"I see. I actually came down to ask you if I could use your bathroom." Inspector Hudson smiled politely.

"Of course, it's up the stairs and then the first door on the right."
"Thank you!"

Übung 92: Bilden Sie positive Sätze!

ÜBUNG 92

1. Prince Vikram didn't stay at the Savoy.

   Prince Vikram stayed at the Savoy.

2. His bodyguards weren't very strong.

3. Inspector Hudson disliked Miss Elliot.

4. Miss Elliot hates the way Inspector Hudson dresses.

5. Nobody knew who stole the Kohinoor diamond.

6. Mrs Drum doesn't have blue eyes.

7. Inspector Hudson didn't find Mrs Drum in the kitchen.

Inspector Hudson turned around and walked in the direction of the stairs.
"Oh, Inspector!" Edith Drum called after him. "Did you find anything interesting?" she asked.

"I'm not quite sure," he replied as he walked up the stairs.
Inspector Hudson went into the bathroom and closed the door.
"The description of the thief could fit, but Mrs Drum has blue eyes," he thought.
The inspector washed his hands. His eyes wandered around. Suddenly he saw a small white container.
"That's it! Contact lenses!" he exclaimed.

! ÜBUNG 93

*Übung 93: Setzen Sie **to** oder **too** ein!*

1. Mrs Drum showed the inspector the way ______ the office.
2. Edith Drum was ______ distressed to have a normal conversation.
3. Inspector Hudson is trying ______ solve the crime.
4. Marc Drum used ______ live in the house ______.
5. Edith Drum did some climbing ______.
6. She told Inspector Hudson where ______ find the bathroom.
7. Inspector Hudson wanted ______ ask some questions.

Inspector Hudson took his phone out of his pocket and called Scotland Yard. It was ringing. Suddenly, the bathroom door opened.
"Put the phone down, Inspector!" Edith Drum said in a cold, hard voice.
Inspector Hudson looked up and saw through the reflection of the mirror that Edith Drum was pointing a gun at him. Someone on the other end of the phone line answered.
"I said put it down!" she *hissed.*
Inspector Hudson slowly put the phone down and turned around.

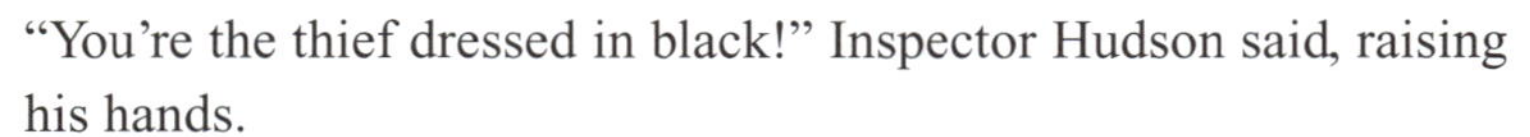

"You're the thief dressed in black!" Inspector Hudson said, raising his hands.
"Well observed, Watson!" she *mocked* him, taking the mobile phone from him.
"Now move into the office, slowly. And don't try any tricks or you're dead!"
Inspector Hudson walked into the office. He did not take his eyes off the weapon that Edith Drum was pointing at him.

Übung 94: Verwandeln Sie die Sätze in direkte Rede!

ÜBUNG 94 !

1. Edith Drum said she used to do gymnastics.

   "I used to do gymnastics."

2. She said she was in the middle of organizing her late husband's funeral.

   ____

3. Inspector Hudson asked where the bathroom was.

   ____

4. Elvira Elliot said she liked working with Inspector Hudson.

   ____

5. Sergeant Wood said he would like to be an inspector one day.

   ____

6. Edith Drum told Inspector Hudson to put down his phone.

   ____

"Sit down on the chair!" Edith Drum commanded.
Inspector Hudson sat down. Edith Drum got some climbing rope out of a drawer and tied him to the chair, all the time pointing the gun at him. After she had tied him up, she stepped a little way back from him.
"You really had us fooled," Inspector Hudson said.
Edith Drum smiled coldly.
"When I was young, I always dreamed of being an actress. It was a good show, wasn't it – all the worrying, the nervous breakdown."
"Yes, very convincing."
Edith Drum *bowed*.
"Thank you!" she said.

! ÜBUNG 95

Übung 95: Setzen Sie ein: ***do*** *oder* ***make****?*

1. Inspector Hudson had to __________ a phone call.
2. Marc Drum could not __________ his wife happy.
3. Edith Drum had to __________ a lot of training before she stole the diamond.
4. She told Inspector Hudson to __________ exactly what she said.
5. By *threatening* Inspector Hudson, Mrs Drum was going to __________ things worse.
6. Sergeant Wood had to __________ some research to find out who the knife belonged to.
7. __________ as I tell you!

“So you actually killed your own husband?”
“Yes!”
“But why, when he obviously helped you?”
“He was a *wimp* and was in the way anyway,” Edith Drum replied dismissively.
“In the way of what?”
The front door opened.
“Edith? Edith? Are you home?” said a man’s voice from downstairs.
“I’m up here, dear!” Edith Drum called.
Craig Gunn *appeared* at the door. He looked *dumbfounded* as he saw what was going on. In disbelief he stared at the weapon Edith Drum was still pointing at the inspector.
“Oh, now I understand why your husband was in the way,” Inspector Hudson remarked. “You started an affair with one of the Tower guards who just happened to be *on duty* the night of the robbery. He helped you as well, I *assume*?”
Edith Drum nodded.
“What on earth are you doing!” exclaimed Craig Gunn. “Have you gone totally mad?”
“No, dear, just *playing it safe*,” she replied *casually*. She did not even look at her lover but kept her eyes fixed on Inspector Hudson.
“But he’s a policeman. You’re making things worse and worse. What are you going to do, kill him?”
“Why not, he’s the only one who knows.”
“You can’t just kill a policeman and expect to get away with it. They’ll hunt us like foxes!” Craig Gunn kept running his fingers through his hair. Obviously, he was very nervous.
“Oh, don’t be such a *wimp*!” Edith Drum *admonished* her lover.
Then, Edith Drum pulled back the *trigger*.

Übung 96: Wählen Sie die richtige Variante!

1. Edith Drum spoke ___________.

   a) cold b) coldly

2. Inspector Hudson answered ___________.

   a) calm b) calmly

3. Marc Drum was ___________ killed.

   a) brutally b) brutal

4. Craig Gunn spoke in a ___________ tone.

   a) hysterical b) hysterically

5. Inspector Hudson was in ___________ trouble.

   a) many b) a lot of

6. Edith Drum was ___________ prepared.

   a) good b) well

7. It couldn't really get any ___________ .

   a) badder b) worse

At the same time, Elvira Elliot was at the Savoy Hotel observing Prince Vikram, who was sitting in the tearoom with his bodyguards. They were joking and playing cards. Miss Elliot's phone rang. It was Sergeant Wood.
"Well, hello Sergeant, to what do I *owe* the pleasure of you calling me for a change?"
"Is Inspector Hudson with you? I must speak to him immediately!" the sergeant exclaimed.

"Then why don't you call him?"
"I can't reach him. His mobile is off."
"Where is he?"
"He's at Edith Drum's house," Elvira Elliot answered.
"Oh!" said the sergeant in a worried voice.
"Why, what is it?"
"I just found out who Major Brian Smith *is related to*."
"Who?"
"He's Edith Drum's father – her *maiden name* was Smith!"
"That means she could be our man…erm…I mean woman!" exclaimed Elvira Elliot.
"Exactly!"
"Oh, I'm so stupid," Miss Elliot said, annoyed at herself. "Here I am watching an Indian prince playing cards with two gorillas!"

Übung 97: Wie lautet das Wort auf Englisch?

ÜBUNG 97 !

1. Mädchenname ______	7. vermuten ______
2. scherzen ______	8. ermahnen ______
3. verblüfft ______	9. Mobiltelefon ______
4. sofort ______	10. Abzug (Waffe) ______
5. Raub ______	11. sich verbeugen ______
6. vornehm ______	12. beiläufig ______

"There's something else I wanted to tell the inspector. Prince Vikram has a *cast-iron* alibi. He was dining with Lady Chatto – the only daughter of the *late* Princess Margaret."

"Well, that's a *firm* alibi." Miss Elliot said as she rushed out of the hotel, nearly knocking over the *bellboy*.
"Yes, there were over thirty people at the dinner party."
"Why didn't he just say so in the first place?" exclaimed the insurance *investigator*.
"I guess we'll see each other at Mrs Drum's – and hurry up, Inspector Hudson might be in danger!"
"Yes, see you there!"
Elvira Elliot hurried out of the hotel lobby.

ÜBUNG 98 !

Übung 98: Sind diese Sehenswürdigkeiten in London? Markieren Sie mit richtig ✔ oder falsch – !

1. Big Ben ☐
2. British Museum ☐
3. No. 10 Downing Street ☐
4. David Livingstone House ☐
5. Shakespeare's House ☐
6. Tate Modern ☐
7. Brick Lane Market ☐

Edith Drum was still pointing the gun at Inspector Hudson.
"Edith, darling, please, let's just pack our stuff and get out of here!" Craig Gunn *pleaded*.
Edith Drum swung the gun around and pointed it at her lover.
"Would you please just shut up, Craig!" she said in an annoyed voice.
Craig Gunn put his arms up defensively.
"Okay, okay, you're the boss!"
Edith Drum turned around again and pointed the gun back at

Inspector Hudson. She smiled *wickedly* and took a step forward. "That's right, I'm the boss!"
"So you planned it?" the inspector asked.
"Yes, every single step."
"How did you manage to persuade your husband to help you?"
"To keep the answers simple", replied Edith Drum, "love makes people blind."
"So does hate," Inspector Hudson remarked.
Edith Drum *frowned*. "Do you think so, Inspector? I think hate gives you *incredible* power, makes you do things you never thought possible."
"Like kill a man," the inspector remarked dryly.
"That's one example! Love, on the other hand, just makes you weak."
Edith Drum looked over to Craig Gunn. By this time, he seemed very confused.

Übung 99: Lesen Sie weiter und unterstreichen Sie im folgenden Abschnitt alle neun Verben im Simple Past!

"Edith, what are you talking about?" he said in a *devastated* voice.
"Shut up!" she *barked*.
"Why the Kohinoor diamond?"
"There was no particular reason, but it is very beautiful, don't you think?"
Edith Drum took the diamond out of a *belt bag* she had tied around her waist and looked at it. It *sparkled* in the light.
Elvira Elliot arrived at Edith Drum's house. Sergeant Wood had not arrived yet. She looked in the living room window, but could not see anything. She carefully *approached* the door.

Back in the house Edith Drum was still admiring the diamond. Craig Gunn suddenly jumped on her and tried to take the gun off her. However, Edith Drum was faster and shot a bullet into his stomach.

"Argghhhh!" he cried. Elvira Elliot *started* as she heard the man's scream.

"Oh, God!" she *mumbled* as she *fumbled* a small, thin tool out of her bag. She put it into the lock.

Craig Gunn was lying on the floor *bleeding*, holding his stomach. He was in great *agony*. Inspector Hudson tried very hard to get up off the chair, but he was tied too tightly. He just *toppled over* and fell to the ground.

Edith Drum turned her attention to the inspector.

"Now it's your turn", she said coldly.

She pulled back the *trigger*. Just as she was about to shoot Inspector Hudson, Elvira Elliot *tiptoed* into the room with a vase in her hand. She *smashed* it over Edith Drum's head. She screamed and fell over. The gun fell out of her hand and onto the floor. Elvira Elliot picked it up.

Edith Drum was lying on the floor holding her head. She was *moaning*. Miss Elliot *bent down* and untied the inspector.

"Well, I'm pleased to see you, Miss Elliot," he said *relieved*.

"That's the first time I've ever heard you say that," she smiled.

Inspector Hudson got to his feet. He took the gun from Miss Elliot and pointed it at Edith Drum, who was still holding her head. The inspector stepped over to Craig Gunn.

"We'd better call an ambulance!"

Outside, police sirens could be heard that were getting closer.

"That will be Sergeant Wood with the cavalry," said Elvira Elliot.

"I bet he'll be disappointed to have missed out on all the action," Inspector Hudson remarked.

Übung 100: Welches Wort ist das „schwarze Schaf“?

1. command, order, obey, demand
2. posh, poor, noble, high-born
3. over, under, above, more than
4. point, tip, end, bottom
5. wicked, kind, furious, evil
6. dumbfounded, amazed, knowing, astonished
7. shoot, bullet, trigger, barrel

A little later, the inspector and Miss Elliot were standing outside the house. Craig Gunn was being carried into an ambulance and Edith Drum sat in a police car.
"It's funny, that," Elvira Elliot said thoughtfully.
"What's funny?" Inspector Hudson asked.
"That the diamond actually lived up to its *reputation* once again."
"What do you mean?"
"Well, you know it has still not been bought or sold and, as usual, it has left a trail of *greed*, murder, *misfortune* and unhappiness behind it."
"You're not getting *superstitious*, are you?"
"No, but it is strange how *fate* has repeated itself after so many thousands of years."
"Hard to imagine that a thing so beautiful can cause so much *harm*," the inspector said. He paused and *sighed*.
"Maybe I should keep it at home for a while and see what happens," he joked.
"You most certainly won't!" Miss Elliot exclaimed, *snatching* the diamond out of his hand. "It's going straight to the Tower of London where it belongs – to be locked up out of everybody's reach."
Inspector Hudson *shrugged*. He waved a constable over. He had a

small iron case with him. Elvira Elliot put the diamond into it.
"Contact Sir Reginald and have him send a security van over to pick up the diamond."
"Yes, Sir!" said the constable. He walked away and gave the diamond to Sergeant Wood. Elvira Elliot and Inspector Hudson watched this happen.
"What a morning, eh?" Inspector Hudson exclaimed. "I didn't even get to finish my tea."
"Have you any plans, Inspector?" Miss Elliot asked.
"Plans?"
"I mean, do you feel like a cup of tea?"
"Yes, why not!"
"Good! I know this quiet place just down the road."
They walked towards their cars.
"I'll drive myself this time, if you don't mind," Inspector Hudson said.
"No problem, Inspector!" Miss Elliot teased him.
She started running towards her car.
"Last one there pays!" she grinned as she opened her car door.
Inspector Hudson smiled and unlocked his car unhurriedly.
"I *owe* you one anyway!" he shouted back.
However, Elvira Elliot did not hear this – she was already *speeding* up the road.

THE END

Abschlusstest

Übung 1: Welche Gegenteile gehören zusammen?

1. slow down	☐ let go
2. weak	☐ always
3. never	☐ whisper
4. stand	☐ strong
5. towards	☐ hurry
6. scream	☐ walk
7. grab	☐ away from

Übung 2: Welcher Satz enthält die richtige Übersetzung?

1. David Bucket war auch am Tower.
   a) ☐ David Bucket was at the Tower to.
   b) ☐ David Bucket was at the Tower too.

2. Die Polizei konnte sie nicht aufhalten.
   a) ☐ The police could not stop them.
   b) ☐ The police could not stop themselves.

3. Sergeant Wood und Inspector Hudson trafen sich.
   a) ☐ Sergeant Wood and Inspector Hudson meeted.
   b) ☐ Sergeant Wood and Inspector Hudson met.

4. Elvira Elliot fuhr gerade mit dem Auto.
   a) ☐ Elvira Elliot drives the car.
   b) ☐ Elvira Elliot was driving the car.

5. Sergeant Wood hat ihnen schon sehr oft geholfen.
   a) ☐ Sergeant Wood helped them a lot already.
   b) ☐ Sergeant Wood has helped them a lot.

Übung 3: Wie heißt das Simple Past der folgenden Verben?

1. hear ____________
2. come ____________
3. do ____________
4. make ____________
5. swim ____________
6. walk ____________
7. lay ____________
8. hide ____________
9. wear ____________
10. dab ____________

Übung 4: Bilden Sie sinnvolle Phrasal Verbs!

1. crouch	☐ out
2. call	☐ down
3. mix	☐ in
4. fill	☐ off
5. back	☐ by
6. drop	☐ on
7. eat	☐ up

Übung 5: Setzen Sie, wenn notwendig, den richtigen Artikel ein!

1. The thief will go to ______ prison.
2. Sir Reginald was in ______ bad mood.

3. Miss Elliot hadn't talked to the inspector for half ______ hour.

4. Inspector Hudson got out of ______ bed.

5. The Kohinoor diamond was no longer in ______ Tower.

6. David Bucket got more than just ______ few hundred pounds.

7. Inspector Hudson tried to get ______ overview of everything that happened.

Übung 6: Wie lauten die typischen Londoner Sehenswürdigkeiten? Ordnen Sie die Buchstaben zu einem sinnvollen Wort!

1. yee nnoodl ______________________
2. gib neb ______________________
3. hmagnibcku lapace ______________________
4. retsnimestw ______________________
5. ts aulps lardehtac ______________________
6. eeilbuj senrdag ______________________
7. emamda sduatsus ______________________
8. retwo dregib ______________________

Lernkrimi English History

Grundwortschatz

Death of a Dandy

Barry Hamilton

Inhalt

Story

Philipp Havisham genießt im viktorianischen London ein abwechslungsreiches Leben. Er trifft seine Freunde im Klub, besucht Ruderrennen und lässt kaum eine Gelegenheit aus, schönen Damen den Hof zu machen. Sein unbeschwertes Dasein nimmt jedoch ein plötzliches Ende: Ausgerechnet in seinem Lieblingslokal wird er ermordet.

Detective Carlyle von Scotland Yard übernimmt die Ermittlungen. Bald deckt er auf, dass Havisham nicht nur Freunde hatte: Mit seinem Buch „Bekenntnisse eines Dandys" hat er die Frommen und Gottesfürchtigen der Gesellschaft gegen sich aufgebracht.
Als Detective Carlyle bei einem unheimlichen Pfarrer und seinem Gefolgsmann schier untrügliche Beweisstücke sicherstellt, scheint der Fall zunächst gelöst. Bis eine neue Spur auftaucht …

Chapter 1: A Dandy's Life

It was a mild morning as Philip Havisham stepped out of his house on Grosvenor Square, a large garden square in the exclusive Mayfair district of *Victorian* London. He picked up a newspaper from his doorstep. It was dated July 6, 1879. The *headlines* said "Zulu War Over!" Philip Havisham looked up. A coach drawn by horses *approached* his house, the horses' *hooves* drumming rhythmically on the *cobbled* street. The coach stopped in front of his gate. A well-dressed man in his late twenties stepped out. He tipped his *top hat.* The two men smiled at each other.
"I say, you're up early my dear friend!" *beamed* Philip Havisham.
"Well, you know what they say: 'The early bird catches the worm'," laughed Simon Manlove. They warmly shook hands.
"So, what brings you here so early, Simon?"
Mr Manlove looked surprised.
"Have you forgotten today's *rowing* competition on the Thames?"
"Oh yes, great, I forgot!" said Philip Havisham excitedly. "Come in, come in!"
The two friends entered the house.
"Wait in the drawing-room. I'll be back in a minute, help yourself to a drink."

ÜBUNG 1 !

Übung 1: Lesen Sie weiter und setzen Sie die Wörter in Klammern richtig ein!
(bright, room, glasses, stairs, pour, peace)

Philip Havisham disappeared up the (1.) __________. Simon Manlove entered the drawing-room. The wallpaper had an extravagant *pattern* of birds and flowers. Its (2.) __________ colours of gold, red and green seemed to lighten up the (3.) __________. On a shiny round rosewood table was a tray with bottles of alcohol. Simon Manlove poured himself a gin. Shortly after, Philip Havisham entered the drawing-room.

"Would you kindly (4.) __________ me some of that exquisite port?"

His friend lifted up the port bottle and *whistled*.

"That must have cost you a pound or two!"

"Three to be precise," he answered ironically.

The *companions* lifted their (5.) __________.

"To my *late* wealthy father, may his soul rest in (6.) __________, if it were not for him I would not be able to live such a wonderful, *breathtaking* and immoral life."

"Yes, let us drink to your old man: one of the most successful *company promoters* of his time."
They laughed and clinked glasses.
"Cheers!"
Simon Manlove took his golden pocket watch out of his waist jacket pocket.
"Drink up then and let's go. The race starts in half an hour." Philip Havisham downed his port.
"Yes, let's go. This is going to be a lot of fun."

Übung 2: Lesen Sie weiter und unterstreichen Sie acht Begriffe, die mit Wasser zu tun haben!

Philip Havisham and Simon Manlove arrived just in time. Mr Havisham was in a very good mood. He rubbed his hands together joyfully.
"I never like to miss a *rowing* competition on the Thames."
"Yes, it's always such a great spectacle."
"And so full of life."
The men got out of the coach, which had stopped right beside the river. The water was full of boats and the riverbank was *crowded*. *Crowds* of *spectators* stood at the different *landing stages* along the Thames. Men, women and children cheerfully and *eagerly* awaited the beginning of the race.
"What a great atmosphere. I could do with a drink, what about you?" asked Simon Manlove.
"You know me, I never say no."
They *swiftly* walked towards a stand selling beer and tobacco. People turned around and looked at Philip Havisham. Some of them whispered or *smirked*, others just shook their heads. This was always the case as Philip Havisham liked to wear extravagant clothes. He never left the house without one of his long, shiny colourful scarves which he wore *boldly* around his long thin aristocratic neck. It fluttered in the mild summer breeze like an exotic flag. His *top hat* was elegantly tipped to one side and he never went anywhere without his shiny white *cane* made of pure *ivory*.
"Just arrived and you are already the centre of the show, Philip."
"Well, one does what one can."
Simon Manlove ordered two beers. The *companions* took their drinks and wandered along the riverbank. Groups of *watermen* had *gathered* at the different stairs which led into the river.

They were *eagerly* discussing the qualities of the individual boat race *participants*.
"Who do you think shall win?" Philip Havisham asked one of the men.
"I think the men *rowing* the boat called 'Sullivan' have a good chance, sir."
"A toast to Sullivan!"
Their glasses clinked. Mr Manlove and Mr Havisham moved on.

ÜBUNG 3 !

Übung 3: Finden Sie das passende Gegenteil und setzen Sie die richtige Ziffer ein!

1. crowded	☐ cold
2. good	☐ move
3. mild	☐ empty
4. bold	☐ lose
5. long	☐ cowardly
6. stop	☐ evil
7. win	☐ short

"Where are John and Stewart?"
"They should be here soon. I told them to meet us at this *landing stage*, and you have the best view from here."
"I hope they hurry up or they'll miss out on all the fun."
Just at that moment a man came hurrying towards them; he was very tall and slim. His long curly *whiskers* were perfectly *groomed*.
"Sorry I'm late, *chaps*. I had some important business to attend to."
Stewart Portman smiled and greeted his friends warmly.
"Where's John?" asked Philip Havisham.
"He didn't want to come to the race. You know he has been trying to *avoid* the Thames ever since Susan *drowned* herself in it."

"Poor soul, that really got to him," said Simon Manlove *sympathetically*.
"It was over a year ago, you would think he might have got over it by now," said Philip Havisham in a less sympathetic tone.
"Now that's not very fair, Philip…"
Suddenly there was a gun shot. The three men *anxiously* turned round and looked towards the distant bridge. As far as one could see, heads were *bent* forward and everybody had stopped talking and was looking in the same direction.

Übung 4: Übersetzen Sie und enträtseln Sie das Lösungswort!

ÜBUNG 4 !

1. Kutsche _ _ □ _ _
2. viktorianisch _ _ _ _ _ □ _ _ _
3. hell _ _ □ _ _ _
4. Pferd _ _ _ □ _
5. es _ □
6. Haus _ □ _ _ _
7. weil _ _ □ _ _ _ _
8. Vater _ _ _ _ _ □
9. Frieden _ _ □ _ _
10. kosten _ _ _ □

Lösung: _ _ _ _ _ _ _ _ _ _

"The boats are coming!" shouted Philip Havisham excitedly without taking his eyes off the bridge. The first boat shot under the bridge; followed by another and another.

"Here they come!" shouted Simon Manlove.
"Hooray!" cried the crowd around them.
The *rowers* came nearer. It was a close race. There was not a boat's length between the leading two. Philip Havisham took off his hat and turned it over.
"Okay, friends, the bets are on!" He threw in a pound note. "One pound on 'Sullivan'!"
Simon Manlove did the same and put his pound in the hat.
"One pound on the blue boat!"
Stewart Portman hesitated.
"What's wrong, Stewart?" asked Philip Havisham.
"You know betting is against the law."
"Oh, come on. It's just for fun. Don't be a *spoil-sport*!"
"If you insist." Stewart Portman looked in the direction of the boats and *reluctantly* placed a pound in Havisham's hat.
"I will bet on the red boat."
"Good on you, old boy."

ÜBUNG 5 !

Übung 5: Welche Wörter gehören zusammen? Setzen Sie die richtige Ziffer ein!

1. rowing	☐ driver
2. horse	☐ net
3. coach	☐ paddle
4. canoe	☐ skate
5. ice	☐ rider
6. fishing	☐ boat

Philip Havisham clapped his friend on the back. By this time the boats were nearly at their level. The shouting became very intense. People

were *hollering*: "Come on Red, you can do it!" or "Sullivan for ever!" The boats *darted* by, Sullivan was leading; its *rowers* were using every muscle in their body to defend the lead they had gained. The men looked very *strained*. Minutes later the race was over. Sullivan had won. Philip Havisham happily took the three pounds out of his *top hat*. "Some you win, some you lose!"
He smiled at his friends. They smiled back.
"Don't worry, your money will be invested in a good cause. After I have bought us another round of drinks, I am going to take you all out for a meal. But first of all let us see if we can find some lady acquaintances."
Simon Manlove grinned knowingly. Stewart Portman smiled *awkwardly*.
"Don't worry my friend. They won't bite!" said Philip Havisham with a laugh and walked ahead. His *companions shrugged* and followed.

Übung 6: Welche Synonyme gehören zusammen?

ÜBUNG 6 !

1. win	☐ succeed
2. smile	☐ far
3. shout	☐ grin
4. enter	☐ near
5. distant	☐ cry
6. good	☐ go in
7. close	☐ excellent

Philip Havisham and his friends eventually arrived at their favourite eating place called "Criterion" in the early evening. The three *companions* managed to persuade John Pirrip to come along. They had picked him up from the Royal Academy of Music, where he studied to play the violin. The Criterion restaurant was located at Piccadilly Circus. Many aristocrats and well-to-do people came to eat there. Philip Havisham liked this expensive establishment very much. He liked everything that was *costly* and luxurious. He just loved to pass time smoking *pricey* cigars, drinking exquisite wines and eating first class food.

"Good evening, Gentlemen," said the director of the Criterion, Mr Green, as the young men walked through the entrance.

"The same table as usual?"

"Yes, please! I do like the East Room. It's so *cosy* and private," answered Philip Havisham.

A waiter came and took their coats.

He noticed John Pirrip's violin case.

"Shall I take your violin case to the cloak-room, too, sir?"

"No, thank you, we never part," answered John Pirrip.

"As you wish, sir," said the waiter and left.

The men passed the *ante-room*. Philip Havisham *glanced* in. The room had green and cream walls and large *brass* mirrors. Its comfortable dark leather chairs looked very inviting. He suddenly stopped. His eye had caught an extremely attractive woman in her early twenties. She also saw him and smiled.

"I will be with you in a minute," he said to his friend Stewart.

Stewart Portman saw the woman and put two and two together. He shook his head *disapprovingly* and said, "But don't take all night, Philip, we're rather hungry."

ÜBUNG 7 !

Übung 7: Beantworten Sie die Fragen zum Text!

1. What is the restaurant called?

2. Where does John Pirrip study?

3. What instrument does he play?

4. What kind of people dine at the Criterion?

5. What does Philip Havisham like about the East Room?

6. Where does the waiter take the men's coats to?

7. Who does Philip Havisham see in the East Room?

The group of friends moved on. Philip Havisham *casually* walked into the *ante-room* towards the young lady.
"Good evening, Patricia. You're looking beautiful as ever."
He kissed her hand.
"Good evening, Philip. And you are as charming as ever."
"What brings you to London? I haven't seen you in a long time."
Patricia Gillian *sighed* and rolled her eyes.
"I know, I know. Ever since my Aunt Dorothy has taken over my *marital* affairs I don't get out a lot." Miss Gillian gave Philip Havisham a *seducing* look. "She is trying to protect me from men of your kind until Mr Right turns up and marries me."
"So where is the old *bat*? She doesn't seem to be doing such a great job."

A *malicious* smile flickered over her face.
"She is right behind you!"
Philip Havisham turned around. An elderly lady stood in front of him. She was very tall. A large diamond necklace *covered* her wrinkled décolleté. The woman looked at Philip Havisham sceptically.
"Mr Havisham, what a pleasure to meet you here."
The way she said this did not sound very convincing.
"How do you do?"
Her voice had a slight *threatening* touch to it.
"Very well, thank you, Lady Broughton. I cannot complain."
"So you have not wasted the fortune of your *late* hard-working father yet?"
Philip Havisham tried to keep smiling. He was just about to say something when Lady Broughton said, "Well, it was nice speaking to you. Have a nice evening."
And with this Lady Broughton took her niece's arm and pulled her discreetly away.
Philip Havisham cleared his throat.
"It was nice speaking to you, too, Madame."
Patricia Gillian turned around and waved. Philip Havisham waved back and then *headed for* the exit.

ÜBUNG 8 !

Übung 8: Welche Wörter gehören in die Lücken?
(boatman, waiter, musician, husband, charm, royal)

1. A ________________ serves in a restaurant.
2. A ________________ plays an instrument.
3. A ________________ is the male equivalent of wife.
4. A ________________ rows a boat.

5. An aristocrat is of ______________ descent.

6. A dandy has a lot of ______________.

Philip Havisham walked along the long corridor leading to the East Room. As he entered he could hear the cheerful voices of his *companions*. This brought back a smile to his face.
"Some you win, some you lose!" he thought.
The East Room in the Criterion only had three tables and his favourite table was hidden by a wooden screen. The group of friends liked their privacy and met there every week to discuss art, literature, philosophy and other pleasures of life. Philip Havisham sat down beside his friends. They were already drinking a bottle of expensive French red wine. Simon Manlove filled up Philip Havisham's glass.
"Any luck?" he asked *casually*.
"No, I am afraid we were disturbed by her most *ghastly* aunt!"
"Lady Broughton?"
"Yes!"
"They say she used to be very beautiful in her time."
"Well, her time is most certainly over," Philip Havisham said bitterly.
"Look, we've already chosen tonight's menu," said John Pirrip changing the subject. He *handed* him the carte.
Philip Havisham's face brightened up. "Oh, lovely!"
Philip Havisham read the menu out loud.
"Caviar, *asparagus* and *leek* soup, *sole* filet, grilled chicken in mustard sauce… Mm, this is delicious!"
Mr Havisham lifted his glass.
"To friendship, the only thing that lasts."
"Hear, hear!" his friends replied.

ÜBUNG 9 !

Übung 9: Übersetzen Sie folgende Sätze!

1. Das Restaurant hatte nur drei Tische.

____

2. Er hörte ihre fröhlichen Stimmen.

____

3. Sie tranken eine Flasche Wein.

____

4. Man sagt, sie sei einmal sehr schön gewesen.

____

5. Er las das Menü.

____

6. Hast du Erfolg gehabt?

____

7. Herr Havisham erhob sein Glas.

____

The four gentlemen had a wonderful meal. They were just waiting for dessert when suddenly a tall young man *appeared* from behind the wooden screen and threw a book on the table. It landed with a loud bang straight in front of Philip Havisham and knocked over his full glass of wine. *Astonished*, the men looked at the rude *intruder*. His face was red with anger and his mouth *twitched* under his long, curled *moustache*.
"This novel is outrageous, absolute *filth*. You should be ashamed of yourself," the stranger shouted.
Philip Havisham calmly *wiped* his wet trousers with his napkin and said with an arrogant *sneer*, "May I know who my *fierce* critic is?"

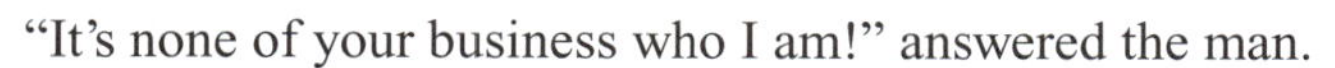

"It's none of your business who I am!" answered the man.
"Well, you obviously don't seem to like my book, do you?"
"You can say that again, it's full of lies! If I didn't know better I would…"

Übung 10: Lesen Sie weiter und unterstreichen Sie die fünf inhaltlich nicht dazugehörenden Sätze!

The man tried to move on Mr Havisham, but his friends got up *straight away* and held him back. "Here's to you, Philip!" they shouted.
"Let me go you *bunch* of *scum*!" the man shouted.
At this moment Mr Green *appeared*.
"Please, gentlemen, this is no place for a *quarrel*!" he whispered.
"I was just leaving!" said the stranger and left hastily. He flew into the evening sky.
Philip Havisham looked at his friends.
"Another one of these ignorant people, who do not appreciate a good piece of fiction," he said.
They all laughed. Mr Green smiled, shook his head and left as if nothing had happened. Stewart Portman pulled his pocket-watch out of his waist jacket pocket. Then he threw it onto the floor.
"It's getting late; I think I'd better go now."
"Me too," said Mr Manlove.
Philip Havisham looked disappointed. He was really happy they were leaving.
"But what about dessert?"
"I'm full as it is. And Mary is expecting me."
"Oh well, that leaves us down to two. Doesn't it, John?"
John Pirrip downed his wine in one. Afterwards his glass was full.
"Guess it does, Philip! But we still have lovely Jane, here." He *stroked* his instrument case.

"Yes, I *assume* that will be the only woman you will be holding in your arms tonight," laughed Philip Havisham.
Simon Manlove and Stewart Portman laughed as well, but John Pirrip just stared at Philip Havisham *grimly*. Everybody felt a little uncomfortable.
"Sorry, John!" he said. "I should watch my silly mouth…I'm really sorry."
"It's okay," said John Pirrip sadly.
Simon Manlove and Stewart Portman gave John Pirrip a *reassuring* clap on the back and said goodbye. Over a year ago John Pirrip's *fiancée* had *drowned* herself in the Thames. Nobody understood why. Her death was a great tragedy and mystery. John said nothing. He seemed to be lost in thought. Philip Havisham felt a little awkward.
"I'll go to the men's room", he said, "I'll be back soon."
John Pirrip lit his pipe, nodded and sat back.

! ÜBUNG 11

Übung 11: Ordnen Sie die Wörter zu sinnvollen Sätzen!

1. with anger red his face was

____

2. calmly he trousers wiped his

____

3. his wine in one downed he

____

4. place a quarrel no is this for

____

5. man to move tried the him towards

____

6. understood why nobody

____

7. awkward he felt

____

Philip Havisham took his time. He was in no hurry to get back to his friend. It wasn't that he really felt sorry. He just hated to have *depressed* people around him. In his view life was too short for depression. He *strolled* around the building and walked by the entrance to the *ante-room*. He looked to see if he could spot any other acquaintances. He saw nobody he knew. Philip Havisham wandered on to the empty Great Hall where the statue of Shakespeare looked meditatively down upon him. He stood in the middle of the room with his back to the door.
"Shakespeare, what a man," he thought.
Suddenly the door behind him closed. Philip *startled* and turned around.
"Are you following me…?"
He had no time to finish his sentence. The last thing Philip Havisham heard was a *dull*, deadly bang.

Übung 12: Welche Adjektive werden gesucht? Setzen Sie ein!
(grim, tragic, awkward, sad, silly, short, dull)

ÜBUNG 12 !

1. He was not happy, he actually looked very ____________.

2. Her face looked fierce and ____________.

3. That was very stupid and __________________ of you.

4. How __________________, I am very sorry.

5. The man's trousers were above his ankles, they were very __________________.

6. It was an __________________ situation.

7. The bang was __________________.

Chapter 2: Tracing Lord Spencer

The London Police arrived at the murder scene shortly after Philip Havisham's body was found. Detective Hamish Carlyle pushed his way through a group of shocked guests blocking the corridor that lead to the Great Hall of the Criterion. The London Police Detective had a very *impressive* appearance. He was a small, *stout* man with thick red hair. His hair was so wild; he even had trouble finding a bowler hat to fit him. His red bushy eyebrows guarded over his clever and flaming blue eyes. This made him look *fierce* and a little rough, but Detective Carlyle was actually a very friendly and good-natured person. All the way up the corridor you could hear him saying: "Excuse me, madame!" or "Oh, thank you, sir!"

ÜBUNG 13

Übung 13: Fügen Sie die Übersetzung der deutschen Wörter ein!

One could tell by his (1. Akzent) ______________ that Detective Carlyle was not originally from London, but (2. aus) ______________ Edinburgh. He rolled the "R" in sir and strongly accentuated the "A" in madame – a sign that he was a native Scot. He was followed by a number of constables. They were not quite as polite as their (3. Chef) ________________.

"Get out of the way!" they *snarled*. "This is a crime-scene, not a tea party!"

Mr Green came running towards Detective Carlyle, he was very *tense*. The men introduced themselves to each other.

"It's a great (4. Tragödie) ________________ ...," he *stammered* nervously as he walked (5. neben) ________________ the detective. "I just don't understand..."

They entered the Great Hall. Philip Havisham lay on the (6. Boden) ________________. His arms were *spread* out and his eyes wide (7. offen) ________________. Blood *trickled* out of the area where his (8. Herz) ________________ used to beat. Detective Carlyle took in the scene thoughtfully.

"Is there anything I can do?" asked Mr Green.

"Yes, close the restaurant for today, but don't let anybody leave before we question them," answered Detective Carlyle.

"But Detective Carlyle, very important people dine here; I just can't force them to stay."

"I know you can't force them, but I can. However, I'm sure your way is more diplomatic."

"What a day!" *mumbled* Mr Green nervously to himself and left.

Detective Carlyle stepped into the room and walked around the body. Sergeant Thompson arrived. He was Detective Carlyle's best man and his *features* showed signs of great intelligence. Detective Carlyle liked him very much and was certain that one day he would become Chief Inspector.

ÜBUNG 14 !

Übung 14: Welches Wort ist das „schwarze Schaf"? Unterstreichen Sie das nicht in die Reihe passende Wort!

1. snarl, bite, bark, smile
2. important, beggar, well-to-do, aristocratic
3. run, walk, stand, move
4. leave, go in, arrive, enter
5. great, terrible, good, super
6. pleased, happy, sad, cheerful
7. speak, talk, chat, silence
8. diplomatic, tactful, careless, careful
9. shocked, upset, happy, troubled
10. secure, vulnerable, safe, protected

"So what do you think?" Sergeant Thompson asked his *superior*.
"Certainly it looks as if the murderer is good with a gun. One shot straight in the heart. He probably died *instantly*."
"How is it that nobody heard the shot?" asked Sergeant Thompson.
Detective Carlyle walked to the corner of the room and pointed at a cushion with a hole in it.
"That's why; the murderer used a cushion to silence the gun."
"That old trick never *fails*, eh?" said the sergeant. "Is the cushion from this room?"
"I don't think so. I can't see any others."
Detective Carlyle looked up at the statue of Shakespeare.
"If only you could speak," he said quietly to himself.

At that moment Mr Green entered the Great Hall again. He was *dabbing* his sweaty bald head with a *handkerchief*.
"I did what you told me, but I must say, many of my guests are not pleased at all…"
Detective Carlyle ignored the last sentence. "Who found Mr Havisham's body?"
"His friend, Mr Pirrip. He's sitting in the *ante-room*. He *appears* to be in a state of shock. They had just dined together shortly before this…eh…incident."
Detective Carlyle looked at his sergeant.
"You *secure* the crime-scene, meanwhile I'll see to Mr Pirrip."

Übung 15: Übersetzen Sie!

ÜBUNG 15 !

1. zu Abend essen ____________
2. zu Mittag essen ____________
3. frühstücken ____________
4. Abendessen ____________
5. Mittagessen ____________
6. Frühstück ____________

The *ante-room* was *crowded*. There were smaller and larger groups of people standing around talking. The main topic was the death of Philip Havisham. A pale, thin man sat on a chair staring into the *blazing* fire. He was drinking a brandy. It was in fact his fifth or sixth. Detective Carlyle sat on the chair opposite him.
"Are you Mr Pirrip?"
"Yes!" he said without lifting his eyes from the fire.

"I thought so. May I introduce myself? I am Detective Carlyle from the London Police."
John Pirrip looked up. Both men shook hands.
"I heard Mr Havisham was a good friend of yours."
"Yes, that is true."
The young man seemed very miserable and sad.
"I know this is not quite the time, but I have a few questions I must ask you."
John Pirrip took a sip of his brandy and turned his face back to the fire.
"Go ahead."
Detective Carlyle took out his notebook and pen.
"Is it true that you found Mr Havisham in the Great Hall?"
"Yes!"
"How did this come about?"
John Pirrip took a deep breath.
"Well, he said he was going to the men's room. After about 25 minutes I started to wonder where he was. So I looked for him and as you know I eventually found him…", John Pirrip *gulped*, "…dead!"
Mr Pirrip downed his brandy.

ÜBUNG 16

*Übung 16: Vervollständigen Sie die Sätze mit **after** oder **before**!*

1. ________ about 25 minutes John Pirrip went to look for his friend.
2. ____________ he went he poured himself another drink.
3. __________ John Pirrip found Philip Havisham he called the police.
4. Some time passed ___________ he started to get worried.
5. __________ he could say another word he was dead.
6. The police arrived soon __________ he had called.

"Since you were close, do you have any idea who could have done such a thing?"
John Pirrip smiled bitterly.
"Philip had a lot of enemies. He wasn't what you would call a respected member of society."
"What do you mean?"
John Pirrip looked surprised.
"Haven't you heard of his book 'Dangerous Confessions of a Dandy'? It caused quite a scandal."
"No, what is it about?"
"It's a fictional story about the life of a dandy in London called Robert Sway and his experiences; it certainly does not *shed a good light on Victorian* society."
Detective Carlyle raised one of his bushy eyebrows.
"Does it not?"
"No, the novel unmasks society's *bigotry* and indirectly criticizes the church and the government. His *debut* has not made him very popular."

Übung 17: Ordnen Sie die Wörter ihrem Gegenteil zu!

ÜBUNG 17 !

1. popular	☐ happy
2. important	☐ true
3. fictional	☐ sweet
4. dangerous	☐ unpopular
5. bitter	☐ unimportant
6. miserable	☐ safe

"What makes you think the book has something to do with the murder?"
"Philip has received a few *death threats* recently…oh, and just half

an hour before he was murdered this *chap* tried to *threaten* him because of the book. You should have seen him, he was very angry."
"Really?" the eyebrow went up again.
"Do you know who he was?"
"No, never seen him before. He just turned up out of nowhere, but maybe Mr Green knows him."
"Okay, thank you Mr Pirrip, that will do for just now."
John Pirrip nodded and stared back into the fire. Detective Carlyle got up, closed his notebook and said goodbye.

ÜBUNG 18 !

Übung 18: Welche der folgenden Aussagen sind wahr? Markieren Sie mit richtig ✓ oder falsch – !

1. Philip Havisham and John Pirrip were good friends. ☐
2. Mr Green found Philip Havisham. ☐
3. Philip Havisham did not have many enemies. ☐
4. Detective Carlyle does not know Philip Havisham's novel. ☐
5. John Pirrip is drinking champagne. ☐
6. Philip Havisham was shot in the East Room. ☐
7. "Dangerous Confessions of a Dandy" is a true story. ☐

The detective fought his way back to the Great Hall. His constables were interviewing the guests one after another. They were listening, nodding and writing down anything that seemed important. "Come to any conclusions?" asked Detective Carlyle as he walked into the room.
"Not really, sir," answered the sergeant. "And I can't find a gun, however I *assume* the victim was taken by surprise."
"Yes, the murderer may have followed him and waited for the right moment…or someone *lured* him to the Great Hall. What have your men found out, Sergeant, did anybody see anything *suspicious*?"

"No, but they have not yet questioned all of the guests."
Detective Carlyle *bent* over Philip Havisham's body.
"His wound is quite big. The gun certainly was not small. Maybe it was a Remington Revolver or a Colt. You certainly can't just walk into a restaurant with one of those in your pocket. Somebody must have seen something *suspicious*."
"We'll see what the autopsy says, sir. Dr Brown should be arriving any minute. He was playing a game of *whist* at Colonel Walkers, but one of my men eventually found him."
"I hope the man is *sober*. He is *notorious* for having a few drinks."
Mr Green entered the room. He was followed by a middle-aged, handsome looking man, who held a small black leather bag in his hand. It was Dr Brown. He seemed a little *unsteady* on his feet.

Übung 19: Verneinen Sie folgende Sätze!

ÜBUNG 19

1. Dr Brown was sober.

2. He lost his balance.

3. Detective Carlyle knows who the murderer is.

4. The constables were listening.

5. The sergeant's men have found a clue.

"Good evening, Gentlemen. What do we have here?"
Dr Brown *approached* the body. He *hiccoughed*.
"Oh dear, if that is not the *notorious* dandy Philip Havisham," he said dryly.
"You know this man?" asked Detective Carlyle.
"Yes, from the newspapers. I read his book. I don't know what all the *fuss* is about, it's great."
Dr Brown smiled and kneeled down beside the body. He nearly stumbled, but managed to keep his balance.
"Have you been drinking, Dr Brown?" asked Detective Carlyle.
"Oh, just the usual *night-cap*."
"I bet!" whispered Sergeant Thompson to himself.
"I would like to know what kind of bullet killed him."
"No problem. I'll have him taken to the hospital as soon as you're finished here and pull it out. Good shot, eh?" *chuckled* Dr Brown.
The others did not think this very funny.
"Show some respect, Doctor!" said Sergeant Thompson.
Dr Brown seemed embarrassed.
"Ehm…well…yes…I guess you're right."
Dr Brown started to take medical instruments out of his bag.
Detective Carlyle shook his head and turned around to Mr Green. He was still very nervous.
"John Pirrip told me that someone had *threatened* Mr Havisham shortly before he was killed. Do you know the man?"
"Yes, his name is Lord Manuel Spencer."
Detective Carlyle wrote this information in his notebook.
"I think we'll visit Lord Spencer tomorrow, Sergeant Thompson."
"Very good idea, sir."

Übung 20: Benutzen Sie die Kurzform!

ÜBUNG 20 !

1. I cannot	______	6. it is	______
2. I will	______	7. could not	______
3. I do not	______	8. I am	______
4. you are	______	9. he is	______
5. we will	______	10. does not	______

Mr Green wanted to leave the Great Hall again.
"Oh, I have one last question, Mr Green."
Mr Green turned around.
"Yes!"
"Is this cushion part of the restaurants *interior*?"
Mr Green *screwed up his face*.
"I should certainly think not! It looks very *shabby* to me."
"Thank you, Mr Green. That will be all for now."
"For now?" said Mr Green *uneasily*. "I must say, I don't like the sound of that at all. This whole affair is a never ending story!"
Sergeant Thompson and Detective Carlyle looked at each other and *shrugged*.
"This is just the beginning," said Detective Carlyle knowingly.
Mr Green did not hear this because he had already gone.

Übung 21: Lesen Sie weiter und übersetzen Sie die Wörter in Klammern!

ÜBUNG 21 !

The next day Detective Carlyle and Sergeant Thompson went to Lord Manuel Spencer's *lodgings*. They stood (1. vor) ______ a *shabby* second class London hotel called "Stephan's" on Hill Street just off Berkley Square.

"Are you sure this is the right place, Sergeant? It doesn't look like the home of an aristocrat to me."

"I see your point, but I'm certain he lives here."

The policemen (2. betraten) ______________ the hotel. A man was sitting at the reception desk smoking a pipe and reading the newspaper. He looked up, *startled* as soon as he saw the policemen coming towards him.

"Good afternoon, can I help you?" he said *apprehensively*.

"We (3. hoffen) ______________ so," answered Detective Carlyle.

"Is there a Lord Spencer staying here?"

"Lord Spencer?" said the landlord (4. überrascht) ______________

"Do you mean Mr Manuel Spencer?"

"Yes!"

"Well he is staying here, but I haven't seen him since yesterday morning."

"He did not come home (5. letzte Nacht) ____________________?" asked Detective Carlyle with great interest.

"No!"

"You seemed surprised that Mr Spencer is of aristocratic *descent*?"

"Well, yes. He sometimes has (6. Geldprobleme) ________________ and can't always pay his rent. Mr Spencer…I mean Lord Spencer certainly is not a wealthy man."

Sergeant Thompson looked around. Suddenly his (7. Auge) ______________ caught something. He walked over to a chair placed in the reception area and lifted up a cushion.

"Look sir, it's the same cushion we found at the crime scene!"

"Well done, Sergeant Thomson!"

"Crime scene?! What crime scene?" asked the landlord nervously.

"We can't talk about it right now, however I am (8. neugierig) ____________________. Are you missing any of these cushions?"

"Ehm…no…I mean…I don't count them," *stammered* the landlord.

"Well maybe you could find out if any cushions of that kind are missing. In the meantime, I and my colleague would like to *inspect* Lord Spencer's room, please."

Detective Carlyle held out his hand. The landlord *grabbed* a key and placed it in the detective's hand.

"Room number 17. It's on the second floor."

"Thank you!"

The policemen unlocked the hotel room door and entered. The room was small and dusty. However, the room was very tidy. In one corner there was a single bed and in the other corner by the window there was a desk and chair. A *typewriter* was placed on top of the desk.

"Not the place you would expect to find a Lord, is it?" said Sergeant Thompson.

"No, it certainly isn't."

Detective Carlyle walked over to the desk and opened the drawers. He did not find anything *suspicious*. He *bent down*. Under the desk was a waste-paper basket full of paper *scraps*. Detective Carlyle emptied it on the floor.

ÜBUNG 22 !

Übung 22: Unterstreichen und verbessern Sie im folgenden Textabschnitt die acht falsch geschriebenen Wörter!

"Let's sea what we have here."
Sergeant Thompson joined his *superior*. They started sorting out the paper *scraps*.
"This is interesting!" said Detective Carlyle and read the content of a letter out loud, which he had just taken out of an envelope.
"Havisham is going to be at the Criterion this evning."
That is what the *entire* message said.
"Looks like somebody *tipped off* Lord Spencer. He new Havisham was going to be at the Criterion."
"That could mean that if Spencer has something to do with the murder he isn't in it alone."
Sergeant Thompson unfolded another peace of paper.
"Luke at this, sir! It's about some campain against Havisham's book."
He shoed it to Detective Carlyle.

1. ____________________ 5. ____________________

2. ____________________ 6. ____________________

3. ____________________ 7. ____________________

4. ____________________ 8. ____________________

It read: "Set an example for moral values now! Come to the book burning on July the 25th of 'Dangerous Confessions of a Dandy' written by Philip Havisham. Meeting place, church of St Andrews."
"I know that church. It's a very conservative Evangelical church near Fleet Street," said Sergeant Thompson.
"It's been typed on a *typewriter*. I wonder if Lord Spencer typed this himself."
Detective Carlyle saw that the letter "W" on the sheet of paper had a very specific *malfunction*.
"Put in a piece of paper in the *typewriter* and see if it types the 'W' in the same way."
Sergeant Thompson put a sheet of paper in the *typewriter* and pressed "W".
"You were right. He wrote the campaign letter on this *typewriter*. He sure hated Havisham's book and probably hated him also as much."
"I'm sure he did, but the question is: Did he hate him so much to want him dead?"
"Good question, sir. But you know what these religious fanatics can be like."

Übung 23: Fügen Sie die richtige Präposition ein!
(in, near, over, at, under, on)

ÜBUNG 23 !

1. The book was ______________ top of the desk.

2. He walked ______________ to him.

3. Scraps of paper were ______________ the waste-paper basket.

4. The waste-paper basket was ______________ the desk.

5. He was sitting ____________ the reception.

6. The restaurant was ____________ the police station.

The policemen went back downstairs. The landlord was expecting them *anxiously*.
"You were right. One of my cushions is missing."
He showed the policemen a chair in the hall near the doorway.
"That's very *suspicious*."
"It certainly is, Sergeant Thompson."
Detective Carlyle turned to the landlord and showed him the message he found in Lord Spencer's room.
"Did anyone give you this message for Lord Spencer?"
The man shook his head.
"No!"
"So Lord Spencer didn't receive any messages yesterday?"
"To be honest, he has never received a message."
"Very strange, very strange *indeed*. Did Lord Spencer have any visitors recently?"
"No, he never had visitors, either. That is…wait a minute! He did have a visitor once, about two weeks ago. The man was a cleric – a minister to be precise."
"Can you remember his name?"
"Sorry, I can't."
"What did he look like?"
"*Scary*!"
"*Scary*, what do you mean by that?"
"It's difficult to say, Detective. He was *creepy*. His face was as white as a sheet; he had very dark thick hair and was at least six foot ten. The man never smiled once."
Detective Carlyle's eyebrow went up.

"Really? Well, thank you for your help. Goodbye!"
"Goodbye!"
Back out on the street the two policemen discussed their next steps.
"Maybe the minister who visited Lord Spencer is the same minister from St. Andrews Church. It can't be a *coincidence* that the campaigners wanted to meet there," said Sergeant Thompson.
"Could well be. Maybe they organized the campaign against Havisham's book together."
The policemen decided to go to St Andrews Church.

Übung 24: Bilden Sie positive Sätze!

ÜBUNG 24

1. Lord Spencer didn't receive a message.

2. He never had visitors.

3. I can't.

4. No, certainly not.

5. No, thank you.

6. I won't come.

7. I don't care.

Chapter 3: The Mysterious Minister Black

By the time Detective Carlyle and Sergeant Thompson arrived at St Andrews Church it was getting dark. The church was very old. On one side there was an *ancient graveyard*. The grave stones were worn and many of them *sloped* to the side. It was overgrown with grass and weeds.

"It's a *creepy* place and look at the *graveyard*; it looks almost like *tombstones* in a jungle."

The sergeant looked up at the roof of the church. *Winged* stone demons looked *fiercely* down upon them. He *shivered*.

"My father used to say: '*Scary* places keep away unwanted guests'," said Detective Carlyle. "Let's have a look around."

The policemen opened the gate of the church yard. It squeaked loudly. Sergeant Thompson jumped with fright. Detective Carlyle smiled at him.

"I think it needs a little bit of oil."

"Yes, absolutely!" said the sergeant trying to play down his fear.

They found the entrance to the church. It was locked. The men moved on. Eventually they came to the minister's house. It looked just as *creepy* as the rest of the place.

"Somebody is at home, sir. There are some lights on in the first floor."

On the door it said: Minister Black. The policemen knocked at the door. They waited for a minute, but nobody answered.

! ÜBUNG 25

Übung 25: Welche Wörter passen inhaltlich zusammen?

1. winged	☐ cleric
2. grave	☐ overgrown
3. church	☐ locked

4. house	☐ yard
5. door	☐ stone
6. garden	☐ demon
7. minister	☐ home

"Knock again, Sergeant, please."

There was still no reaction. The men looked up at the first floor.

Sergeant Thompson knocked at the door again, this time longer and harder. Eventually the door opened.

A very tall, pale man with thick black hair stood in front of them. He was dressed in ministers' clothes. The detective and the sergeant exchanged *acknowledging* looks.

"What do you want?" asked the minister in an unfriendly tone.

"Good evening, Minister," said Detective Carlyle nicely. "My name is Detective Carlyle from the London Police and this is my colleague Sergeant Thompson. We would like to ask you a few questions."

"Question's about what? I don't think I can help you!"

"That's up to us to decide. We are looking for a man called Lord Manuel Spencer. Do you know him?"

"Never heard of him!" he replied *harshly*.

"But we have a *witness* who *claims* you visited him at Stephan's Hotel."

"Stephan's Hotel? Never heard of the place and now if you would excuse me, I am a busy man."

The minister tried to close the door, but the sergeant put his foot in the way.

"Get your foot out of my door! You have no right to question me!" he said angrily.

"As I said, we have a *witness*," said Detective Carlyle calmly.

"A *witness*? Ha, whose word do you believe more: that of a landlord of some second class hotel or a man of God?"
The bushy red eyebrow went up again.

ÜBUNG 26 !

Übung 26: Bilden Sie die Pluralformen!

1. witness	....	6. half	....
2. door	....	7. sheep	....
3. dress	....	8. scarf	....
4. lady	....	9. day	....
5. wife	....	10. tooth	....

"I don't believe anybody *more,* Minister. I just believe the truth. How do you know that Stephan's is a second class hotel?"
For a short second the minister looked irritated.
"It was a good guess, nothing more. Now if you would excuse me!"
The minister *slammed the door in the* policemen's *faces*. Sergeant Thompson *whistled*.
"What a *bad tempered* person."
"Yes, and what a bad liar, too. He definitely knows more than he is *letting on*. We'll have to come back another time."
The policemen *made their way* back to the gate. Just as they were passing the church they heard a loud crashing noise. Sergeant Thompson *was startled*.
"What was that?"
"I don't know. It came from inside the church."
The policemen went to the entrance.
"Open the door, please, Sergeant."

Übung 27: Setzen Sie ***to*** *oder* ***too*** *ein!*

1. He is not only a thief, he is a bad liar ____________.
2. Minister Black lied ____________ the policemen.
3. The minister ought ____________ tell the truth.
4. Detective Carlyle has far ____________ much work to do.
5. Lord Spencer used to be rich ____________.
6. The case is getting ____________ complicated.

The sergeant took out a long metal instrument with a hook at the end. He put it in the lock then twisted and turned it. There was a loud clacking noise and the church door opened. It was very dark inside, a lamp hung beside the door on the wall. Sergeant Thompson took it down and pulled a box of matches out of his pocket.
"This should brighten things up a little," smiled Sergeant Thompson and lit the lamp.
Detective Carlyle and Sergeant Thompson went in carefully. In a far corner the men could see *piles* of boxes. One of them had fallen against the altar.
"Do you think someone is in here?" whispered the sergeant.
"Maybe, keep your eyes open. First of all let's see what's in the boxes."
The policemen moved slowly towards the boxes; the sergeant keeping a watchful eye on everything around them. Detective Carlyle opened a box.
"Look, it's full of Philip Havisham's novel 'Dangerous Confessions of a Dandy'."
The detective opened another box and another. Sergeant Thompson followed him all the time with the lamp.

"Looks like Minister Black ordered a great amount of Philip Havisham's book and I doubt he did this because he is a great admirer," Detective Carlyle remarked.
"Probably for the book burning, sir," said Sergeant Thompson.
"Yes, I wonder how Minister Black is going to talk himself out of this one," said Detective Carlyle triumphantly.

ÜBUNG 28 !

Übung 28: Wählen Sie die richtige Variante!

1. The minister ______________ opened the door.
   a) ☐ scarcely b) ☐ immediately c) ☐ eventually
2. He was a ______________ - tempered person.
   a) ☐ well b) ☐ bad c) ☐ good
3. There were ______________ of boxes.
   a) ☐ miles b) ☐ masses c) ☐ piles
4. Sergeant Thompson __________ a box of matches out of his pocket.
   a) ☐ pulled b) ☐ placed c) ☐ put
5. Keep your eyes ______________.
   a) ☐ wide b) ☐ large c) ☐ open
6. Sergeant Thompson ______________ Detective Carlyle.
   a) ☐ shadowed b) ☐ trailed c) ☐ followed

Suddenly the policemen heard another noise.
They turned around in the direction of the noise. Sergeant Thompson held up the lamp trying to *cast* more light.
"Is there anybody there?" he shouted. "This is the London Police. Come out and show yourself now!"

The sergeant's voice echoed and *bounced off* of the cold stone walls. There was no answer. The policemen held their breaths and listened.
"Maybe it was just a mouse or something, sir?"
"You could be right, but let's take a look."
The men moved slowly over to the corner where the noise had come from. Sergeant Thompson pulled out his *truncheon*.
"Nobody here!" The sergeant moved the lamp up and down, lightening up the walls and the floor.
"Wait a minute, Sergeant!" said Detective Carlyle all of a sudden. "Shine the light back onto the wall…no, not there, a little more to the left…yes, that's it."
"What is it, sir?" asked the sergeant *astonished*.
Detective Carlyle walked over to a stone in the wall that *stuck out* more than the others and pushed it. It *gave way* and part of the stone wall swung open.
"A secret passage!" said Sergeant Thompson *bewildered*. "But how did you know?"
Detective Carlyle smiled at him knowingly.
"I have come across the *odd* secret passage in my time and some things just never change."
The door opened up to a winding spiral wooden staircase.
"After you, Sergeant!"

Übung 29: Enträtseln Sie die folgenden Definitionen!

1. a place you pay to stay in: ______________________ (telho)

2. an aristocratic title: ______________________ (uked)

3. a large church: ______________________ (thcaraled)

4. a thing you can write letters with: ________________ (pyteertwri)

5. something that happens by chance: _____________ (ecnedicnioc)

6. a police rank: ____________________ (gresaetn)

7. an undisclosed corridor: __________ _________ (cesssterpaega)

8. something which creates light: ____________________ (malp)

9. an element of time: ____________________ (eminut)

10. the opposite of before: ____________________ (ertfa)

The men slowly walked down the staircase. The wooden stairs creaked under their feet. At the bottom of the steps the sergeant suddenly cried out loud: "Arrrggghhh!"
Detective Carlyle jumped with fright. He nearly fell down the stairs, but caught the *railing* in time.
"Are you alright, Sergeant?"
Detective Carlyle's voice was *shaky*, but he tried to keep calm.
"Sorry, sir, I'm alright. I didn't want to frighten you, but look at this…"
Sergeant Thompson shone his lamp along a long, thin corridor.
"Skeletons!" *gasped* Detective Carlyle.
As far as their eyes could see skeletons lay on stone platforms alongside both walls.
"This must be some kind of crypt," said Detective Carlyle.
The two men walked on, passing by the *motionless* bones that once had belonged to living human beings. Sergeant Thompson *shivered*.
"These lads could do with a bit of sunlight, might *ease* the old bones a little," he joked, trying to laugh away his fear.
At the end of the corridor the policemen reached a door. Detective Carlyle opened it carefully. The men entered a small, square-shaped

chamber. It consisted of a desk and several shelves full of books. On the floor lay a mattress. A plate with fruit and food lay beside it.
"Looks as if someone has been sleeping here."
"Yes, probably somebody who does not want to be found." remarked Detective Carlyle thoughtfully and looked over to the desk.
"Shine the lamp over to the desk please, Sergeant."

Übung 30: Lesen Sie weiter und unterstreichen Sie die fünf inhaltlich nicht dazugehörenden Sätze!

The desk was untidy. Everything was neat. Sheets of paper were *spread* all over it. A *fountain pen* lay on top of the desk. Detective Carlyle lifted up one of the sheets and read it.
"What does it say?"
"It's a *death threat* and it's addressed to Philip Havisham." Detective Carlyle's red bushy eyebrow went up. He took a sip of tea. "I think we have a *lead* here, Sergeant – I definitely do! The books, the *death threats*; I think the minister has a lot to explain!"
"Do you think he has something to do with the murder?"
"I'm not quite sure yet, but something is certainly very *fishy* about the man. The boxes of books definitely prove that he knows Lord Spencer. They probably organized the book burning session together. If you ask me somebody has been hiding out here and I bet it was Lord Spencer."
Detective Carlyle looked up and saw a bell hanging from the roof.
"Look Sergeant, a warning system. The minister most likely informed Lord Spencer of our presence."
"I think Minister Black certainly has a few things to explain," said Sergeant Thompson.

With that the policeman *headed back* to the staircase. Just as they got to the top of the stairs they could here somebody running up the church isle. Detective Carlyle closed the secret passage.
"There's somebody in the church after all. I'll get him, sir!"
The sergeant run up the rest of the steps and shot out into the church. Detective Carlyle followed him in time to see a shadow *dart* out of the church door. It suddenly *bent down* and plucked a flower.
"Stop, in the name of the law!" shouted Sergeant Thompson as he ran in the direction of the exit. The bright sun almost blinded him.

The sergeant managed to catch up with the person fast. He was about 15 feet behind him. Sergeant Thompson jumped over a grave stone. The *pursued* man shot around to the right and *headed for* the church gate. Sergeant Thompson was very close now; he jumped and caught the fleeing man by the *collar*. They both fell to the ground. Sergeant Thompson got on top of the *struggling* man and held him down.
"Let me go, let me go!" he cried.
Shortly after Detective Carlyle arrived, he was *puffing* and *panting*.
"Good evening, Lord Spencer," he *panted*.
"You have no right...," he tried to throw the sergeant off of him. "Get this *rogue* off of me..."
"Now, now, now, Lord Spencer; you don't want us to charge you for offending a policeman, do you?" said Detective Carlyle friendly. "If you stop *struggling* I'm sure he will let go of you."
Lord Spencer calmed down. Sergeant Thompson got off of him and helped him to his feet. However, he still *had a good grasp of* his arm just in case Lord Spencer tried to run away.
"Let me introduce myself: I'm Detective Carlyle from the London Police and the gentleman who is making sure you don't try to run away is my colleague Sergeant Thompson."

Übung 31: Übersetzen Sie und enträtseln Sie das Lösungswort!

1. Treppe ☐ _ _ _ _ _
2. Grab _ _ _ _ ☐
3. anzeigen _ _ _ ☐ _ _
4. gut ☐ _ _ _
5. ankommen _ _ _ _ _ ☐
6. Kragen _ _ _ _ ☐ _
7. vorstellen _ ☐ _ _ _ _ _ _ _
8. schnell _ _ _ ☐

Lösung: _ _ _ _ _ _ _ _

Sergeant Thompson tipped his police hat. Lord Spencer looked away in *disgust*.
"So what do you want from me then? I have not done anything wrong!"
Detective Carlyle's eyebrow went up *disapprovingly*.
"You *are charged with murder*!"
"Murder?" Lord Spencer *spat* the words out. "That is *ridiculous*!"
The detective ignored this and took out his notebook. He *flicked through* the pages.
"Is it true you were at the Criterion on Sunday evening?"
Lord Spencer nodded.
"Is it also true you *threatened* Mr Havisham because you dislike his recently published book?"
"Yes…'dislike' is not quite the right word; I *detest* it!"

"Do you *detest* it enough to have murdered him?" asked Detective Carlyle.

"Most certainly not, murder is absolutely against my Christian *faith*!"

"And what about the *death threats*?"

"They were just meant to scare him and force Havisham to stop publishing the book. We did not want to kill him."

" '*We*'? Are there more people in on this?"

ÜBUNG 32 !

Übung 32: Welcher Satz enthält die richtige Übersetzung?

1. Die Männer gingen langsam die Treppe hinunter.
   a) ☐ The men gradually walked down the stairs.
   b) ☐ The men slowly walked down the stairs.

2. Er war im Criterion.
   a) ☐ He was on the Criterion.
   b) ☐ He was at the Criterion.

3. Die Polizisten machten sich auf den Weg zurück zur Treppe.
   a) ☐ The policemen headed back to the stairs.
   b) ☐ The policemen directed back to the steps.

4. Lord Spencer beruhigte sich.
   a) ☐ Lord Spencer combed down.
   b) ☐ Lord Spencer calmed down.

5. Lord Spencer verabscheute das Buch.
   a) ☐ Lord Spencer disliked the book.
   b) ☐ Lord Spencer detested the book.

6. Sergeant Thompson ließ ihn los.
   a) ☐ Sergeant Thompson let him be.
   b) ☐ Sergeant Thompson let him go.

At this moment Minister Black came hurrying along.
"What is going on here? Let Lord Spencer go at once!" he said angrily.
"I'm afraid that will not be possible, Minister. I'm going to arrest Lord Spencer for the murder of Philip Havisham. To be honest, I should really take you in as well."
The minister laughed out loud. It was not a real laugh, it sounded more like *mocking*.
"Take me in, what in heavens name for?"
"You lied to us. You have been hiding a murder *suspect*. For all I know you could be in on the murder, too. I *assume* the *death threats* were not just Lord Spencer's idea."
"Okay, I lied and I helped Lord Spencer hide. However, not because he is guilty, but because we knew the police would *suspect* him. I just wanted to keep him out of the way until the real murderer was found. Anyway, you cannot prove anything!"
Sergeant Thompson smiled triumphantly at his *superior*.
"Tell him about the cushion, sir."
The minister looked back and forth between the two men.
"Cushion, what cushion?" he asked nervously.
"The murderer used a cushion to silence his gun and the cushion is from Stephan's Hotel."
"I did not take a cushion out of the hotel – I swear!" Lord Spencer protested.
"We'll have to *carry on* our conversation at the police station, Lord Spencer. Sergeant, if you would kindly escort Lord Spencer to the gate."

"Yes, sir!"
"But you cannot do this!" shouted Minister Black. "I can *testify* that Lord Spencer came straight to the church right after his *quarrel* with Mr Havisham."

ÜBUNG 33 !

Übung 33: Welche Synonyme gehören zusammen?

1. hurry	☐ suggestion
2. honest	☐ argue
3. mock	☐ talk
4. assume	☐ killer
5. murderer	☐ suppose
6. conversation	☐ annoyed
7. quarrel	☐ bear witness
8. testify	☐ truthful
9. angry	☐ rush
10. idea	☐ scorn

Detective Carlyle looked at the minister *sympathetically*.
"I'm afraid you have lied once too often this evening, how am I to believe you now."
"It is true and I also know another ten *God-fearing* people who will be able to *confirm* what I told you."
"Did one of these so-called '*God-fearing*' persons inform Lord Spencer that Philip Havisham would be dining at the Criterion on Sunday evening?"
"I do not know what you are taking about!"
"We found a note addressed to Lord Spencer telling him where he could find Mr Havisham."

"Somebody slipped the note through my door. Neither the minister nor anybody else from this church has anything to do with it!"
Detective Carlyle *sighed*.
"Oh, really?" he said in an ironic tone.
The detective tipped his bowler hat.
"Good evening, Minister Black."
The minister was *trembling with* anger and shook his fist at the policemen.
"This is going to have *repercussions*, believe me!" Then he said in a more gentle tone: "Don't worry, Manuel; I will get you out of there as fast as I can."
Detective Carlyle walked to the gate where the sergeant was waiting for him. Lord Spencer stood in silence, his head hanging *sullenly* towards the ground.

Übung 34: Unterstreichen Sie die richtige Variante!

The (1.) next/after day Detective Carlyle was (2.) called/named into his *superior's* office. Chief Inspector Gatsby was a very fat man and his face was as grey (3.) like/as the sky on a rainy day. The chief inspector was sitting behind (4.) him/his untidy desk drumming his fingers impatiently on the wood. He was not amused.
"What is this I hear (5.) about/over you locking up Lord Spencer? People, *very important* people have been in and out of my office the whole morning! They all *testified* that Lord Spencer was with them in the church (6.) whole/all evening."
"But Philip Havisham was murdered in the early evening. He could have killed him and then joined them (7.) at/on the church."

"When was Mr Havisham murdered?"
"Around seven o'clock."
"And at what time did the *quarrel* between Havisham and Spencer take place?"
"Half past six."
"So we have half an hour between the two incidents."
"Yes, I know that, but…"
Inspector Gatsby did not let him finish his sentence.
"The *witnesses testified* that Lord Spencer arrived at St Andrews Church at a quarter to seven; meaning that it could not have been him."

! ÜBUNG 35

Übung 35: Schreiben Sie die Uhrzeit aus!

1. 06:30 pm *half past six*
2. 08:00 pm ______
3. 04:15 am ______
4. 07:10 pm ______
5. 10:25 am ______
6. 17:45 ______
7. 19:35 ______
8. 15:50 ______
9. 02:05 pm ______
10. 16:20 ______

Detective Carlyle was getting angry. He *clenched* his fist under the table. Nevertheless, he tried to keep calm.
"But these people are *covering for* him. They had been sending Havisham *death threats* and wanted to burn his books publicly. For all I know they could all be in on the murder."
Chief Inspector Gatsby slammed his fist on the table.
"That is outrageous, Detective Carlyle. Do you know who these people are?"

"No, sir, but do tell me," said Detective Carlyle with a *smirk* on his face.
"I most certainly will not! I don't want you round terrorising innocent citizens. However, the one thing I can tell you is that they are all very respectable and credible citizens of London."
"I can prove Lord Spencer is the murderer. The cushion from the scene of the crime is from the hotel where he lives."

Übung 36: Welche Wörter passen inhaltlich zusammen?

ÜBUNG 36

1. hesitate	☐ calm
2. slam	☐ wait
3. burn	☐ door
4. police	☐ crime
5. murder	☐ flame
6. ocean	☐ coach
7. horse	☐ detective

Chief Inspector Gatsby hesitated for a second to think about what Detective Carlyle had said, and then he shook his head.
"Not enough, Carlyle, that is just not enough. Did you find the gun?"
"No, my men searched the church *premises* and the hotel but they could not find it."
Inspector Gatsby took a deep breath.
"We're letting him go!"
"But…"
"No buts! Go and find the real murderer and leave these innocent people alone."
Detective Carlyle stood up shaking his head. He was about to say something, but changed his mind and *headed for* the door.

"Good day, sir!"

"I want you to go to Havisham's house. See if you find any *clues*."

Detective Carlyle did not answer.

"That is an order, Detective!" he shouted after him as he closed the door.

ÜBUNG 37

Übung 37: Lesen Sie weiter und ordnen Sie die Buchstaben in Klammern zu sinnvollen Wörtern!

Sergeant Thompson was (1. pmiateityln) ________________ waiting for Detective Carlyle outside Inspector Gatsby's office.

"What was all the (2. gnitohus) ________________ about?"

"Gatsby wants to let Lord Spencer go (3. refe) ________________."

"What? But the *evidence* against him is (4. vgnilmewhoer) ________________."

"I know - that's why I want one of your men to follow him around. Maybe (5. osoern) ________________ or later he will give himself away or lead us to the *hiding place* of the (6. ung) ________________."

"Will do, sir! What do we do in the meantime?"

"I guess we should go to Philip Havisham's house or we'll be in big trouble."

"What do you mean?" asked the sergeant *puzzled*.

Detective Carlyle nodded in the direction of Chief Inspector Gatsby's office.

"Oh, I see!" said Sergeant Thompson and shook his head.

Übung 38: Wählen Sie die richtige Variante aus!

1. Detective Carlyle was getting ________.
   a) ☐ lucky b) ☐ angry c) ☐ happy
2. The note ________ him where to find Mr Havisham
   a) ☐ said b) ☐ told c) ☐ claimed
3. The minister was trembling with ________.
   a) ☐ fear b) ☐ joy c) ☐ anger
4. Somebody slipped the note ________ Lord Spencer's door.
   a) ☐ through b) ☐ over c) ☐ into
5. Chief Inspector Gatsby took a deep ________.
   a) ☐ gasp b) ☐ breath c) ☐ pant
6. Lord Spencer was let ________.
   a) ☐ free b) ☐ in c) ☐ over
7. Chief Inspector Gatsby ________ his fist on the table.
   a) ☐ smashed b) ☐ slammed c) ☐ hammered

Chapter 4: The Man behind the Dandy

Sergeant Thompson *whistled*. He and Detective Carlyle were standing in the hall of Philip Havisham's house. The doors to the rooms off the hall were wide open: The furniture had been *turned upside down*; drawers were open and their content hanging out.
"Somebody has certainly turned this house into a *pig-sty*, sir!" said Sergeant Thompson.
"Yes, I don't think Philip Havisham left his house like this."
"Do you think it was burgled?"

"I'm not quite sure yet. It certainly looks like a burglary, but it is also possible the person was looking for something – maybe something to do with the murder."
"I wonder why nobody has reported this yet. Philip Havisham must have had relatives or at least servants."
"As far as I know he had no living relatives. However, I don't know if he had servants. I think it is best to contact his close friends Simon Manlove, John Pirrip and Stewart Portman. Maybe they can explain why nobody has reported this yet and tell us if something has been stolen."
"I'll get one of my men to contact them."
"Good, Sergeant, in the meantime I'm going to look around the house."

ÜBUNG 39 !

Übung 39: Markieren Sie mit richtig ✓ oder falsch – !

1. Victorian upper-class people had servants. ☐
2. Philip Havisham had servants. ☐
3. Chief Inspector Gatsby was a very slim man. ☐
4. Philip Havisham's house was burgled. ☐
5. Lord Spencer is the main suspect. ☐
6. The furniture had been toppled onto the street. ☐
7. Philip Havisham's house looked like a horse-stable. ☐

About three quarters of an hour later the sergeant arrived at the house with Philip Havisham's friends. They were all dressed in black as they had just been to Philip Havisham's *funeral*.
"What has happened here?" cried out Simon Manlove.
"We are not quite sure at the moment, but I thought, gentlemen, you could help us find out," said Detective Carlyle calmly.

The men looked at each other. They all looked very sad. Then John Pirrip looked towards Detective Carlyle.
"*With all due respect*, Detective, we have just been to Mr Havisham's *funeral* and are not really up to being questioned just now. Are you sure we can really help you?"
"At least I hope so. What interests me most is why nobody has reported this? Mr Havisham has been dead for nearly three days now."
"Mr Havisham does not have any living relatives", answered Stewart Portman, "but Mr Pirrip has a key and wanted to come and check on things…"
"I just have not been able to make myself do it. There are so many good memories attached to the house," said John Pirrip finishing Stewart Portman's sentence. He sounded very sad.
"I see, and did Philip Havisham not have any servants either?"
The three friends laughed in a soft and *rueful* way.
"Philip…I mean Mr Havisham hated servants. He believed they were far too *inquisitive* and corrupt," said Simon Manlove.
The three men smiled and shook their heads. Detective Carlyle waited a few seconds and then said:
"Gentlemen, I would like you to walk around the house with me and tell me if you think anything is missing. I am sure nobody knows this place better than you."

Übung 40: Ordnen Sie das passende Reflexivpronomen zu!

ÜBUNG 40 !

1. I could not make *myself* do it.

2. You could not make ________________ do it.

3. He could not make ________________ do it.

4. She could not make ________________ do it.

5. It could not make ________________ do it.

6. We could not make ________________ do it.

7. You could not make ________________ do it.

8. They could not make ________________ do it.

Together with them, Detective Carlyle looked in every room of the house, but nothing *appeared* to have been stolen. They all came back down the stairs and stood in the hall by the front door.
"That is strange!" said a perplexed Simon Manlove. "Why should someone break into a place and not steal anything?"
"If I knew that I could solve the case *in no time*," answered Detective Carlyle. "But I *assume* the murderer was looking for something."
"For what?" asked John Pirrip.
"I don't know. Maybe he was looking for whatever he killed Mr Havisham for."
The three friends looked even paler and more shocked than in the beginning.
"I think I have *strained* your nerves enough for today. You may go home now. I will keep you up to date with the investigation."
"Yes, please do so. The sooner you find this terrible murderer the better," Stewart Portman said with a *shaky* voice.
Philip Havisham's friends shook the policemen's hands, said goodbye and left.

! ÜBUNG 41

Übung 41: Welche Verben und Substantive gehören zusammen?

1. solve	☐ a fuss
2. knock	☐ a steak
3. commit	☐ an interview

4. conduct	☐ a murder
5. eat	☐ at the door
6. make	☐ the case

"What shall we do now, sir?" *sighed* Sergeant Thompson.
"Maybe the murderer has not found what he was looking for. So let's have a look around and see if we can find anything *suspicious*."
Detective Carlyle and Sergeant Thompson began searching Philip Havisham's home. After a while Sergeant Thompson came into Philip Havisham's bedroom. Detective Carlyle's feet were *sticking out* from under the bed. It had a *brass* golden *bedstead* which shone brightly in the summer sun coming through the bedroom window.

Übung 42: Lesen Sie weiter und unterstreichen Sie vier Begriffe, die Erstaunen ausdrücken!

"Find anything, sir?" Sergeant Thompson *smirked*.
Detective Carlyle's feet *wobbled* about as he pushed himself back. He *surfaced*. His hair was quite a mess and he had a very large box in his hand.
"Yes!" he said triumphantly to the sergeant.
The detective laid the box on the bed and opened it. It was full of small black books.
"Diaries!" exclaimed Sergeant Thompson. "What shall we do with them?"
"Read them!" and with this Detective Carlyle gave the sergeant a couple of books.
"Read them?" *gasped* the sergeant unenthusiastically. "There must be about 40 or 50 in the box!"
"Well, you had better get started then. We don't want to take all day," said Detective Carlyle in a friendly, casual tone.

The sergeant looked *baffled*.
"If you say so, sir."
He took his *share* of the diaries and sat on the corner of the bed. Detective Carlyle sat on the other side. After some time the sergeant said: "This *chap* is unbelievable! Do you know that he had the nerve to *con* Simon Manlove *out of* 150 pounds! He wrote here he just did it for pleasure!"

Detective Carlyle shook his head *disapprovingly*.
"And I just read that he sold two bottles of port to John Pirrip for four times as much as he had paid."
"What was wrong with this man, sir? He *betrayed* his best friends!"
Sergeant Thompson paused and thought for a second.
"Wait a minute, do you think…"
"No, Sergeant! I don't think that gives a man enough motivation to cold-bloodedly shoot his friend in the heart; even though his behaviour towards them was very shameful. I doubt his friends know of this, but what this information does tell us is that Philip Havisham was not a very *honourable* man."
"He most certainly wasn't!" said the sergeant in *disgust*.
Suddenly the doorbell rang.
"I'll answer that," *volunteered* Sergeant Thompson.

ÜBUNG 43 !

Übung 43: Welche viktorianischen Wörter entsprechen heutigen Ausdrücken?

1. Sir	☐ talk
2. chap	☐ living-room
3. Madame	☐ guy
4. drawing room	☐ womanizer

5. lady's man ☐ foyer
6. anteroom ☐ Mr
7. patter ☐ Mrs

He went down the stairs and opened the door. Constable Taylor, a young new recruit, was standing in front of the door. He was out of breath.
"Sergeant Thompson, we've just followed Lord Spencer to something which *appears* to be a *hide-out*."
"Where is it?"
"Blackwall, on the north bank of the Thames. We followed him to a *shed* located at the West India Docks."
"Good work, Constable. I will be with you in just a minute."
Sergeant Thompson walked towards the stairs and called to his *superior*. Detective Carlyle was still reading the diaries when he heard the sergeant's voice: "We have a *lead*, sir!"
The detective quickly packed the diaries back into the box.
"Very interesting material," he *mumbled* to himself. "I'll read the rest later."

Übung 44: Setzen Sie die richtige Zukunftsform in die Lücken!

ÜBUNG 44 !

1. We're in a hurry, I'm afraid you ________________ have to read the diaries later.

2. Okay, I ________________ read them when I get home.

3. This time tomorrow we're ________________ know more.

4. I'm ________________ read the rest of the diaries tonight.

5. I'm actually ________________ get through all of them tonight if it's the last thing I ever do.

Detective Carlyle hurried down the stairs with the large box in his hands. The men ran towards the police coach awaiting them at the gate. "Oh, I nearly forgot to tell you that Dr Brown has identified the bullet which belongs to the murder weapon: Havisham was killed with a Remington Revolver," Constable Taylor *panted*.
"Just as I thought! Maybe Lord Spencer has led us to its *hiding place*."
They hastily climbed into the coach, the coachman cracked his *whip* and the coach shot off.

ÜBUNG 45 !

Übung 45: Was ist gemeint? Setzen Sie ein!
(hide-out, diary, bedroom, murder weapon, constable, volunteer, a mess)

1. a book to document appointments: ________________
2. a remote hiding place: ________________
3. a place to sleep in: ________________
4. lowest police rank: ________________
5. to do something of free will: ________________
6. something someone is killed with: ________________
7. in a very bad condition: ________________

Detective Carlyle, Sergeant Thompson and Constable Taylor *approached* two other policemen. They were hiding behind an old

dock container and were observing the *shed* which was close to the water.
"Is he still in there?" asked Detective Carlyle.
"Yes, sir!" answered one of the constables. "I wonder what he has been doing all this time."
"We'll soon find out. I'll count to three and then we'll *sneak* over, but be careful, the *suspect* could be *armed*."
The policemen moved carefully towards the *shed* keeping their heads down low. As they reached the *shed* they *crouched* down. Detective Carlyle carefully looked into one of the windows. What he saw surprised him. His eyebrow went up.
"Looks like a game of *whist*!" he said *astonished*.
"*Whist*, sir?!" asked Sergeant Thompson.
Everybody looked *puzzled*.
"Yes, Lord Spencer is sitting in there with three other men. I think I've seen one of them before, I just can't remember where."
"What shall we do?"
"I say we take them in. Unofficial *gambling* is against the law!"
"I'll count to three again and then I want two of your men to kick the door down…one…two…three…"
Two constables kicked the door down and blew their *whistles*.
"The game is over!" they cried.
They were followed by the sergeant and the detective. There was a lot of *turmoil*.

Übung 46: Setzen Sie die passende Mengenbezeichnung ein! ***(a lot of, much)***

! ÜBUNG 46

1. The case is not solved yet. There still are __________ things to be done.

2. Lord Spencer is in ______________ trouble.

3. Detective Carlyle asked ______________ questions.

4. But he did not really have very ______________ time.

5. Lord Spencer did not say very ______________.

One of the men tried to escape, but he was quickly caught by a young and *swift* constable. Lord Spencer looked surprised.
"Detective Carlyle, I had hoped I had seen the last of you. Did Chief Inspector Gatsby not give you orders to leave me alone?"
"Chief Inspector Gatsby believes you are innocent, but I don't." Detective Carlyle turned to the two constables. "Search the hut and Lord Spencer for the gun, please!"
The policemen went to work.
Lord Spencer smiled *mockingly*.
"I have no gun, why do you not believe me?"
"Gun? What gun?" one of the gamblers asked Lord Spencer nervously.
He was a very well-dressed man, as were all of the gentlemen present.

ÜBUNG 47 !

*Übung 47: Vervollständigen Sie die Sätze mit **good** oder **well**!*

1. Detective Carlyle is a very ____________ policeman.

2. Sergeant Thompson does his job really ____________.

3. Lord Spencer appears to be ____________ at lying.

4. Sir James is a ____________ whist player.

5. All of the gentlemen were very ____________ dressed.

6. Some people are just __________ for nothing.

7. Just as __________ Detective Carlyle caught them gambling.

"Nothing to worry about, Sir James. It's just some kind of misunderstanding," said Lord Spencer.
"I bloody well hope so!" he said angrily. "Bad enough them catching us here playing a game of *whist*. If this is made public…"
"…Nobody is going to make anything public!" interrupted the man Detective Carlyle thought he knew from somewhere.
"I think that is up to me to decide, Mr…," Detective Carlyle made a gesture for the man to finish his sentence.
"Lord Fellowes!" he said in a *threatening* tone.
"Lord Fellowes? I am sure that rings a bell."
"I most certainly would hope so. I am First Lord of the Admiralty – as you know a very high position in the British Parliament."
Lord Fellowes paused to let his great words sink in. Detective Carlyle looked at him *pensively* and *sighed*. He knew what he was about to do could get him into great trouble with his *superior*.
"Lord Fellowes, gentlemen – I am afraid I will have to arrest you for illegal *gambling*."
There was *uproar* in the *shed*. The constables started taking the men outside. They protested loudly. Constable Taylor came over to Detective Carlyle.
"I'm afraid we could not find the gun."
"Never mind, I'm sure we'll find it sooner or later."
Just at that moment Lord Fellowes was being escorted out. He gave Detective Carlyle a very angry look.
"You will pay for this!" he shouted.
"I know, I know!" said Detective Carlyle with a distinctly *gloomy* tone to his voice.

ÜBUNG 48 !

Übung 48: Welches Wort ist das „schwarze Schaf"?

1. find, discover, ascertain, mislay
2. hope, crave, dread, anticipate
3. worry, fret, exasperate, wish
4. right, wrong, incorrect, false
5. innocent, guilty, guiltless, blameless
6. believe, trust, doubt, rely
7. hide, reveal, conceal, mask
8. angry, fuming, glad, furious

The last man to be taken out of the *shed* was Lord Spencer. His *seeming* confidence had disappeared. He was feeling very sorry for himself. He looked sadly at Detective Carlyle.
"You caught me *gambling*, but that does not mean I am a murderer. I want to be honest with you: I *am addicted to gambling*. Why do you think I live in such a poor hotel? It is because I waste all of my money on *gambling*."
Detective Carlyle looked him straight in the eye. For some reason his police-instinct was telling him to believe Lord Spencer.
"Is that how you ended up in the hands of that religious fanatic Minister Black?"
"Yes, I was looking for *spiritual guidance*. I had really wanted to stop. It is not much of a life you know, losing all your money at a silly game."

Tears welled up in Lord Spencer's eyes. He was very embarrassed by this and quickly *wiped* them away. Detective Carlyle looked at him *sympathetically*.
"Well, by the looks of it the Minister seems to have got you into even more trouble and he has apparently not been able to help you fight your *addiction* either."

"I had stopped for a while", Lord Spencer insisted, "however, after all the trouble you caused me, accusing me of murder and all that, I started to *gamble* again."
"I am sorry to hear that, but a lot of the *evidence* does seem to make you *appear* guilty. We will just have to wait and see how the further investigations turn out."
Detective Carlyle nodded in the direction of the exit. The constable escorted Lord Spencer out of the *shed*.

Übung 49: Mit oder ohne Artikel? Setzen Sie, wenn nötig, ***the*** *ein!*

ÜBUNG 49 !

1. They were walking in ______ same direction.

2. Such is ______ life.

3. Lord Spencer got out of ______ bed early to play cards.

4. Lord Spencer liked to go to ______ church.

5. Sir James knows a lot about ______ history of England.

6. ______ life Mister Black leads is very boring.

"So what do you think, sir; do you believe him?"
"He seems to be telling the truth. If he isn't he sure is a very good liar. What does seem plausible to me is that my long experience with the police has taught me that someone with a *gambling addiction* would not break into a house with so many *riches* as Havisham's and *resist* stealing something."
"You do have a point. Do you think someone has tried to *set* Lord Spencer *up*?"

"It is a possibility. Lord Spencer was easy *bait* as he *detested* Philip Havisham's book. He was probably just waiting for a chance to confront him."

"So maybe the poor man just walked right into a trap?"

"Yes, it's possible. The person who *allegedly* passed the note through his door could easily have taken a cushion from the hotel; leading us straight to Lord Spencer."

The detective and the sergeant walked slowly towards the police coach.

"I think we've had enough excitement for today. It's time we went home; I've still got those diaries to read through. Who knows, maybe I'll find something that might help us solve this most puzzling case."

ÜBUNG 50 !

Übung 50: Welche Bedeutung haben folgende Sätze?

1. Lord Spencer was looking for spiritual guidance.
   a) ☐ Lord Spencer needed more fun.
   b) ☐ Lord Spencer needed a drink.
   c) ☐ Lord Spencer needed help.

2. Minister Black is a religious fanatic.
   a) ☐ Minister Black is narrow-minded.
   b) ☐ Minister Black is open-minded.
   c) ☐ Minister Black is immoral.

3. He walked into a trap.
   a) ☐ He got lost.
   b) ☐ He got caught.
   c) ☐ He got hit.

4. Detective Carlyle was sympathetic.
   a) ☐ Detective Carlyle was a nice person.
   b) ☐ Detective Carlyle was considerate.
   c) ☐ Detective Carlyle disapproved.

5. Lord Spencer appears to be guilty.
   a) ☐ Lord Spencer is unlikely to be guilty.
   b) ☐ Lord Spencer admitted he was guilty.
   c) ☐ Lord Spencer is probably guilty.

Chapter 5: The Beautiful Baroness McKee

Detective Carlyle and Sergeant Thompson met early at the police station the next day. The two policemen sat themselves down in Detective Carlyle's office. They had steaming cups of tea in front of them. The detective had not slept much, but reading all of Philip Havisham's diaries had been worth staying up most of the night.
"What did you find out, sir?" asked Sergeant Thompson trying to hide his excitement.
"Philip Havisham had a relationship with a woman named Baroness McKee."
The sergeant looked disappointed.
"If you will excuse me saying so – but that's not really very surprising, sir; the man had a few affairs in his time!"
Detective Carlyle smiled *wisely* at Sergeant Thompson and lent back on his chair.
"Let me finish, Sergeant. As St Augustine said: '*Patience is the companion of wisdom*'."
Sergeant Thompson looked like a school boy who had been told off by his teacher.

"Sorry, sir – I'm just very curious!"
"*Indeed* you are, and that is a quality a job like ours needs."
Detective Carlyle tipped his nose with his finger.
"Anyway, Baroness McKee must be a very beautiful woman; in fact the most beautiful woman in London, if we want to believe Philip Havisham – and I guess, as we know by now, the man knew what he was talking about."
Sergeant Thompson *chuckled*.
"But the thing about Baroness McKee was", Detective Carlyle *carried on*, "that she was not interested in Philip Havisham in the least – she was a very conservative Lady and did not like Mr Havisham's way of life."
"So what made her change her mind?" asked Sergeant Thompson impatiently.

ÜBUNG 51 !

Übung 51: Ordnen Sie die Wörter auf der rechten Seite den Begriffen auf der linken zu!

1. gasp	a) ☐	handle, cope, run
2. wisdom	b) ☐	lure, attract, tempt
3. guess	c) ☐	wants, requirements, desires
4. life	d) ☐	consider, think, trust
5. needs	e) ☐	pant, puff, breath
6. bait	f) ☐	make-up, play, make-believe
7. manage	g) ☐	presume, assume, estimate
8. pretend	h) ☐	mayhem, upheaval, turmoil
9. believe	i) ☐	being, existence, mortal
10. uproar	k) ☐	insight, understand, knowledge

Detective Carlyle's bushy red eyebrow went up *disapprovingly*. This gesture silenced Sergeant Thompson.

"She changed her mind because he managed to make her believe he was a new person; for weeks he played the perfect gentleman and *pretended* to be a newborn man. In the end he eventually won her heart."
"That is unbelievable, sir!" *gasped* Sergeant Thompson. "Philip Havisham was a very *devious* man!"
"It gets worse," said Detective Carlyle *grimly*.
"How much worse can it get?"
"Well, he did all of it because of a bet…"
"A bet?" Sergeant Thompson could not believe his ears.
"Yes, he bet with a friend he could win her heart."
"But that means he did not really care about her. The only thing that really attracted him was that she was hard to get."
"I *assume* so."
"That is outrageous!"

Übung 52: Enträtseln Sie die fünf Begriffe, die man stellvertretend für ***outrageous*** *sagen könnte!*

! ÜBUNG 52

1. lufemsha ______________
2. kingoshc ______________
3. racegulfsid ______________
4. ablepicdes ______________
5. ppallniga ______________

Detective Carlyle nodded with a sigh.
"It certainly is, Sergeant."
"What happened after he won her heart?"
"He broke it."
"What did he do – just left her and that was it?"
"Yes!"
"But a woman of her rank and moral integrity must have been *shattered*!"

Sergeant Thompson paused and thought for a moment.
"She definitely has a motive," he remarked.
"She sure has, but the question is if a lady of such integrity could really cold-bloodedly murder another person?"
"But Philip Havisham did treat Baroness McKee very badly and *hurt* her to a great *extent* – the lies, *deceit* and dishonesty she experienced were terrible!"
"Exactly! That is why I think we should pay Baroness McKee a visit."
The two policemen took a last sip of their tea and left the office.

! ÜBUNG 53

Übung 53: Bilden Sie sinnvolle Sätze!

1. relationship Baroness he McKee woman a with called a had

2. had cups front in steaming they them of tea of

3. place more fortress if looks ask you me this like a

4. left he her won after heart he her

5. really could Baroness McKee murder person a

6. is Philip Havisham man devious a

7. share took of sat corner at bed of diaries a he the the and the

8. Thompson Sergeant read want books did not to the

Detective Carlyle and Sergeant Thompson arrived at Baroness McKee's house. It was extremely large and located in Mayfair – a very aristocratic district. The crème de la crème of *Victorian* London's high-society lived there. A long, high iron fence protected the *property* from unwanted visitors. Each *bar* was *spear-shaped* and looked very sharp. Sergeant Thompson looked *bewildered*.
"That place looks more like a fortress than a house, if you ask me!"
"Yes, but it still couldn't protect the baroness from Philip Havisham," Detective Carlyle remarked.
The policemen got out of the coach and climbed the steps to the doorway bridge which led over a six foot deep *ditch* on either side. Sergeant Thompson opened the small gate at the top of the steps and let his *superior* pass. Detective Carlyle used the knocker – an iron *loop-shaped device* which hung on the door. Shortly afterwards a butler opened the door.

Übung 54: Lesen Sie weiter und setzen Sie das passende Wort ein!
(wish, home, investigating, unnoticeable, luck, message, statue, observed, contact)

"You (1.) ________________?" he asked in a monotonous and almost bored tone. "Who may I announce?"
"My name is Detective Carlyle from the London Police. I wish to speak to Baroness McKee. It is very important; I am (2.) ________________ the murder of Philip Havisham."

The detective (3.) ________________ a slight *twinge* at the corner of the butler's mouth. *Apart from* this almost (4.) ________________ movement, the butler's face did not *alter* – it reminded the detective of a (5.) ________________ made of stone

"I am afraid Baroness McKee is not at (6.) ________________ at the moment. Do you wish to leave a (7.) ________________?"

"Could you please tell her I was here and that I would be very grateful if she would (8.) ________________ me as soon as possible."

"I will most certainly do so," replied the butler and closed the door.

Sergeant Thompson *shrugged*:

"No (9.) ________________, eh?"

The policeman turned away from the door. In that moment Detective Carlyle *glanced* sideways to the window at the front of the house. He saw a curtain move slightly. He looked away as if nothing had happened.
"I wouldn't say that," he *mumbled* to himself while they walked back down the stairs.
Detective Carlyle and Sergeant Thompson got back into the coach. As soon as it turned the corner Detective Carlyle asked the coachman to stop.
"Why are we stopping, sir?" asked Sergeant Thompson *puzzled*.
"Because Baroness McKee is probably at home."
"How do you know?"
"I saw a curtain move in one of her windows. I *assume* she was watching us, to see who we were."

Sergeant Thompson was impressed. He smiled at his *superior* and tipped his nose with his finger. Detective Carlyle smiled back. The men got out of the coach and walked back to the entrance of the street where Baroness McKee's house was. There was a wall they could hide behind allowing them to observe the baroness's home.
"What are we going to do now, sir?"
"I suggest we wait and see what happens. She might leave the house sooner or later. Then we'll follow her."

Übung 55: Unterstreichen und verbessern Sie im folgenden Textabschnitt die sieben falsch geschriebenen Wörter!

After one and a half hours stil nothing had happened. Sergeant Thompson was getting impatient.
"Maybe she isn't at home after all," he said.
Detective Carlyle gave his sergeant another one of his *disapproving* looks.
"I know, I know: '*Patience is the companion of wissdom*'!" he said in a slightly irritated tone.
All of a suden the baroness's front door opened and an astonishingly beautiful and elegant woman *appeared*. Sergeant Thompson was speechless. He just watched her descend the steps in amazement. Detective Carlyle looked to the side and observed the open-mouthed sergeant.
"Sergeant Thompson?" he said amuced.
"Sir?" said the sergeant without taking his eyes off the baroness. His voice had a *distracted* and remot ring to it.
"We have work to do?"
"Oh…yes…of course…you are absolutely right!" replied the sergeant as if he had just been awoken from a beautiful dreem.

The policemen started to follow Baroness McKee. They followed her to the neighbourhood of Berkley Square.
"I don't think such a beautiful lady could just have walked in and out of the Criterion Restaurant without being noticed, do you?" Sergeant Thompson asked Detective Carlyle.
"No, I don't, but she could have disguised herself or perhaps she paid someone to kill Philip Havisham."
Sergeant Thompson looked at Detective Carlyle in disbelief.
"I think she is innocent. I meen, she must be…such an attractive and delicate-looking being…she probably couldn't *hurt* a fly!"
"Time will tell, Romeo!" laughed Detective Carlyle.

1. ______________________
2. ______________________
3. ______________________
4. ______________________
5. ______________________
6. ______________________
7. ______________________

Sergeant Thompson looked a little embarrassed and went red.
Just off Berkley Square Baroness McKee entered a café. The policemen waited on the other side of the road. They could see what she was doing through the large glass window. She greeted a man with a nod and sat down at his table. He was well-dressed, however, he had a cruel and rough-looking face, which did not seem to match his exquisite and expensive outfit.
"Don't seem to be the best of friends," said Detective Carlyle.
"Wait a minute, I know that man from somewhere!" exclaimed Sergeant Thompson. "Well, I'll be damned, that's William Butcher!"
"William Butcher? That man has been in and out of jail more times than the prison director himself!"

"You can say that again. He has worked through the catalogue of offences like others through a restaurant menu: *assault*, dealing with opium and many other offences – you name it, he's done it."
"Murder?"
"I'm not quite sure about murder, sir. What I want to know is why in heavens name Baroness McKee keeps such bad company!"
"Maybe our baroness is not as innocent as she looks."
Sergeant Thompson was about to protest when she suddenly passed an envelope under the table to William Butcher.
"What do you think is in the envelope?" asked Sergeant Thompson.
"I'm not quite sure, certainly not any good news. As soon as William Butcher leaves the café, we'll follow him and wait for the right moment to get a hold of him."
"And what about the baroness?"
"We'll leave her for just now. I don't want her to know we are on to her quite yet."

Übung 56: Welche Bedeutung haben die Sätze? Kreuzen Sie an!

1. Well, I'll be damned!
   a) ☐ That really surprises me.
   b) ☐ I am going to hell.
   c) ☐ The water pressure is high.

2. He has been in and out of jail more times than the director himself.
   a) ☐ He is more important than the jail director.
   b) ☐ He has been in jail very often.
   c) ☐ He likes going to jail very much.

3. He has worked through the catalogue of offences like others through a restaurant menu.
   a) ☐ He likes good food.
   b) ☐ He likes to read.
   c) ☐ He has a long criminal record.

4. You name it, he's done it!
   a) ☐ He will do anything you say.
   b) ☐ There is not a crime he has not committed.
   c) ☐ He has great knowledge of things.

5. She is in bad company.
   a) ☐ She is with someone or people, who are dangerous.
   b) ☐ She works for a terrible firm.
   c) ☐ She dislikes good company.

Shortly after, both the baroness and William Butcher left the café. The policemen followed William Butcher for a while. The criminal had no idea he was being followed. He turned into a small narrow lane.
"Let's try and get ahold of him now."
Sergeant Thompson and Detective Carlyle ran into the lane after William Butcher. He heard the steps and turned around, the policemen were very close. The criminal took to his feet. Sergeant Thompson finally caught up with him. Detective Carlyle was still a bit further behind. The sergeant held William Butcher by his *collar* and pushed him against the wall. William Butcher did not move and did not say a thing. He seemed very calm.
"Now, no funny tricks!" said Sergeant Thompson.
William Butcher just smiled *mockingly*. His smile looked *creepy* because his front teeth were missing. Sergeant Thompson put his

hand into the inside pocket of William Butcher's jacket and took out the envelope.
"So what have we got here?" said Sergeant Thompson triumphantly. At that moment Detective Carlyle arrived. He was breathing heavily. The sergeant turned around and *handed* the envelope to his *superior*. William Butcher used this moment of *distraction* to his advantage. He *punched* Sergeant Thompson in the stomach and pushed him away. The *blow* was very hard and the sergeant *toppled over*. William Butcher ran as fast as he could. Sergeant Thompson got back on his feet.
"Come back, you *scoundrel*!" he shouted in anger and started to run after him, but William Butcher managed to escape.

Übung 57: Füllen Sie die Lücken mit dem passenden Wort!
(under, used, about, down 2x, at, up, behind, to 2x)

ÜBUNG 57 !

1. Philip Havisham worked ____________ the menu.
2. Lord Spencer was ____________ to protest.
3. The policemen started ____________ follow him.
4. She passed the envelope ____________ the table.
5. Detective Carlyle ____________ the door knocker.
6. The baroness was not ____________ home.
7. The policemen crouched ____________.
8. They finally caught ____________ with him.
9. William Butcher took ____________ his feet.
10. Sergeant Thompson hid ____________ a wall.

"Are you all right, Sergeant?" asked Detective Carlyle as the former returned back to the lane.
Thompson was holding his stomach and was out of breath.
"Yes, but if I ever catch that man he will be sorry!"
"I'm sure we'll get him sooner or later," said Detective Carlyle.
"So what's in the envelope?" asked Sergeant Thompson as he leaned against the wall still *puffing* and *panting*.
"Money – a lot of money!"
Detective Carlyle waved a bundle of notes in the air.
"I hate to ask this: Do you think the baroness paid him to kill Philip Havisham?"
"It's possible, Or can you think of any other reason why she met up with such a person and gave him a lot of money?"
Sergeant Thompson shook his head.
"Well, let's get back to her house and I won't let her arrogant butler blow us off this time."

ÜBUNG 58 !

Übung 58: Setzen Sie im folgenden Text die richtigen Fragepronomen ein!
(whose, whose, who, who, which, what, where)

1. ____________ is Baroness McKee?
2. ____________ did she meet William Butcher?
3. ____________ money was in the envelope?
4. In ____________ café did Baroness McKee and William Butcher meet?
5. ____________ is the name of the square in which Philip Havisham's house is located?

6. .... is the main murder suspect?

7. .... servant opened the door?

Detective Carlyle knocked at the baroness's door. The butler opened the door.
"Oh, it is you again!" he said in his arrogant tone. "I told you the baroness is not in at the moment."
Sergeant Thompson shot forward.
"Now listen, you. I've had enough of your nonsense! We know the baroness is at home, now let us in!" he said angrily.
The butler's mouth *twitched* again. Detective Carlyle gave his sergeant a slight, calming push to the side.
"I'll *deal with* this, Sergeant."
He looked the butler straight in the eye.
"We have reason to believe that Baroness McKee is involved in the murder of Philip Havisham. Just tell her we followed her to the Café Royal and let her make up her own mind whether or not she wants to talk to us after all."
The butler disappeared without a word and came back to the door shortly afterwards. He let the policemen in – his face showing a slight look of *disgust*.
"Thank you!" said Detective Carlyle triumphantly and lifted his bowler hat in a greeting gesture. Sergeant Thompson gave the butler an angry look. The butler did not seem to care – he did not look at the policemen once and stared straight ahead in the direction of the wall. He closed the door.
"If you will kindly follow me," he said and walked down the long, bright hall in front of the policemen. Sergeant Thompson could not hide that he was impressed by the thick red carpet, the paintings of long dead *ancestors* and the gold framed mirrors, which decorated

the hallway. The corridor seemed to be endless until they eventually reached a door – the butler opened it and entered the room. Detective Carlyle and Sergeant Thompson could not get a proper look of the inside because the butler had only left the door half open.

"Madame, the two gentlemen from the police I told you about."

"Yes, let them in," a soft female voice answered.

ÜBUNG 59

Übung 59: Übersetzen Sie!

1. Die Baronin hatte eine geheimnisvolle Ausstrahlung.

2. Sie konnten nicht richtig in das Zimmer sehen.

3. Sergeant Thompson griff in seine Innentasche.

4. Sobald William Butcher das Café verlässt, werden wir ihm folgen.

5. Die Polizisten näherten sich vorsichtig den Kisten.

6. Detective Carlyle sah, dass der Vorhang sich bewegte.

The doors opened and the policemen stepped into a large drawing room. The baroness lay on a chaise longue – a couch in the shape of a chair. She was leaning *gracefully* against the sofa's arm supporting her head with her hand. She looked almost like a Roman *empress*. The chaise longue was *covered* in white satin and in front of it was a huge Persian *rug*. The butler *bowed*, left the drawing room, closing the doors behind him.

"How may I help you, Gentlemen?" asked the baroness. There was something about her voice that did not seem right. It sounded slow and *drowsy*. Detective Carlyle and Sergeant Thompson looked at each other.

"I am Detective Carlyle and this is my colleague Sergeant Thompson – we are from the London Police," the detective said with his most formal voice.

Baroness McKee *glanced* at Sergeant Thompson standing in his police uniform.

"Well, that would be hard to guess!" she said in a dry, sarcastic tone. "So what does the London Police want from me?"

Detective Carlyle cleared his throat. The baroness *exuded* a bizarre, *secretive* aura and her beauty combined with her aristocratic self-confidence had a disarming effect on both policemen.

"We are investigating the murder of Philip Havisham – he was shot dead a few days ago in the Criterion."

"Yes, I have heard of that. What a shame," said Baroness McKee sarcastically.

Detective Carlyle cleared his throat again.

"Well, what I would like to know is where you were on Sunday the 6th of July."

The baroness laughed. It was a loud, almost hysterical laugh. The policemen exchanged looks again. Sergeant Thompson *shrugged* helplessly.

Übung 60: Lesen Sie weiter und unterstreichen Sie im Text die Synonyme der Wörter in Klammern!
(1. condemning, 2. lack discretion, 3. did you find that out, 4. that is typical of him, 5. assume)

"Where I was? You are not really accusing me of the murder, Detective Carlyle?"
"To be honest, Madame, we do have reason to *suspect* you."
"And what may that be?" she asked coldly.
"I do not want to be indiscreet, but we know you had a relationship with Mr Havisham…"
"…But you *are* being indiscreet," interrupted Baroness McKee angrily. "How did you find out about this? And if it is true, how does that make me a murder *suspect*?"
"We also know that Mr Havisham treated you…how shall I say…very badly."
This time the baroness laughed hysterically.
"Badly? I like that, I like that very much! Very good, Detective, very good!" Then she all of a sudden stopped laughing. Her face became very serious. "Now, how do you know of this?" she asked *grimly*.
"Mr Havisham wrote diaries, I read about it in one of them."
"Trust him!" *sighed* Baroness McKee. "And now you believe I shot him because of all he did to me."

"Yes!"
"Well, I wish I had, but I must disappoint you, I did not."
"That could be true, however, we have reason to believe you paid William Butcher to kill him. We saw you meeting him at the Café Royal," said Sergeant Thompson.
"Yes, I know you know that, but what does that prove?" asked the baroness impatiently. "For all you know he could be my new *fiancé*

– I seem to have been quite *keen on* dishonest men lately," she *chuckled*.

Detective Carlyle tried to ignore this remark. He was beginning to feel very sorry for Baroness McKee. She seemed to *be in great* emotional *distress*.

"Why did you pay him so much money then?"

Baroness McKee looked at the policemen. She seemed to be thinking hard about something. For a few seconds there was nothing but silence in the room. Then the baroness moved into a sitting position. In the process of this she nearly lost her balance. Sergeant Thompson was about to hurry over and catch her, but she managed to stabilize herself. "I take opium! I take it because it is the only thing on earth that helps me forget what Philip Havisham did to me."

Detective Carlyle and Sergeant Thompson looked a little embarrassed.

Übung 61: Welches Wort ist das „schwarze Schaf"?

ÜBUNG 61 !

1. dishonest, good-natured, deceitful, devious
2. meet, gather, leave, congregate
3. mention, remark, unspoken, say
4. money, riches, penniless, wealthy
5. book, newspaper, novel, sign
6. letter, stamp, address, account
7. evening, breakfast, morning, afternoon
8. week, month, age, year

"I meet William Butcher every two weeks at the Café Royal and pay him for his deliveries – he sells me opium! I am not sorry in the least that Philip Havisham is dead, however, believe me I did not kill him."

"Why did you meet with him yourself? You could have sent one of your servants."
"I never send a servant. I want to keep my problem as secret as possible – you know how much people *gossip* nowadays."
Baroness McKee laid her head in her hands and began to *sob*.
Sergeant Thompson looked helplessly across to his *superior*.
"So what do you think?" he whispered.
"I believe her," Detective Carlyle whispered back. "But I still want one of your men to find William Butcher and question him – see if he has an alibi for Sunday evening."
"What shall we do about…?" Sergeant Thompson nodded in the direction of the baroness.
"I think its best just to go and leave the poor woman alone."
Detective Carlyle looked over at the baroness. She had not moved. He shook his head, feeling very sorry for her. Then he turned around and walked towards the door.
"We can't just leave her like this!" Sergeant Thompson whispered.
"I'm afraid there is nothing we can do! It would be very indiscreet to do anything else," replied the detective and walked on.
Sergeant Thompson looked at Baroness McKee and then looked towards his *superior*. He was not quite sure what to do. He eventually decided to follow his *superior*.

ÜBUNG 62 !

Übung 62: Finden Sie die weibliche Entsprechung für die männlichen Adelstitel!

1. Baron	______	4. Viscount	______
2. Lord	______	5. Duke	______
3. King	______	6. Prince	______

Detective Carlyle and Sergeant Thompson stood in front of the baroness's house. The sergeant was pale.
"Where do we go from here, sir?" he asked a little *weary*, looking at the detective.
"Well, we don't have much. If Baroness McKee really had nothing to do with the murder then all we know is that whoever killed Philip Havisham must have had it well planned. We also know the murderer was looking for something in his house."
"What could it be?"
"I don't know – possibly something worth killing a man for. Let's go back to Havisham's house – perhaps we overlooked something the first time. That gives us at least something to do until William Butcher has been questioned."

Übung 63: Welche Relativpronomen gehören in die Lücken? Vervollständigen Sie die Sätze!
(who, who's, that, whose, which)

1. Baroness McKee's fiancé, ____________ from London, was a very devious man.
2. Sergeant Thompson ____________ truncheon fell on his foot felt great agony.
3. The house ____________ the policemen went to was like a fortress.
4. Dandies ____________ treat women badly should be sent to jail.
5. The Criterion, ____________ usually opens on a Sunday evening, was closed.

Chapter 6: Who is Miss SW?

Just as Detective Carlyle and Sergeant Thompson were walking across Grosvenor Square to Philip Havisham's house they met John Pirrip. He smiled when he saw the policemen.

"Detective Carlyle, Sergeant Thompson, what a pleasure to meet you here," he said *casually*.

"Good day, Mr Pirrip – on your way to the Music Academy?" asked Detective Carlyle. John Pirrip looked surprised. Detective Carlyle pointed at the violin case and smiled.

"Oh, yes of course. I thought there for a minute you could read my mind, Detective."

"If I could read minds, Mr Pirrip, I would solve every police case *in no time*," *chuckled* Detective Carlyle.

"Are you on your way to Mr Havisham's house?" asked John Pirrip in a more serious tone.

"In fact we are," answered Detective Carlyle.

"Are you making any progress in the murder investigation?"

"We have a few *leads*, however, nothing we can talk about at the moment."

"That I understand, Detective Carlyle. Well then, I have got to hurry, my class starts soon, please keep me informed."

The men said goodbye to each other and went their separate ways.

ÜBUNG 64 !

Übung 64: Wofür stehen die folgenden Abkürzungen?

1. a.s.a.p. ____________________

2. ch. ____________________

3. sen. ____________________

4. GB ____________________

5. ca. ____________________

6. BC ____________________

As soon as the policemen entered Philip Havisham's house, Detective Carlyle checked the inside of the drawing room door.
"What are you doing, sir?" asked Sergeant Thompson *puzzled*.
Detective Carlyle smiled triumphantly.
"It's gone!"
"What has gone?"
"My hair!"
"Your hair? You still have *all* your hair, if you ask me!" exclaimed a perplexed Sergeant Thompson.
"No, no!" said the detective laughing. "I used an old police trick: I stuck one of my hairs between the door's wooden frames."
"Why did you do that?"
"So that I could tell if somebody had been here and had opened the door."
"Oh, and now it's gone?" said the sergeant who was beginning to understand what was going on.
"Exactly – this probably proves that the murderer returned; meaning he had not found what he was looking for the first time!"
"That would mean there was or still is something in the house which is connected in some way to the murder."
"Yes, and if it's still here we're going to find it this time. Let's start looking, Sergeant. We must be more accurate. Don't leave anything out. Look behind pictures; search for loose panels and *floorboards*."

ÜBUNG 65 !

Übung 65: Übersetzen Sie und enträtseln Sie das zusammengesetzte Lösungswort!

1. Minute ___ □ __
2. Fortschritte □ _______
3. blass □ ___
4. verblüfft _ □ _______
5. verstehen ____ □ _____
6. kichern ___ □ ___
7. Eifersucht ___ □ ____
8. eifrig _ □ ___
9. Opfer (Plural) _______ □
10. Fall __ □ _

Lösung: ______ - ______

The policemen began their searching. Sergeant Thompson worked his way down the hall. He lifted back every picture and knocked against the wall to check if it was *hollow*. The sergeant was just getting to the last picture when he saw something lying on the floor. He went to see what it was and discovered a wallet. Sergeant Thompson picked it up and opened it. He *whistled*. There was a name on the inside. It read: Manuel Spencer. He hurried with it to the kitchen and found Detective Carlyle on his hands and knees trying to pull up a loose wooden plank.

"Oh, Sergeant, you're just in time, come and help me with this, please."

"Sir, look what I found!" Sergeant Thomson exclaimed and gave Detective Carlyle the wallet. "It belongs to Lord Spencer!"

Detective Carlyle *inspected* it and *scratched* his head thoughtfully.

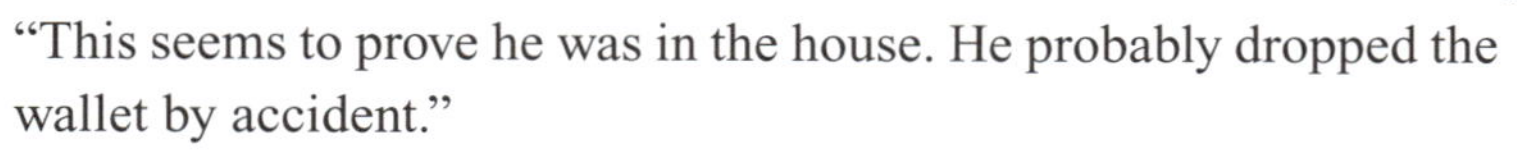

"This seems to prove he was in the house. He probably dropped the wallet by accident."

"So he is the murderer after all!"

"The *evidence* is certainly *overwhelming*. Funny though, I believed the *chap*. My instinct doesn't usually let me down," wondered Detective Carlyle.

"Maybe you're getting old!" joked Sergeant Thompson.

Detective Carlyle did not laugh. He gave the sergeant a *disapproving* look.

"Sorry, sir, it was just a joke! I was getting a little exited about solving the case."

"I wouldn't quite call it solved yet. There are still many questions to be answered. For example: What is under this loose *floorboard*. Would you be so kind and help me pull it up?"

Übung 66: Beantworten Sie die Fragen zum Text!

1. What were Detective Carlyle and Sergeant Thompson doing when they met John Pirrip?

....

2. What did John Pirrip think Detective Carlyle could do?

....

3. Whose wallet did Sergeant Thompson find?

....

4. Why is John Pirrip in a hurry?

....

5. What did Detective Carlyle do with one of his hairs?

---

6. Where did Sergeant Thompson find Detective Carlyle?

---

7. What was Detective Carlyle doing as Sergeant Thompson entered the kitchen?

Sergeant Thompson knelt down beside Detective Carlyle and helped him loosen the *floorboard*. The men pulled it up and found a bundle of letters underneath. Detective Carlyle removed them.
"This fellow Havisham sure liked to write," stated Sergeant Thompson.
"Let's see if the letters are actually written by Havisham first before we *jump to* any *conclusions*."
Detective Carlyle opened an envelope and looked at it. He opened another and then another.
"They're not written by him; they *appear* to be from someone with the initials SW."
"SW? Who could that be?"
"I don't know, but they seem to be love letters."
Detective Carlyle read a part of one out aloud:
"...Why do you not want me to leave him? We could be so happy together. I don't care what the others say as long as I can be with you..."
The detective picked up another letter and read from it:
"...Oh, please do not *reject* me like this. You said you loved me and we would be together for ever. If it has anything to do with him, I promise you he means nothing to me..."

Übung 67: Lesen Sie weiter und unterstreichen Sie die richtige Variante!

"Do none of the letters (1.) say/tell who her *fiancé* is?" asked Sergeant Thompson.
"No, she always addresses (2.) him/his as 'he' or 'him'."
Detective Carlyle opened another envelope and began to read aloud:
"…I am pregnant and very sure the child is (3.) yours/your's. I am going to leave him and come to you. This child is definitely a sign that we belong together…"
Sergeant Thompson looked shocked.
"I don't like the sound of (4.) when/where this story is going," he said and started to read a new letter:
"…An *abortion*…how *dare* you propose such a terrible thing…once you said you loved me…we need to talk, I suggest we (5.) meat/meet at our special meeting-place, Vauxhall Bridge."
Sergeant Thompson's hands were shaking.
"Well, if that man wasn't dead I would certainly kill him!" he said in an angry voice. "He must have been the reincarnation of the Devil!"
"Now, now, Sergeant Thompson; don't get carried away (6.) by/with your emotions. I don't like what we have found out (7.) on/about Havisham either, but we have got to stay professional," said Detective Carlyle *firmly*.

Sergeant Thompson took a deep breath and tried to calm down:
"Do you think SW could have been or even still is Lord Spencer's *fiancée* and he found out about the affair?"
"Maybe, we'll need to find that out. That would mean he killed Philip Havisham more out of *jealousy* than because of his book, or perhaps because of both."

"There is one thing I don't understand: If Lord Spencer had planned to kill Philip Havisham all along why did he cause such a *fuss* at the Criterion? He must have surely expected to be our main *suspect*."
"Good question, Sergeant. There are a few things which don't quite fit into the picture yet. If SW happens to be his *fiancée* then it would certainly explain why he had so *eagerly* searched for the letters – he was in danger of being discovered. For some reason he must have known or at least *assumed* that they existed. In the meantime, though, I think the *evidence* we have is enough to put him into jail."

ÜBUNG 68

Übung 68: Was ist gemeint? Finden Sie den passenden Begriff!

1. something you put a letter into: ____________
2. something you put money into: ____________
3. a place for criminals: ____________
4. to be born again: ____________
5. another word for to be: ____________
6. to look for: ____________

"There is also one more thing I don't quite understand."
"And what might that be, Sergeant?"
"Why did Philip Havisham *go to* so *much bother* as *to* hide these letters?"
"That is also a very good question. You are a born detective."
Sergeant Thompson grinned from ear to ear.
"I'm sure Lord Spencer will be able to explain a thing or two. Let's get back to the police station and question him. He should still be in jail where we left him yesterday evening after we caught him *gambling*."

As soon as Detective Carlyle and Sergeant Thompson entered the police station, Chief Inspector Gatsby came *thundering* towards them. Detective Carlyle noticed his face was redder than its usual colour. He knew he was in for some trouble.

"Detective Carlyle, into my office now!" yelled Chief Inspector Gatsby pointing his finger in the direction of his office door.

"And as for you, Sergeant Thompson, you'll be lucky if you're not *demoted* to the rank of constable…for life!" he shouted, now pointing his finger at him.

The two policemen just looked at each other. Sergeant Thompson *shrugged* and went over to greet his colleagues. Detective Carlyle disappeared into Chief Inspector Gatsby's office.

Übung 69: Übersetzen Sie die Imperative!

ÜBUNG 69 !

1. Hinsetzen! ______________________
2. Geh doch weg! ______________________
3. Bleib da! ______________________
4. Mache es richtig! ______________________
5. Genug davon! ______________________
6. Tu es nicht! ______________________
7. Kommen Sie her! ______________________
8. Nicht laufen! ______________________
9. Hören Sie damit auf! ______________________
10. Nicht jetzt! ______________________

"Sit down!" Chief Inspector Gatsby said in a *harsh* tone. "So what's this I hear about you arresting Lord Fellowes and several other highly decorated citizens of London?"

"They were *gambling*, sir, what was I to do? It's against the law."

"What are you talking about? It was just a harmless game of cards amongst friends – that's what they told me!"

Detective Carlyle's eyebrow went up.

"A harmless game of cards in an old *shed* out in the docks, sir?"

Chief Inspector Gatsby thought the detective had a point.

"Maybe it's quiet out there. You know, away from wives and children," he said a little less *harshly*.

"Then why didn't they just go to the men's club?"

Chief Inspector Gatsby was not the most intelligent of persons. He felt he was beginning to lose ground and was starting to see that the explanation his club friends had given him was possibly not very plausible. He decided to slam his fist on his desk.

"Enough, I let them go this morning. I saw no reason to keep them here."

"You let them go?" Detective Carlyle could not believe his ears.

"Yes!" he replied as if it was the most normal thing in the world.

"How are you getting on with the Havisham case?" asked Chief Inspector Gatsby, trying to *casually* change the subject.

"Well, you've just let my main *suspect* go!"

"What – Lord Fellowes is your main *suspect*! Now listen to me…"

"No, no!" interrupted Detective Carlyle. "Lord Spencer is my main *suspect*."

"That isn't really much better!" *growled* Chief Inspector Gatsby. "I thought I told you to leave him alone."

"I found his wallet in the victim's house."

Chief Inspector Gatsby was lost for words.

Übung 70: Welche polizeilichen Begriffe werden gesucht?

1. the person who has been murdered:

....

2. the person who is thought to have committed a crime:

....

3. the general name for the process involved in solving a crime:

....

4. the general word used for a person who is not guilty:

....

5. the place where a criminal receives his sentence:

....

"What did you say?"
"I said I found his wallet in Havisham's house. That proves he must have been there recently. It certainly wasn't there the last time I was there. We also have reason to believe his *fiancée* was having an affair with Mr Havisham."
Detective Carlyle's *superior* was now *stunned*.
"Oh…well…that seems to put things into a new light," he said a little more reserved.
"It's just a shame he's not around to question anymore. Would you mind if I just went back out to round up some men to go and arrest him?" asked Detective Carlyle in a casual, *sardonic* tone.
"No, I wouldn't mind!" answered Chief Inspector Gatsby unnerved. "Go and bring him in!"
"My pleasure, sir!" grinned Detective Carlyle.
Chief Inspector Gatsby *sighed* and *motioned* for him to leave.

Chapter 7: The Great Escape

Detective Carlyle, Sergeant Thompson and four constables arrived at Stephan's Hotel and went in. The landlord looked very *astonished* as the six policemen came towards him.
"Can…can…I help you?" he stuttered.
"Is Lord Spencer in his room?" asked Detective Carlyle.
"Yes!"
The landlord was going to ask something, but Detective Carlyle turned around and signalled his men to follow him up the stairs.
"He's in room 17," whispered Detective Carlyle. "I want you all to be as quiet as possible, I don't want him to escape."

! ÜBUNG 71

Übung 71: Lesen Sie weiter und setzen Sie die Wörter ein!
(gradually, sneaked, fault, hurt, carefully, approaching, him, hysterical, want)

The policemen (1.) __________________ up the stairs. One of the constables stood on a *rotted* wooden step, it cracked. Everybody else looked at him. Sergeant Thompson shook his head. The young man just *shrugged* as if to say: "It's not my (2.) ________________! How could I know?" The policemen moved on carefully until they reached Lord Spencer's room. Detective Carlyle signalled two of the constables to break down the door. He counted using his fingers: one, two, three…the policemen kicked the door open. Lord Spencer was sitting at his desk. He shot out of his chair with fright.

"What do you (3.) ________________!" he cried and hastily opened one of the desk drawers and took something out. Detective Carlyle saw him doing this.

"Watch out! *Seize* him!" he shouted.

But it was too late – Lord Spencer was pointing a gun at them all. The policemen (4.) ________________ moved back a little. Detective Carlyle stood closest to Lord Spencer. He held up his hands in a calming gesture.

"Put the gun down, Lord Spencer," he said *firmly*. "You do not want anybody to get (5.) ________________, do you?"

Lord Spencer *wiped* sweat from his brow with his free hand.

"What do you want?" he asked again; this time in a more (6.) ________________ tone. "Why can you not just leave me alone?"

"Now, calm down, Lord Spencer. We just have a few questions."

"Ha, a few questions, you say? Why did you bring half the London Police with you, if you just want to ask me a few questions?"

Lord Spencer was (7.) ________________ moving backwards towards a window at the back of the room. One of the constables moved slightly towards his direction. Lord Spencer pointed the gun at (8.) ________________. "Do not move or I will shoot you!" he shouted. Detective Carlyle signalled the policeman to stay where he was. Lord Spencer was (9.) ________________ the open window.

"You are only making things worse," said Detective Carlyle.
"Making what worse, Detective? I did not do anything. You and your colleagues are *driving me mad*! Do you still believe I am the murderer?"
Detective Carlyle *sighed* and pointed at the gun.
"Well, Philip Havisham was shot dead with a gun similar to the one you are now pointing at us."
"I have had enough of your *accusations*, Detective," and with this Lord Spencer fired a shot into the air. The policemen ducked, *plaster* fell from the ceiling.
"I am not going back to jail!" he exclaimed and jumped out of the window.

! ÜBUNG 72

Übung 72: Setzen Sie ein: ***do*** *oder* ***make****?*

1. His behaviour is going to ______________ things worse.
2. Sergeant Thompson had to ______________ some research.
3. Lord Spencer said he did not ______________ anything.
4. Detective Carlyle asked Sergeant Thompson to ______________ him a cup of tea.
5. The baroness wanted Philip Havisham to ____________ her happy.
6. The policemen had to ______________ a lot of running.

"Is the man mad!" exclaimed Sergeant Thompson as the policemen rushed towards the window. They looked down. Lord Spencer had landed softly in the bushes that surrounded the hotel's *premises*. He freed himself from the bushes and ran. He *accidentally* dropped the gun and left it lying.

"Get him!" exclaimed Detective Carlyle.
The constables quickly left the hotel room. Sergeant Thompson wanted to join them, but Detective Carlyle held him back.
"Leave the chase to your men, Sergeant – I need you here."
Sergeant Thompson looked disappointed.
"But sir, that means I'm losing out on all the excitement," he *sighed*.
Detective Carlyle raised his eyebrow.
"I think we've had enough excitement for one day!" he said dryly. "I saw Lord Spencer drop the gun. If it's a Remington Revolver then we have our murderer for sure. Let's go down and get it."

Übung 73: Wählen Sie die richtige Variante!

ÜBUNG 73 !

1. The baroness laughed ___________.
   a) ☐ hysterical   b) ☐ hysterically
2. Detective Carlyle was ___________ prepared.
   a) ☐ well   b) ☐ good
3. Sergeant Thompson was ___________ punched into the stomach.
   a) ☐ brutally   b) ☐ brutal
4. He said it in a ___________ tone.
   a) ☐ dryly   b) ☐ dry
5. The policemen ___________ ran down the stairs.
   a) ☐ fast   b) ☐ quickly
6. Lord Spencer was in ___________ trouble.
   a) ☐ deeply   b) ☐ deep
7. The suspect ___________ dropped the gun.
   a) ☐ accidental   b) ☐ accidentally

The two policemen walked out of the room. You could hear the constable's loud *whistles* in the distance. Some of the hotel guests had left their own rooms to see what all the *commotion* was about. They were standing around talking to each other. Some of them looked rather shocked. Just as Detective Carlyle and Sergeant Thompson were hurrying down the stairs, the landlord of Stephan's Hotel came running towards them.

ÜBUNG 74 !

Übung 74: Lesen Sie weiter und unterstreichen Sie im Text die gegenteiligen Begriffe der Wörter in Klammern!
(1. whispered, 2. brand new, 3. in front of, 4. doubtful, 5. far away from, 6. less, 7. everybody)

"What in heavens name is going on here? Who was shooting in my hotel?" he cried out.
"Oh, just the usual police affairs," answered Sergeant Thompson *matter-of-factly*.
"Who is going to pay for all the damage?" asked the landlord as he pointed at one of the *rotted* steps which now had broken under the weight of the running policemen.
"I'm sure Lord Spencer will pay for the damages," answered Detective Carlyle.
"Spencer?" laughed the landlord. "He never even has enough money to pay his rent!"
"Well, once he's behind bars I'm sure he will have enough time to save a pound or two."
"Jail – what do you mean by that? That man still *owes* me two weeks' rent," said the alarmed landlord.
"I'm more than certain you will read all about it in tomorrow's newspaper," answered Detective Carlyle.

The landlord sat down on a chair near the hotel exit. He shook his head and looked very worried.
"This is not good at all," he said more to himself. "After half of London has heard about this, no one is going to want to stay at my hotel."

Sergeant Thompson gave him an encouraging clap on the back and followed his *superior* out of the door. The policemen crossed the road. Detective Carlyle picked up the gun and examined it. He *scratched* his head thoughtfully.
"It's not a Remington Revolver," he said disappointedly.
"I think you're right, sir. It looks more like a Colt."
"And a Colt it is," *sighed* Detective Carlyle. "However, the fact the gun is a Colt still does not prove Lord Spencer's innocence in any way – but it sure would have made things easier if it had been a Remington."
Detective Carlyle gave Sergeant Thompson the gun.
"If you would kindly hold on to it, Sergeant?"
"Certainly, sir!"
The sergeant took the gun from Detective Carlyle and put it in his belt. Detective Carlyle gave him a *disapproving* look.
"Maybe you could be a little more discreet," said the detective.
Sergeant Thompson looked *puzzled*.
"Discreet? What do you mean, sir?"
Detective Carlyle nodded in the direction of the gun.
"We don't want the public to think that the London Police are now *armed*, do we?"
Sergeant Thompson looked down at the gun.
"Oh, yes, of course!" he answered feeling a little stupid.
He removed the gun from his belt and put it in the inside of his police uniform jacket.
Detective Carlyle nodded in a satisfied manner and smiled.

"That looks better – a policeman with a gun doesn't look like a friend and helper."
Sergeant Thompson smiled back.
"Now, Sergeant, let's get back to the police station and wait for your men to bring in Lord Spencer. He most certainly has a lot to answer for."

ÜBUNG 75 !

Übung 75: Setzen Sie die erste oder zweite Steigerungsform des Adjektivs ein!

1. Detective Carlyle wanted Sergeant Thompson to be (discreet) ____________________.
2. Detective Carlyle was (clever) ____________________ than Chief Inspector Gatsby.
3. Sergeant Thompson was (funny) ____________________ of all.
4. The case was (difficult) ____________________ than Detective Carlyle had thought.
5. Things were not getting (good) ______________ for Lord Spencer.
6. Stewart Portman was (thin) _______________ than Philip Havisham.
7. The lane was (narrow) _________________ than the road.
8. Philip Havisham was the (nice) _________________ person she had ever met.

Detective Carlyle was drinking a cup of tea in his office when suddenly the door opened. Constable Taylor entered:

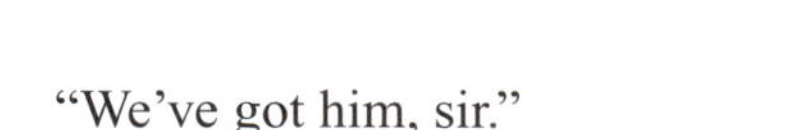

"We've got him, sir."
"Very good work, Constable – would you kindly bring Lord Spencer into my office."
"Yes, sir!"
The constable turned around and was about to leave.

Übung 76: Setzen Sie das passende Pronomen ein!
(mine, his, your, them, him, me)

ÜBUNG 76

1. Detective Carlyle was drinking tea in ________ office.
2. "Shall I bring Lord Spencer, Baroness McKee and Simon Manlove into ________ office?"
3. "Oh no, not all of ________ at once!"
4. "I like Sergeant Thompson. He's a good colleague of ________."
5. "I tried to speak to him, but Lord Spencer did not want to talk to ________."
6. Constable Taylor said they had caught ________ soon after he had fled.

"Oh, Constable, *due* to all the *commotion* I nearly forgot: Did you find William Butcher to question him?"
"No, we didn't. He seems to have *disappeared into thin air*.
However, I talked to a colleague from Hyde Park Police Station, he told me they had locked up William Butcher the day Philip Havisham was murdered. He was behind bars all night because he had started a fight and had *assaulted* a policeman."

ÜBUNG 77

!

Übung 77: Lesen Sie weiter und fügen Sie das passende Wort ein!
(handcuffed, take, again, best, dangerous, cause, returned)

"Well, if that's not the (1.) ____________ alibi a man can have," Detective Carlyle laughed.

"You can surely say that (2.) ____________, sir," *chuckled* Constable Taylor. "I'll bring Lord Spencer in then?"

"Yes, please do, Constable."

Constable Taylor (3.) ____________ shortly afterwards with Lord Spencer. He pushed him carefully into the detective's office. Lord Spencer's hands were behind his back as he was (4.) ____________. The policemen and the main *suspect* were followed by Sergeant Thompson. "You can (5.) ____________ the *handcuffs* off," said Detective Carlyle. "But, sir, this man is (6.) ____________!" protested Constable Taylor. "It's okay, Constable – I don't think Lord Spencer is going to (7.) ____________ us any trouble…are you now?"

Detective Carlyle looked at Lord Spencer. He shook his head. Lord Spencer's face was dirty and his clothes were *ripped* – his attempt to escape had left some traces. Constable Taylor unlocked the *handcuffs* and sat Lord Spencer down on the chair at the opposite side of Detective Carlyle's desk. Constable Taylor stood there waiting for further instructions.

"You can leave now, Constable. Wait by the door in case Sergeant Thompson and I need any further help."

"Yes, sir! If you need any help with this *rogue* I'll be more than happy to lend a hand."
Constable Taylor gave Lord Spencer an angry look and left the office. Lord Spencer did not see this because his head was hanging down in resignation. He looked like a wild animal that had just been caught and given into its *fate*. Detective Carlyle felt very sorry for Lord Spencer. He looked over to Sergeant Thompson. He did not seem to share the same feeling. All the detective could read in his face was professional interest. Detective Carlyle opened a drawer, took out Lord Spencer's wallet and laid it on top of the desk.

Übung 78: Beantworten Sie die Fragen zum Text!

1. Why was the landlord of Stephan's Hotel so upset?

2. How did Lord Spencer escape?

3. How many times did Lord Spencer fire into the air?

4. Did Sergeant Thompson catch Lord Spencer?

5. What was Detective Carlyle doing before Lord Spencer was brought into his office?

6. Did Sergeant Thompson feel sorry for Lord Spencer?

---

7. What did Detective Carlyle lay on his desk?

"We found your wallet in Philip Havisham's house; could you possibly explain how it got there?"
Lord Spencer looked at Detective Carlyle for the first time. He *shrugged* helplessly.
"I have no idea," he answered. "It was stolen from me two days ago."
"Did you report it to the police?"
"No!" *sighed* Lord Spencer.
"Why not?"
"Well, to be honest, I had had more than enough of the police. As far as I was concerned I did not want to see the inside of a police station again for the rest of my life," he answered tiredly.
"That didn't keep you out for long, did it?" said Sergeant Thompson.
Lord Spencer ignored this and *carried on*:
"Secondly, there was not much money in it. Reporting it was not really worth the bother. As you can see for yourself, the wallet is not very new either." Lord Spencer paused for a moment and then said in a *self-pitying* tone: "Anyway, what use is a wallet to someone who has nothing to put in it."
"I'll just go and get the violin players, shall I?" said Sergeant Thompson *sardonically*.
Detective Carlyle silently signalled to the sergeant to keep statements like that to himself.

"So you say it was stolen?" Detective Carlyle *proceeded* with the questioning.
"I *assumed* so. I certainly do not understand how it got into Mr Havisham's house – I swear I was never there in my life!"
"Do you know a woman who has the initials SW?" asked Detective Carlyle, changing the subject.
"SW? No idea! Who is that *supposed* to be?"
"That is exactly what I am trying to find out. We found hidden love letters in Philip Havisham's house. I *assume* you were looking for them when you lost your wallet."
"I do *not have the foggiest idea* what you are talking about," said Lord Spencer in a more irritated tone.
"Coming back to life, are we?" asked Sergeant Thompson.
Detective Carlyle gave the sergeant a *disapproving* look. Sergeant Thompson made a gesture that he was sorry.

Übung 79: Setzen Sie das passende Adjektiv ein!
(difficult, sad, dishonest, helpful, low, narrow, immoral, unlucky, angry, lazy)

1. A person who kills is ________________.

2. A person who cries is ________________.

3. A person who lies is ________________.

4. A person who shouts is ________________.

5. A person who is out of luck is ________________.

6. A lane that is not very wide is ________________.

7. A task that is hard to solve is ________________.

8. A person who always gets up late is ________________.

9. A person who likes to help is ________________.

10. A wall that is not very high is ________________.

Lord Spencer was nervously playing with his hands. He looked up at Detective Carlyle:

"Would you please have the kindness to explain to me exactly what you are getting at?"

"We have reason to believe SW was or still is your *fiancée*...she had an affair with Philip Havisham…you eventually found this out and murdered him…"

Detective Carlyle could not finish his sentence as Lord Spencer was laughing out loud.

"Ha, ha, ha!" he did not seem to be able to stop. He gradually calmed down: "You should be writing crime stories, Detective Carlyle. This is getting better all the time: First you say I killed Mr Havisham because of his book and now you are saying I killed him out of *jealousy*. You certainly have a great imagination."

"Now, that's enough of your *cheek*!" protested Sergeant Thompson.

"It is okay, Sergeant. Let me *deal with* this," said Detective Carlyle calmly.

"So you are telling me you have never heard of a woman with the initials SW?"

"No! And she certainly was not my *fiancée*."

"You do know we can easily find out if you are lying to us."

"Go and find out!" *spat* Lord Spencer in *disgust*: "The sooner, the better!"

"If you are as innocent as you insist, why did you try and escape from the police? You did seem in great distress."

"Of course I *was in great distress*!" shouted Lord Spencer and rose up from his chair. It *toppled over*. Sergeant Thompson put his hand on his *truncheon* and moved closer.
"You just won't leave me alone. I tell you someone is trying to *put the blame on* me, can you not see that!" Lord Spencer cried.
The door opened. Constable Taylor looked in.
"Is everything all right?"
"Yes, thank you, Constable. Lord Spencer was just going to sit down again. I'm sure he doesn't want the *handcuffs* back on."
Lord Spencer sat back down and Constable Taylor closed the door again.

Übung 80: Welche Wörter gehören zusammen?

1. blame	☐ with
2. sit	☐ in
3. eat	☐ to
4. involved	☐ down
5. escort	☐ on
6. black	☐ up
7. stay	☐ out

"And what about my alibi?" asked Lord Spencer more calmly. "I do have an alibi, remember?"
"Yes, I remember very well. The problem with your alibi is that I do not trust the people connected to it. I believe they are trying to protect you. Minister Black lied to me many times, you know." Detective Carlyle paused. The office was absolutely silent. One could hear the voices and laughs of the policemen outside.
"I will ask you one more time: Who is SW?"

"I do not know, you must believe me!" *pleaded* Lord Spencer.
Detective Carlyle stood up and *sighed*:
"I'm afraid we're not really getting anywhere here, Sergeant. Would you kindly ask Constable Taylor to escort Lord Spencer back out."
Lord Spencer looked alarmed back and forth between Sergeant Thompson and Detective Carlyle.
"So that's it; you are locking me back up?" asked Lord Spencer.
"For the meantime anyway. There is just too much *evidence* against you, and your adventurous escape earlier today did not help to *bolster* your *pleas* of innocence."
Constable Taylor entered the office and led Lord Spencer back out. He did not protest or say another word.
"Poor *chap*", said Detective Carlyle *regretfully*, "what if he is innocent?"
"Looks like a liar to me, sir. I mean, he could have shot one of us today!" exclaimed the sergeant.
"He was *aiming at* the roof, Sergeant."
"How do you know for sure? Maybe he's just a bad *marksman*."
"Well, if he is a bad *marksman*, he certainly can't be the murderer of Philip Havisham – he was killed with one direct shot to the heart."
Sergeant Thompson *scratched* his head.
"You have a point there sir; maybe Lord Spencer was just lucky. You know, first time lucky sort of thing."
Detective Carlyle rolled his eyes.
"Where do we go from here?" asked Sergeant Thompson.
"We need to find out if Lord Spencer ever had or has a *fiancée* with the initials SW."
"Right, I'll get one of my men to make some *inquiries* – anything else?"

"Yes, ask Philip Havisham's friends, Simon Manlove, Stewart Portman and John Pirrip round to the police station – maybe they heard Philip Havisham talk about a woman with the initials SW."

Sergeant Thompson suddenly looked at Detective Carlyle as if he had been enlightened.

"I've got it!" he exclaimed.

"You've got what?" asked Detective Carlyle *puzzled*.

"I know what SW stands for!"

Detective Carlyle sat up in excitement.

"What?"

"Silly Woman!" laughed Sergeant Thompson.

Detective Carlyle smiled and made a half-heartedly *disapproving* gesture with his hands.

"Oh, get to work, Sergeant Thompson!" he laughed.

Übung 81: Enträtseln Sie die folgenden Definitionen!

ÜBUNG 81

1. the opposite of getting better: ______________ (orsew)

2. another word for stupid: ______________ (lilys)

3. a lot of action: ______________ (nitocmomo)

4. during the investigation it is collected: ______________ (viedecne)

5. to look into something: ______________ (qiuerni)

6. not on purpose: ______________ (cacdietnla)

7. owner of a hotel for example: ______________ (droldnal)

Chapter 8: A Tragedy Unfolds

Simon Manlove, Stewart Portman and John Pirrip sat in Detective Carlyle's office waiting for him to arrive. The door opened and Sergeant Thompson looked in.
"Would anyone like a cup of tea?"
"No, thank you!" they all answered at once.
"Oh, well, fine with me. The detective will be with you in a minute."
Sergeant Thompson closed the door. The three friends looked a little out of place sitting in Detective Carlyle's office. Their exquisite clothes and upper-class behaviour stood out in contrast to his *tatty* and *scarcely* furnished office. The men's body language expressed a slight feeling of *disgust*. Stewart Portman especially showed great dislike of the place. He was sitting on the edge of his chair just touching the seat with his bottom. It looked as if somebody had forced him to sit on something very horrible.

ÜBUNG 82

Übung 82: Setzen Sie ein sinnvolles Synonym ein!
(maybe, disgusting, hot, certainly, discussion, shocked, replied)

"It's a *ghastly* place, is it not?" remarked Stewart Portman. "I have never been in a police station before."

"Well it is not quite Buckingham Palace," said Simon Manlove.

"Most (1. definitely) ________________ not!" *smirked* Portman.

"Look at the furniture: The desk and chairs are populated with wood worm," he said *screwing up his face*.

"Yes, (2. revolting) ________________! And look at the ceiling. It looks as if it might come down any second," said Simon Manlove.

"I wonder what Detective Carlyle wants?" asked John Pirrip, who *was fed up* with his friends (3. talk) ________________ about the police station's *interior*.

"I have no idea – (4. perhaps) ________________ he has found the murderer", (5. answered) ________________ Simon Manlove.

"It is about time, if you ask me", stated Stewart Portman, "I wonder if it was that *chap*…ehm…Lord…what was his name again?"

"Lord Spencer," replied John Pirrip.

"Ah yes, Lord Spencer. I know his aunt. She must be absolutely (6. *shaken*) ________________. Lord Spencer was always bad news, as far as I can remember anyway," said Stewart Portman in a matter-of-fact tone.

The office door opened and Detective Carlyle walked in. He had a (7. steaming) ________________ cup of tea in his hand.

"Good afternoon, Gentlemen. I hope I did not keep you waiting too long."

Detective Carlyle sat down and smiled at the men. He looked over at Stewart Portman, who was still sitting on his chair in an awkward way.

"Comfortable?" asked Detective Carlyle.

"Most certainly, thank you", said Stewart Portman not very convincingly, "we were actually just talking about how *cosy* your little office is."

"Were you now," replied Detective Carlyle in a slightly *suspicious* tone.

Detective Carlyle opened one of his drawers and took out some biscuits.

"Does anybody want a biscuit?"

The three friends *declined*. The way they *declined* Detective Carlyle's offer one might have thought he had just offered them grilled *ants*. Detective Carlyle *shrugged* and took a bite of his biscuit and then took a sip of his tea.

ÜBUNG 83 !

Übung 83: Lesen Sie weiter und tragen Sie die Vergangenheitsform der angegebenen Verben ein!

"I guess, Gentlemen, you are wondering why you are here?"

"Yes, that is correct. We (1. think) ___________ that maybe you had identified Philip Havisham's murderer," said John Pirrip.

"Well, we have a main *suspect*, we are just *gathering evidence* to make sure there is no doubt that he is guilty."

"Does the *suspect* have a name?" asked Simon Manlove.

"Yes, we have (2. arrest) _________________ Lord Spencer."

"I knew it!" exclaimed Stewart Portman. "Don't like the man – never (3. do) _______________!"

"Did you just call us into the police station to tell us that?" (4. ask) ___________ John Pirrip.

"Well, as I was saying we still need to put some pieces together: I was wondering if Philip Havisham had ever (5. mention) __________________ a woman with the initials SW?"

"SW?" asked Stewart Portman thoughtfully.

"Yes!"

"Our *late* friend had so many…how shall I say…lady friends…let me think…No, sorry, does not ring a bell."

"What about you, Mr Pirrip?"

John Pirrip (6. look) ________________ a little pale.

"Is everything okay?" asked Detective Carlyle.

"Pardon?" he asked in a distant tone.

"I asked if everything is okay."

"Oh, yes, sorry, everything is fine. It is just a little *stuffy* in here. To answer your question: No, I am afraid not."

"It is strange, though," (7. remark) ________________ Simon Manlove.

"What is strange?" asked Detective Carlyle.
"It is strange he never mentioned her. He always *boasted* about his lady acquaintances."
"That is interesting your saying that because we have reason to believe he was trying to keep this affair a secret."
"I wonder why?" said Stewart Portman. "That really was not like him."
The office door opened and Sergeant Thompson looked in.
"Do you have a minute, sir?"
Detective Carlyle nodded and said:
"If you would excuse me for a moment, Gentlemen."
Detective Carlyle went out of the office and closed the door behind him.

ÜBUNG 84 !

Übung 84: Setzen Sie, wenn notwendig, den richtigen unbestimmten Artikel ein!

1. Do you know ______ woman with the initials SW?
2. Philip Havisham was shot half ______ hour ago.
3. Sergeant Thompson had ______ good news for Detective Carlyle.
4. Lord Spencer has run away from the police many ______ time.
5. Detective Carlyle is keeping ______ eye on Lord Spencer.
6. Stewart Portman has never been in ______ police station.
7. Simon Manlove is wearing ______ new pair of trousers.
8. Lord Spencer would pay ______ hundred thousand pounds to get out of jail.
9. Detective Carlyle needs ______ information.
10. Baroness McKee needs ______ advice.

"What is it, Sergeant?"
"My men just came back from their *inquiry* concerning the initials SW. It seems to be that Lord Spencer never had a *fiancée* with those initials. There was a Cassandra Anderson, however, nobody whose name consists of an S and a W."
"Oh dear!" exclaimed Detective Carlyle. "Maybe we have the wrong man after all."
"Or maybe the burglary and the letters are not connected to each other – a pure *coincidence*."
"But Lord Spencer's wallet was in the house and the house was broken into more than once."

Detective Carlyle *scratched* his head and *sighed*.
"This is a very tricky case. There is something missing…I just don't know what it is…something that is staring us right in the face, but we can't see it."
Detective Carlyle looked a little frustrated.
"I'll get back to my royal guests," he said *sardonically*. "I'll be with you in fifteen minutes."

Übung 85: Ordnen Sie die Begriffe einander zu!

ÜBUNG 85 !

1. pure	☐ life
2. real	☐ love
3. reality	☐ bread
4. plain	☐ bites
5. true	☐ mind
6. open	☐ coincidence

Sergeant Thompson nodded. Detective Carlyle opened his office door and entered. Just as he walked in John Pirrip nearly *bumped into* him.
"Oh, sorry!" he said.
"Are you leaving us, Mr Pirrip?" asked Detective Carlyle surprised.
"No, no! I just need some fresh air. I will be back soon."
John Pirrip walked out of the office. Detective Carlyle looked at Simon Manlove and Stewart Portman.
"Is everything all right with Mr Pirrip? He did seem somewhat *upset*."
"I do not know, Detective. He really has never been the same since his *fiancée* died last year and now Mr Havisham's death – maybe it is all getting a bit too much for him," replied Simon Manlove.

"How tragic!" said Detective Carlyle.
"Yes, very", stated Stewart Portman, "his *fiancée* actually *drowned* herself in the Thames."
"Oh dear, but why?"
"That is part of the tragedy – nobody really understands why."

ÜBUNG 86 !

Übung 86: Übersetzen Sie!

1. John Pirrip sah sehr blass aus.

2. Die drei Männer wollten keinen Tee.

3. Simon Manlove hat noch nie von einer Frau mit den Initialen SW gehört.

4. Er ist nicht mehr richtig derselbe, seitdem seine Verlobte gestorben ist.

5. Stewart Portman fand das Büro von Detective Carlyle scheußlich.

6. Nein, tut mir Leid, das sagt mir nichts.

7. Detective Carlyle verließ das Büro und schloss die Tür hinter sich.

Detective Carlyle paused for a minute and stared thinking into his cup of tea. Simon Manlove and Stewart Portman exchanged looks. Suddenly Detective Carlyle looked up; his eyes were *sparkling* under his red, bushy eyebrows.
"Tell me, what was this woman's name?"
"Susan White," answered Simon Manlove.
"Susan White you say…SW…Susan White…that's it!" exclaimed Detective Carlyle.
The two men looked irritated.
"That is what?" asked Stewart Portman.
"The woman who wrote the letters to Philip Havisham was Susan White."

Übung 87: Welche Ausdrücke gehören zusammen?

ÜBUNG 87 !

1. cup of	☐ chips
2. plate of	☐ boxes
3. pile of	☐ beer
4. bunch of	☐ wine
5. glass of	☐ tea
6. barrel of	☐ flowers

"What letters?" asked Simon Manlove perplexed.

"We found love letters in Philip Havisham's house. They were signed SW," replied Detective Carlyle.

"You can not possibly believe Mr Havisham had something going on with one of his best friend's *fiancées*? I believe this to be a tragic *coincidence*!" exclaimed Stewart Portman.

"Yes, so do I!" said Simon Manlove. "Not even Philip could have done such a thing!"

"I would not be too sure there, Gentlemen," *mumbled* Detective Carlyle more to himself.

"Pardon, what did you say?"

Detective Carlyle shook his head.

"It was not important. Where exactly did Miss White *drown* herself?"

"She jumped from Vauxhall Bridge."

Detective Carlyle shot up.

"A most unlikely *coincidence*!" he exclaimed and hurried to the door. Simon Manlove and Stewart Portman got up. They looked very *puzzled*.

"But Detective Carlyle – I do not quite understand," said Simon Manlove.

"I will explain everything to you later."

ÜBUNG 88 !

Übung 88: Welcher Satz enthält die richtige Zeitform? Kreuzen Sie an!

1. Simon Manlove setzte sich hin.
   a) ☐ Simon Manlove had sat down.
   b) ☐ Simon Manlove sits down.
   c) ☐ Simon Manlove sat down.

2. Ich werde Ihnen alles später erklären.
   a) ☐ I will explain everything to you later.
   b) ☐ I will be explaining everything to you later.
   c) ☐ I was going to explain everything to you later.

3. Detective Carlyle starrte gerade nachdenklich aus dem Fenster.
   a) ☐ Detective Carlyle stares thoughtfully out of the window.
   b) ☐ Detective Carlyle was staring thoughtfully out of the window.
   c) ☐ Detective Carlyle stared thoughtfully out of the window.

4. Früher ging Philip Havisham ins Criterion.
   a) ☐ Philip Havisham was going to the Criterion early.
   b) ☐ Philip Havisham used to go to the Criterion.
   c) ☐ Philip Havisham went to the Criterion early.

5. Sergeant Thompson hat schon viele Lügen gehört.
   a) ☐ Sergeant Thompson has heard many lies.
   b) ☐ Sergeant Thompson heard many lies.
   c) ☐ Sergeant Thompson hears many lies.

Detective Carlyle hastily left his office. Outside he looked for Sergeant Thompson. Eventually he found him.
"Have you seen John Pirrip?" he asked urgently.
"The last time I saw him he was walking out onto the street; said he was going to get some fresh air."
Detective Carlyle ran out onto the street. He was closely followed by Sergeant Thompson. John Pirrip was gone.
"What's going on, sir?" he asked perplexed.
"I know who the murderer is!"
"Who?"
"John Pirrip!"

Sergeant Thompson looked very *puzzled*.
"John Pirrip?"
"Yes! Get your men together, Sergeant. We must find him – I'll explain everything to you later."
Sergeant Thompson hurried back into the police station.

ÜBUNG 89 !

Übung 89: Füllen Sie die Lücken mit ***do*** *oder* ***does****!*

1. ________ Philip Havisham really have many lady acquaintances?
2. ________ Detective Carlyle find John Pirrip?
3. ________ I know you?
4. ________ Detective Carlyle have a suspect?
5. How ________ you ________?
6. What ________ Philip Havisham say?
7. Why ________ Lady McKee hate Philip Havisham?

Detective Carlyle and Sergeant Thompson sat in the police coach. They were on their way to John Pirrip's house. The coach was travelling very fast. The two men were being *jerked* back and forth. Sergeant Thompson's police hat almost flew off. He caught it just in time.

ÜBUNG 90 !

Übung 90: Lesen Sie weiter und setzen Sie den gegenteiligen Begriff der Wörter in Klammern ein!

"So you believe SW and Susan White are the same person?" (1. whispered) ____________ Sergeant Thompson.

He had to speak very loud in order to make himself heard properly. The noise of the coach's wheels hitting the *cobbled* street and the rhythmic crack of the *whip* made a conversation very (2. easy) ________________.

"Yes! John Pirrip must have found out about his *fiancée's* affair with Philip Havisham after her (3. life) ________________. I *assume* if he had known about it (4. later) ________________ he would have reacted sooner."

"He must have been shocked to hear of such (5. faithfulness) ________________ – both his best friend and the woman he loved *betraying* him."

"You can say that again. Now we also understand why Philip Havisham hid the letters: He wanted to make sure his good friend John Pirrip would never find out."
"But how did he find it out eventually then?"
"I'm not quite sure. He possibly found something in his dead *fiancée's belongings* that made him *suspicious*; maybe even a letter. He obviously *assumed* there were more or he wouldn't have searched Havisham's house so often."
"Yes, he feared they would give him away, I believe."
"And he was right!"
"Remember the day we met him at Grosvenor Square?"
"Yes, he said he was on his way to the Royal Music Academy."
"I know, and how stupid of us not to realize that the academy is nowhere near Grosvenor Square."
"That's right. He probably had just been in Havisham's house to search for the letters again."
"And he left Lord Spencer's wallet there as well."

Übung 91: Lesen Sie weiter und setzen Sie das passende Wort ein!
(reason, blame, hindsight, fooled, into, investigations, credit, exclaimed, assume, violin)

"He certainly had us (1.) ________________, sir," said Sergeant Thompson angrily.

"He certainly did, Sergeant. For some (2.) ________________ he must have found out that Lord Spencer was no longer our main *suspect* and tried to lead us back to him. He had planned all along to put the (3.) ________________ on him."

"But how did he smuggle the gun and the cushion from Lord Spencer's hotel (4.) ________________ the Criterion?"

"That is a good question: John Pirrip used his violin case – he had it with him all evening."

"His violin case…well, I'll be damned!" (5.) ________________ Sergeant Thompson.

"I most certainly hope not," smiled Detective Carlyle.

"But, sir…how do you know that he did not hand in the (6.) ________________ case?"

"I remember it lying by the fireplace beside the chair he was sitting on. He didn't have his coat or anything else with him; so I (7.) ________________ he must have had it with him all evening."

"Come to think of it, that is very *suspicious*."

"Yes, in (8.) ________________ it does. However, he had us very well *distracted*."

"He certainly did. We were concentrating the (9.) ________________ far too much on Lord Spencer – the *evidence* was *overwhelming* though."

"Yes, I must give (10.) ________________ to John Pirrip for that; he had everything very well planned."

"There is still just one thing I do not understand, sir."
"And what might that be, Sergeant?"
"How on earth did John Pirrip manage to leave the East Room of the Criterion unnoticed shortly after Philip Havisham with a violin case in his hand?"
"I thought about that too, Sergeant. Do you remember that Philip Havisham's favourite table was *secluded* from the rest of the room by a wooden screen?"
"Yes!"
Detective Carlyle took a piece of paper out of his pocket and unfolded it.
"The same night of the murder I got one of the constables to draw me a rough *sketch* of the Criterion…now look here…"
Detective Carlyle pointed at a room which was labelled "East Room". His finger moved along the paper.
"Do you see this small door? It's located right behind the table Philip Havisham and his friends dined at. You can't see it from the other tables because it is hidden behind the wooden screen."
Sergeant Thompson looked *astounded*.

ÜBUNG 92

Übung 92: Welche Wörter passen inhaltlich zusammen?

1. dinner	☐ clothes
2. jacket	☐ smoke
3. waiter	☐ cigarette
4. paper	☐ lane
5. Victorian	☐ document
6. dark	☐ London
7. matches	☐ table
8. pipe	☐ pocket
9. case	☐ dine

"I see; the wooden screen *prevented* the other guests *from* seeing John Pirrip leave the room."

"Exactly! And nobody noticed he was gone."

"That was risky. A waiter could have come or theoretically someone could have seen him go through the door."

"That is absolutely correct, Sergeant. However, never forget: Crime is always connected to risk. There is no such thing as the perfect murder."

ÜBUNG 93

Übung 93: Sind die folgenden Aussagen korrekt? Markieren Sie mit richtig ✓ oder falsch – !

1. Susan White was pregnant. ☐
2. John Pirrip smuggled the gun into the Criterion in his violin case. ☐
3. One of the doors in the East Room was hidden by a wooden screen. ☐
4. John Pirrip gave his violin case to the waiter. ☐

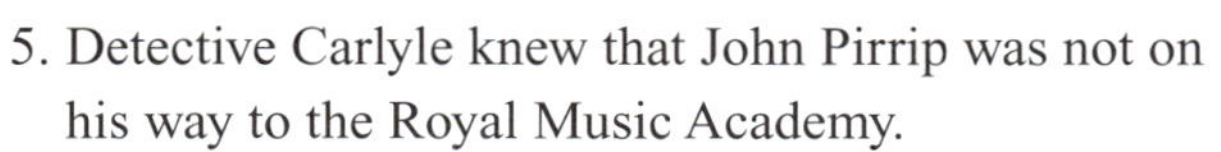

5. Detective Carlyle knew that John Pirrip was not on his way to the Royal Music Academy. ☐
6. John Pirrip's murder plan was perfect and not risky at all. ☐

Detective Carlyle's eyes *sparkled* when he said this. He moved his finger onwards to the hall, drawn behind the door.
"Now, the side door leads to a quieter corridor of the restaurant – but nevertheless it also leads to the men's room and the Great Hall. John Pirrip was probably waiting for the right moment: He knew his friend liked to stay longer than the others; he also knew he would go to the men's room sooner or later."
"Well, sir, I must say you're a genius!" exclaimed Sergeant Thompson. Suddenly the coach went over a large *bump*. Sergeant Thompson fell on top of Detective Carlyle.
"Now, now, Sergeant; there is no need to get that exited!" Detective Carlyle laughed.
"Sorry, sir!" said Sergeant Thompson embarrassed and sat back on his side of the seat. Just then the coach came to a *halt*.
"That's us arrived!" called the coachman.

Übung 94: Lesen Sie weiter und fügen Sie die Übersetzung der angegebenen Wörter ein!

ÜBUNG 94 !

Detective Carlyle and Sergeant Thompson hurried out of the coach and ran towards the (1. Eingang) ________________ of John Pirrip's house. They were followed by two other policemen, who had been travelling (2. neben) ________________ the coachman. The door had not been properly closed.

"All right men, let's go in. But be (3. vorsichtig) ______________,

John Pirrip could be *armed*."

The policemen carefully entered the house and searched the rooms.

All of a sudden one of the constables called his *superiors*.

"Over here!" he whispered.

The door to the bedroom was slightly open. John Pirrip was sitting on a chair looking out the (4. Schlafzimmer) ______________ window. He was holding a (5. Pistole) ______________ to his head – it was the Remington Revolver. Detective Carlyle took a deep breath and entered the room.

"Mr Pirrip, at last we (6. gefunden) ______________ you," he said *casually*.

"What do you want?" asked John Pirrip turning around on his (7. Stuhl) ______________ nervously. "Leave me alone or I shall shoot myself!"

Detective Carlyle signalled his men not to come into the room. He carefully took a chair (8. in der Nähe von) ______________ the door and sat down.

"Do not do anything *rash*, Mr Pirrip," he said calmly.
Sweat was running down John Pirrip's face and he was breathing heavily.
"But you know everything – I am going to be hanged sooner or later anyway!"
"Well, under the circumstances, you have a good chance escaping the *death penalty*."
"And spend the rest of my life in jail! I am better off dead!"
John Pirrip's finger pressed hard against the *trigger*.
"Goodbye, Detective!" said John Pirrip with a *weary* smile.
"No!" cried Detective Carlyle and jumped up from his chair. It was too late, John Pirrip had pulled the *trigger*, but nothing happened; the gun *jammed*. Detective Carlyle ran over to John Pirrip and pulled the gun from him. John Pirrip was going to attack him. Detective Carlyle's men came to his assistance. The two constables held John Pirrip back.

Übung 95: Ordnen Sie die Ausdrücke einander zu!

ÜBUNG 95 !

1. pull	☐ the coach
2. press	☐ the whip
3. push	☐ the menu
4. crack	☐ the button
5. throw	☐ the gun
6. fire	☐ the ball
7. read	☐ the trigger

"Let me go!" he shouted. "Let me go!"
Suddenly he stopped *struggling* and fell back onto the chair. He had no strength left in him.

ÜBUNG 96 !

Übung 96: Welche Wörter gehören zusammen?

1. drive	☐ deeply
2. smile	☐ highly
3. done	☐ friendly
4. recommended	☐ wearily
5. wink	☐ well
6. sing	☐ slowly

"Well, thank you very much for saving my life, Detective!" he said in a *sardonic*, *weary* tone. "Now I can either rot in jail or wait to be hanged."

"Let us wait and see what the court has to say to all of this."

"Tell me how you found out that Philip Havisham and your *fiancée* had had an affair."

John Pirrip took a deep breath.

"It was about a month ago. *By chance* I took one of her favourite books out of the library. I found a letter inside the book. It was addressed to Philip…"

John Pirrip's voice was *shaky*. He was trying hard not to cry.

"What did the letter say?" asked Detective Carlyle.

"Susan was…Susan was…writing to Philip *threatening* to kill herself, if he did not come back to her…she was scared he would leave her alone with the baby…"

ÜBUNG 97 !

Übung 97: Welche Wörter bezeichnen ähnliche Dinge?

1. dumb	☐ preferred
2. try	☐ positioned
3. shake	☐ attempt

4. deep	☐ novel
5. attack	☐ opportunity
6. located	☐ warn
7. favourite	☐ bottomless
8. book	☐ assault
9. threaten	☐ tremble
10. chance	☐ stupid

John Pirrip was fighting back his tears. The policemen standing around felt very sorry for this man. One of them shook his head. He could not believe what he was hearing.
"Did you have no idea this was going on?" asked Detective Carlyle. John Pirrip shook his head.
"Not in the least. I still cannot really believe it. I thought Susan loved me…after reading the letter the whole picture came together. Until then I just could not understand why she had killed herself…"
"When did you decide to kill Philip Havisham?"
"More or less *straight away* – he was an arrogant, *self-centred*, *devious* man and *deserved* nothing better. I wanted to revenge Susan…poor, dear Susan…and made a plan: I knew how much Lord Spencer hated Philip because of his book and I thought he would make a good *suspect*."

Übung 98: Vervollständigen Sie die Aussagen!

ÜBUNG 98 !

1. Sergeant Thompson hurried out of the coach and ran towards
   a) ☐ the entrance of John Pirrip's house.
   b) ☐ the back door of John Pirrip's house.
   c) ☐ the beautiful Baroness McKee.

2. Detective Carlyle signalled his men to
   a) ☐ come into the bedroom.
   b) ☐ keep out of the bedroom.
   c) ☐ overwhelm John Pirrip.

3. John Pirrip was fighting hard
   a) ☐ against his fears.
   b) ☐ against his anger.
   c) ☐ against his tears.

4. Detective Carlyle tried to stop John Pirrip
   a) ☐ from running away.
   b) ☐ from killing himself.
   c) ☐ from shooting him.

5. John Pirrip found one of his late fiancée's letters
   a) ☐ in Philip Havisham's house.
   b) ☐ whilst walking home one night.
   c) ☐ in one of her favourite books.

"So you *shoved* the note under his door telling him where to find Mr Havisham?"
"Yes!"
"And *whilst* you were at the hotel you also took one of the hotel's cushions!"
"Yes, it would have been a perfect plan…"
"…If it had not been for the letters," interrupted Detective Carlyle.
"Exactly, I knew some kind of correspondence must have existed, but I just could not find the letters. That shows you how afraid Philip was of anybody finding out about the affair; especially after Susan's death. My plan would have worked if you had not found the letters."

"Yes, that is the biggest weakness of committing a crime: Everybody believes they will never get caught."
Detective Carlyle looked at the two constables.
"Take Mr Pirrip back to the police station for further questioning. Sergeant Thompson and I will walk back. After the last few turbulent days we could do with some fresh air and a short break."
"Yes, sir!"

Übung 99: Ordnen Sie die Buchstaben zu einem sinnvollen Wort!

The constables (1. eld) __________ John Pirrip out of the bedroom and down the stairs. Detective Carlyle and Sergeant Thompson followed them. The constables seated John Pirrip in the (2. acohc) __________. One *accompanied* him inside and the other climbed up beside the coachman. The (3. piwh) __________ cracked and the coach shot off. John Pirrip looked very tired, but also somehow (4. lerieedv) ______________. He waved wearily at the policemen standing at the side of the road. Detective Carlyle (5. ppitde) ______________ his hat.
"Well, Sergeant, that's another (6. seca) __________ solved," he said watching the coach disappear into the (7. ecnastdi) ________________.
"Yes, who would have thought it was him – he (8. yeanlr) ______________ had us fooled into believing poor Lord Spencer had done it."

"It is the very perfection of a man, to find out his own imperfections," said Detective Carlyle thoughtfully.
"Who said that, sir?"
"St Augustine!"
"Oh, him again!" remarked Sergeant Thompson with a shrug.
He thought hard about something for a moment.

ÜBUNG 100

Übung 100: Was gab es bereits im Jahre 1879? Kreuzen Sie an!

1. street lamps ☐
2. roller-skates ☐
3. radio ☐
4. telephone ☐
5. fish'n'chips shops ☐
6. bicycle ☐
7. car ☐
8. steam-boat ☐

"Come to think of it, St Augustine might have made quite a good detective himself," said the sergeant smiling at his *superior*.
"That could possibly be true, Sergeant," replied Detective Carlyle.
At the same time both policemen pointed to their noses – they laughed and began walking up the road.

THE END

Abschlusstest

Übung 1: Welche Synonyme gehören zusammen?

1. win	☐	go in
2. enter	☐	rush
3. hurry	☐	argue
4. quarrel	☐	smile
5. shake	☐	attempt
6. try	☐	succeed
7. grin	☐	tremble

Übung 2: Fügen Sie die gesuchten Begriffe ein!

1. A person who serves in a restaurant is a ________________.
2. ________________ is the female equivalent of husband.
3. Detective Carlyle was ________________ Edinburgh.
4. ________________ John Pirrip left the East Room he killed Philip Havisham.
5. Something that happens by chance is a ________________.
6. The opposite of after is ________________.
7. They could not make ________________ do it.
8. A place someone hides is also called a ________________.
9. Lord Spencer was in ________________ of trouble.

Übung 3: Was gehört zusammen? Bilden Sie sinnvolle Paare!

1. rowing	☐ stone
2. grave	☐ door
3. church	☐ flame
4. slam	☐ the case
5. burn	☐ guy
6. solve	☐ a fuss
7. make	☐ flowers
8. chap	☐ beer
9. barrel of	☐ boat
10. bunch of	☐ yard

Übung 4: Welcher Satz enthält die richtige Übersetzung?

1. Ich werde Ihnen alles später erklären.
   a) ☐ I will explain everything to you later.
   b) ☐ I was going to explain everything to you later.

2. Kommst du auch?
   a) ☐ Are you coming to?
   b) ☐ Are you coming, too?

3. Das gehört ihm.
   a) ☐ That belongs to him.
   b) ☐ That belongs to himself.

4. Philip Havisham war sehr gut angezogen.
   a) ☐ Philip Havisham was very good dressed.
   b) ☐ Philip Havisham was very well dressed.

5. Baronin McKee war nicht zu Hause.
   a) ☐ Baroness McKee was not in home.
   b) ☐ Baroness McKee was not at home.

Übung 5: Welches Wort ist das „schwarze Schaf“?

1. guy, man, chap, boy
2. poor, penniless, wealthy, broke
3. book, poster, notice, sign
4. lunch, dine, dinner, breakfast
5. tramp, beggar, well-to-do, poor
6. pale, white, ashen, blue
7. exit, leave, enter, go

Übung 6: Wandeln Sie die folgenden Ausdrücke in ihre weiblichen Pendants im Plural!

1. man ....
2. husband ....
3. baron ....
4. policeman ....
5. waiter ....
6. host ....
7. actor ....

Übung 7: Welche Gegenteile gehören zusammen?

1. brand new	☐ less
2. more	☐ bold
3. empty	☐ near
4. cowardly	☐ reveal
5. far away	☐ dangerous
6. safe	☐ crowded
7. cover	☐ old

Übung 8: Unterstreichen Sie die richtige Variante!

1. Chief Inspector Gatsby took a deep breath/gasp.
2. John Pirrip pulled/shoved the trigger.
3. Lord Spencer is nice/nicer than Philip Havisham.
4. Let us meet/meat at the hotel.
5. A piece/peace of paper lay on the ground.
6. Someone is trying to put the blame in/on him.
7. He rowed the boat onto/into the bridge.

Übung 9: Wie lauten die typisch viktorianischen Begriffe? Ordnen Sie die Buchstaben zu einem sinnvollen Wort!

1. moor-ntea ....
2. pach ....
3. terpat ....
4. ris ....

5. meadma ____________________

6. ylads nma ____________________

7. ginward-moro ____________________

Übung 10: Setzen Sie, wenn notwendig, den passenden Artikel ein!

1. He warned him many _____ time.

2. Sergeant Thompson was _____ hour late.

3. John Pirrip was in _____ Great Hall.

4. Sergeant Thompson has got _____ news for his superior.

5. Lord Spencer needed _____ hundred pounds.

6. Philip Havisham did not like to get out of _____ bed.

7. Detective Carlyle ate _____ apple for breakfast.

Lernkrimi Englisch

Aufbauwortschatz

THEFT AT DAWN

Duncan Glan
Nach einer Idee von Bianca Mux

Inhalt

Story

James Hudson arbeitet als Inspector bei der legendären Polizeibehörde Scotland Yard. Er ist einer der fähigsten Männer und wird immer dann zu Rate gezogen, wenn seine Kollegen mal wieder vor einem Rätsel stehen. Diesmal sieht er sich mit einem ungewöhnlichen Fall konfrontiert:

Der erfolgreiche Krimiautor Geoffrey Auberon Carmody steht nach einer durchzechten Nacht vor einem Rätsel. Wem gehören der hochhackige, schwarze Damenschuh und die teure Unterwäsche in seiner Küche und wieso liegen im Flur schwarze Nylonstrümpfe? Doch damit nicht genug – wenige Zeit später bringt ihm ein Kurier eine Karte mit der rätselhaften Aufschrift Central/8.
Carmody beschließt den Rat von Inspector Hudson hinzuzuziehen, doch dann begibt er sich selber auf Spurensuche. Die rätselhafte Unbekannte entpuppt sich als junge und attraktive Frau, die nicht nur Carmodys Gefühlsleben ganz schön durcheinander bringt, sondern seine gesamte Existenz aufs Spiel setzt …

Chapter 1: A Dangerous Offer

Geoffrey Auberon Carmody, a distinguished writer of crime novels, climbed out of the taxi with some difficulty. At his age, pub crawls which ended at discotheques, though great fun, tended to have a somewhat *detrimental* effect on his *equilibrium*. The early morning air was freezing cold, and the pavement was slippery with icy rain. Still, years of practice enabled Carmody to reach the door of his house with his dignity intact. Knowing that the only thing he needed at the moment was a good day's sleep, once inside he *staggered* directly upstairs. Had he been less preoccupied with safely climbing the stairs, he might have noticed a shadow moving in his living room. As it was, Carmody was *relieved* to finally reach his bed. Within seconds, he was fast asleep.

Übung 1: Lesen Sie weiter und setzen Sie die Verben in Klammern in die richtige Zeitform!
(decide, be, freeze, swallow, convince, meet, ache, awake)

ÜBUNG 1

When he (1.) ____________, it (2.) ____________ shortly after lunchtime. His head (3.) ____________, and walking to the bathroom he felt *dizzy*. One look in the bathroom mirror (4.) ____________ Carmody that social calls were out of question. He (5.) ____________ a couple of aspirins and (6.) ____________ to make some really strong coffee. Lots of it. He had just begun descending the stairs, when his eyes (7.) ____________ an extraordinary sight. He (8.) ____________ on the third step.

There, on his *landing*, lay a *pile* of *discarded* women's clothes. A black evening dress was carefully laid out, as if whoever had put it there hadn't wanted it to get wrinkled. Next to it lay silk stockings and expensive-looking undergarments, all *neatly* arranged. On top lay a single, black, high-heeled shoe. Of course, in the ordinary course of events, Carmody would have welcomed a woman of such *impeccable* taste undressing in his house, but he could not begin to imagine why she should have chosen the bottom of his stairs to do so. Whoever she was, though, he couldn't have thought of a more agreeable place for her to *allow* her exhibitionist instincts *free rein*. Unfortunately, Carmody was nearly positive he had come home alone. *Puzzled*, he decided to search downstairs for some answers.

ÜBUNG 2 !

Übung 2: Welches Wort ist das „schwarze Schaf"? Unterstreichen Sie das nicht in die Reihe passende Wort!

1. mound, pile, stack, mind
2. night, afternoon, evening, midnight
3. impeccable, ferocious, perfect, flawless
4. exhibitionist, shy, introvert, timid
5. normal, ordinary, open, usual

What he found, however, was something even more *bewildering*. To be sure, after his activities the previous evening he would not have been surprised to see a few unusual things. A smiling pink elephant would have been absolutely normal. But the fact remained that despite his wide experience in the field, he had never yet hallucinated anything that came close to what he was seeing at that very moment. *Spread out* on his living room table, glinting in the winter light, was an assortment of delicately crafted jewels. Carmody saw about a dozen gold and silver rings softly shimmering. Next to them lay two ornate necklaces, half a dozen *pendants*, several earrings, pearls and a *jewel-encrusted* brooch. Carmody was no expert, but he thought these items looked genuine. It seemed that, for reasons he could not even begin to *fathom*, somebody's crown jewels had materialised in his living room.

Übung 3: Finden Sie das passende Gegenteil! Setzen Sie die richtige Ziffer ein!

! ÜBUNG 3

1. materialise	☐ next
2. expert	☐ plain
3. ornate	☐ disappear
4. common	☐ amateur
5. expected	☐ bewildering
6. previous	☐ unusual

Of the owner there was apparently no trace, which was something of a disappointment for Carmody since he knew where her clothes were. A quick check once again convinced Carmody that he was quite alone in the house. The windows were still closed and locked, and there was no sign that a break-in had taken place. Carmody could feel that he was beginning to lose his concentration. I definitely need that coffee, he thought.

Half an hour later, he was sitting in his armchair with a large cup of coffee, thinking as hard as he could in his condition. He knew any reasonable person would have called the police. On the other hand, Carmody would have been gravely offended had anyone called him "reasonable". Moreover, he did not altogether like the idea of the police arriving at his house to find a hungover writer informing them that in his living room he had just found a small fortune in jewellery which *appeared* to have been left behind by some unidentified high-class stripper. And what she had worn upon leaving Carmody's home was also a mystery, since she had left behind her evening clothes – perhaps she had decided that the winter air would be good for her skin, he thought. Or perhaps she had made off in one of his suits. Something told Carmody that despite its obvious literary potential the police would not find this story the least bit amusing.

ÜBUNG 4 !

Übung 4: Lesen Sie weiter und fügen Sie die richtigen Präpositionen ein! ***(in, in, in, of, of, at, to)***

He remained seated (1.) ______ his favourite armchair another few minutes, until the thought (2.) ______ calling Inspector Hudson, (3.) ______ Scotland Yard, popped into his head. He had called Hudson several times (4.) ______ the past, in order to get details (5.) ______ police methods and past crimes that might make his stories more realistic. He and Hudson had not exactly hit it off, however, possibly because one evening he had paid too much attention (6.) ______ Hudson's friend, Elvira. But perhaps he should call Hudson just the same. He reached into his pocket and pulled out his mobile phone. It's right here, so I don't even have to go into the other room, he thought. Carmody looked up Hudson's home number (7.) ______ his address book and dialled the number.

"Hudson."
"Inspector Hudson, this is Geoffrey Carmody. I wonder if I might have a word with you."
There was a sigh at the other end.
"I don't have time for you right now, Carmody."
"I understand, but I have something that might be of great interest to you. This afternoon, after waking up–"
"'This afternoon'? Stop there, Carmody, I have no time for this. I don't want to be impolite, but I have more important matters at hand. *With all due respect* I would ask you not to call me again. I wish you a good day."

Übung 5: Wie heißt das Wort auf Deutsch oder auf Englisch?

ÜBUNG 5 !

1. Beleidigung ______
2. unhöflich ______
3. unidentified ______
4. Anzug ______
5. gravely ______
6. vernünftig ______

The phone went dead. Carmody thought of calling back and trying to tell Hudson the story before he had a chance to hang up again, but then he put his mobile phone down. This is going to be a *riddle* that I have to solve myself, he thought. He spent the next fifteen minutes carefully examining his *treasure*. The clothes were *devoid* of any laundry marks or labels which were always so helpful to the detectives in his books. Nor were there any telling engravings on the rings.

Carmody noticed that there was no designer watch or anything at all which looked as though it came from the 20th century. This jewellery was old, family *heirlooms* perhaps, or even museum pieces. He *fervently* hoped it wasn't the *latter*. His only *clue* so far seemed to be that his night visitor had left behind one shoe – and one shoe only. As she – if it was a she, because he couldn't be absolutely certain it was – had done everything else with apparent care and precision, Carmody could only conclude that she had left the shoe behind *deliberately*. Had this *mischievous* Cinderella kept the second shoe as a sign of recognition? Carmody *chuckled*. He rather liked the idea of himself as a prince on a *quest*, though after ten hours of non-stop drinking he felt more like an old man than a prince.

ÜBUNG 6 !

Übung 6: Lesen Sie weiter und bilden Sie sinnvolle Wörter aus dem Buchstabenchaos!

He was not overly (1. rrespuisd) ________ when a short while later the (2. lloordeb) ______ rang and a courier *handed* him a (3. tteerl) ________. Cinderella had put too much (4. troffe) ________ into arranging the scene not to want to communicate with him. Carmody *ripped* open the (5. eeplevno) ________ and removed a postcard. He read it and (6. denwrfo) ________. In bold handwriting someone had written **Central/8** and nothing more.

What on earth is that *supposed* to mean? he wondered. Perplexed, Carmody turned the card over. It was one of those would-be artistic cards you buy in bookshops, a colour photograph of a single branch of a Japanese cherry tree. Against the dark wood, the white cherry blossoms stood out; raindrops were glistening in the sunlight. The photographer had obviously tried hard to create a particular atmosphere. This, thought Carmody sarcastically, is a card intended for secretaries with a taste for the esoteric – *incense* and Zen Buddhism. In the context of *stray* jewellery and mysteriously *appearing* underwear and clothing, it seemed very much out of place. For some time Carmody stood very still, *racking* his brains. When at last the solution *struck* him, it came so suddenly that he laughed aloud. What he was looking at were "*petals* on a wet black *bough*". He felt slightly ashamed that it had taken him so long to figure this one out. A poem by Ezra Pound had provided the title for his last novel, "Faces in the Crowd". It was a short poem, consisting of only two lines:

"The apparition of these faces in the crowd;
Petals on a wet, black *bough*."

Übung 7: Übersetzen Sie und enträtseln Sie das Lösungwort!

ÜBUNG 7 !

1. Blätter _ _ □ _ _ _
2. Ast _ _ □ _ _
3. Stiel _ □ _ _
4. Baumstamm _ _ _ _ _ _ □ _ _
5. Blüten _ _ _ _ _ _ □ _
6. Dornen _ _ _ _ □ _

Lösung: _ _ _ _ _ _

More significantly, the poem's title read "In a Station of the Metro". Remembering this, Carmody felt certain that his unknown lady-friend was asking him to take the underground, the Central line, and to go eight stations – but in which direction? In considerable excitement, he gripped his rucksack and coat, and made for the station, suddenly forgetting his hangover. He was beginning to like Cinderella's playful sense of humour.

I'll just have to try one direction and then the other until I see something interesting, he thought. He didn't have to wait long for the Central, but he was so busy wondering what other *insanities* the day might possibly bring that he almost missed the eighth station. At the very last moment, he woke from his *musings* and jumped onto the platform – minding the *gap*, as all the warnings requested – before the doors closed. He looked around. Nothing *struck* him as extraordinary. There was only the usual crowd of passengers, carrying plastic bags or rucksacks with their Saturday shopping. About the only thing of a criminal nature that Carmody could spot were the *lurid* colours of some umbrellas. There ought to be a law against pink in public, he thought.

Spotting nothing further of interest, he climbed the stairs. Outside a *gust* of rain blew in his face, but he didn't care. He had found what he had been looking for. On his right, there was a showcase displaying posters advertising various cultural events. Among them, a particularly colourful one *stuck out.* It was advertising a Christmas pantomime: Cinderella.

ÜBUNG 8 !

Übung 8: Wie lauten die Sätze in der richtigen Reihenfolge?

1. wrote stories simple he very

____

2. one late morning got home he

____

3. mean that does word what?

---

4. already the was he train on

---

5. off her all woman took a clothes

---

6. Cinderella woman is young a beautiful

The poster listed an address, so Carmody *waved down* a taxi. Fifteen minutes later, he stood in front of a *multi-purpose hall* which, according to the bronze plate next to its door, belonged to a church. Wondering what to do next, Carmody began to walk slowly round the building, taking in his surroundings. He had obviously come to an affluent part of the city. Around him stood large, neat houses with well-kept lawns and tasteful Christmas decorations. There were no garden gnomes anywhere, and expensive cars were parked in front of the houses. Carmody was on his second round when his attention was caught by something strange – something in the lawn next door looked almost like a cat, perhaps a kitten, but he could see no head. Curious, he went to investigate. Almost at it, he grinned. On one of the low walls that surrounded the front, in the shadow of an ornamental porch, stood a single, black, high-heeled shoe. He picked up the shoe and examined it: it was without a doubt the twin of the one in his house. He turned around.

So this is it, he thought. *Glancing* at the house, Carmody couldn't help feeling slightly disappointed. For the final destination of a *treasure* hunt, it seemed altogether too ordinary, smaller and less *impressive* than the other buildings around it. Still, he thought, I've come this far, I might as well see it through. She must live here. Walking up the garden path, he noticed that all the *shutters* were down. There were no sounds coming from the house. He rang the bell once, then a second time. Nobody answered. Hesitantly, he tried pushing the door. It opened. Uncomfortably aware that he was just crossing the line between a harmless *lark* and criminal behaviour, he entered.

ÜBUNG 9 !

Übung 9: Lesen Sie weiter und unterstreichen Sie die Wörter, die falsch geschrieben sind! Geben Sie die richtige Schreibweise an!

The house was dark. There was nobody to be seen or heard. Ignoring an increasing sense of *unease*, Carmody called out:
"Hello! Is there anybody here?"
Silents. He decided to risk turning on a light and found a light *switch*. In the bright light that suddenly came from a chamdelier, he saw that he was standing in a *marble* corridoor with inlaid mosaics. There were doors on both sides, and a staircase at the end. Large paintings on the wall *depicted* dark landscapes. On tiptoe, Carmody entered a room on the right which turned out to be the living room. There was no dout that whoever had furnished the room was not lacking in money. It looked like a picture from some glossy magazine on intereor decoration, but otherwise there was nothing of particular interest – no outstanding oil paintings or pieces of furniture. Carmody returned to the corridor. Looking around, he saw something he hadn't sported before. Hanging from the *banisters*, as if dropped carelessly, was a black silk scarf. Smiling despite the *odd* feeling in his stomache, Carmody collected the scarf and went up the stairs, where he came to three other rooms. The door to one

of them stood wide open. It was a bedroom, large and as luxurusly furnished as the living room downstairs. What immediately caught Carmody's eye, however, was not the wonderful antiq bed, nor the exquisite wooden table with matching chairs, but an oil painting of a nude stretched out on a divan. The painting was lying on the bed, but it was obvious that until recently it had hung on the wall right over the bed; you could see the spot on the wallpaper. In its *rightful* place, it had been used to hide a safe – a safe which was now open and conspicuously empty. On the pilow under the safe, Carmody saw something glitter. He took an involuntary step forward – and jumped back in fright.

1. ______________ 6. ______________

2. ______________ 7. ______________

3. ______________ 8. ______________

4. ______________ 9. ______________

5. ______________ 10. ______________

An ear-splitting *howl* filled the air. For a moment, Carmody stood frozen, unable to move, unable to think; he almost dropped the shoe and scarf from his hand. Then, with a rising sense of panic, he realised that the sound was a burglar alarm. He was now wide awake and completely *sober*, and within fractions of a second he understood the impossibility of his situation. He was standing in a strange house which had apparently been robbed, and it did not take much imagination to guess where, if the police caught him, they would find the *loot*. Carmody knew that interrogating officers were unlikely to be impressed by a tale which involved coded messages sent by a Cinderella leaving clothes all over London.

ÜBUNG 10 !

Übung 10: Beantworten Sie die Fragen zum Text!

1. What kind of novels does Geoffrey Carmody write?

____

2. What article of women's clothes (but not an undergarment) does Carmody notice on his stairs?

____

3. What colour is the item of clothes from question 2?

____

4. What kind of picture is on the postcard?

____

5. What animal does the shoe remind Carmody of?

____

6. The single shoe reminds Carmody of which character from a children's book?

____

As quickly as he could, he ran downstairs. The front door was still open, but the noise from the alarm would no doubt *arouse* the neighbours so he could never escape without notice. Hoping against hope for another exit, Carmody hurried towards the door next to the stairs and opened it. It led into what, had he had time to think about it, he would have called a smoking room. On one side, the room opened into a large, beautiful winter garden. Carmody had no eye for the *lush* green of the exotic plants, however. The only thing of interest to him was a door which led from the winter garden to a terrace. It stood slightly *ajar*. Without thinking, he pushed the door open with his elbow and ran out into the garden and into the shadow of the high hedge surrounding it. Looking *frantically* for an escape route, he eventually spotted another gate, practically hidden under a growth of ivy. It turned out to be closed. Carmody shook it violently, but the gate would not *budge*. Finally, he had no alternative but to climb over, an action complicated by the shoe in his hand. From the street behind him, he could hear police sirens *approaching*. He made one last effort and threw his leg over the gate and slipped down the other side.

Übung 11: Markieren Sie mit richtig ✔ oder falsch – !

ÜBUNG 11

1. Geoffrey Carmody comes home drunk. ☐
2. He wakes up later in the morning. ☐
3. He is intrigued by the single shoe in his house. ☐
4. He takes the tube to solve the mystery. ☐
5. The postcard refers to a poem in one of his books. ☐
6. Someone was in his house when he got home. ☐

He found himself on a small footpath leading along the garden hedges. Focused only on getting away as quickly as possible, he ran, *thanking the fates* for his relative physical fitness. Eventually, the footpath led to a border path surrounded by high trees. Carmody saw that he had come to a park. In the distance, he spotted a pond. Some children were feeding ducks; their *squeals of delight* could already be heard ringing through the cold air. He was completely out of breath, but there were a couple of joggers about, and nobody seemed to notice anything unusual – though a man carrying a single high-heeled shoe might be considered a bit *peculiar*. With his last strength, he walked to a nearby bench and sat down.

ÜBUNG 12 !

Übung 12: Wie heißen die folgenden Tiere auf Deutsch?

1. duck ____________
2. eagle ____________
3. snake ____________
4. owl ____________
5. donkey ____________
6. squirrel ____________
7. mule ____________
8. bat ____________

It took nearly half an hour for Carmody to get his breath back and for his heart to stop beating like mad. At last, he got up. He began to slowly cross the park and find a way home from the opposite end. He was still weak-kneed, and he now had a vicious headache, but somewhere deep inside him and half suppressed he also felt something else. Was it triumph because of his escape? If the truth be told, that first rush of adrenaline had not been an altogether unpleasant sensation. Carmody was ashamed to admit it, but the simple fact was that he had thoroughly enjoyed the day's adventures – which were a bridge between his normal, quiet life and the life described in his books. And his narrow escape had only intensified his desire to find out how that jewellery had come to be in his living room. He walked on, throwing the shoe into the air and catching it.

Übung 13: Lesen Sie weiter und unterstreichen Sie die Wörter oder Wendungen im Text mit denselben Bedeutungen!
(across from, plunging in, observe, afterwards, excited, shattered)

ÜBUNG 13 !

An hour later, he was back on his doorstep. Tired and yet wound up, he did not notice the sports car parked opposite his front door. But when he had opened the door and entered, *his ears pricked up.* Music was coming from the living room. Somebody was playing his favourite CD, Genesis' "The Lamb Lies Down on Broadway". Taking a deep breath, Carmody went into the room. He knew without asking who was in his living room.

"Hi, Cinderella", he said. "So nice to meet you".
A slender woman in her late twenties was sitting comfortably on his couch. She was wearing a black silk dress and a marvellous necklace Carmody knew all too well, having examined it carefully earlier that day. Her black silk stockings were shimmering in the lamplight. No shoes, though. There was no trace of nervousness about her. For all the calm she was showing, she might have been sitting on a sundeck at home rather than in the living room of someone she had almost sent to prison. Looking up from a book she had taken from his shelf, she smiled brightly.

Übung 14: Setzen Sie die Verben ins Simple Past!

ÜBUNG 14 !

1. cut ....

2. buy ....

3. seek ....

4. can ....

5. wear ____________________

6. stand ____________________

"Good afternoon, Mr Carmody", she said in a soft, deep voice, "I am glad to see you made it."
"Your shoe," Carmody said, leaning down and *handing* it to her.
"Thank you, darling," she said with a smile, laying it next to her on the couch. Carmody looked at her hard; he was thinking of playing the hard guy and slapping her face. She must have sensed this, so she added,
"I suppose I *owe* you an explanation."
The contrast between his excitement and this woman's *sober* and casual tone *struck* Carmody so hard that he had to fight not to burst into hysterical laughter. The next moment he began to feel his age.
"I don't know about you", he replied, trying to sound relaxed, "but I for one could do with a glass of wine."
"That would be lovely."

ÜBUNG 15 !

Übung 15: Lesen Sie weiter und fügen Sie jeweils die passenden Begriffe in die entsprechenden Lücken ein!
(dawn, tone, fetch, smile, real, handed)

He left the room to (1.) ____________ two glasses and a bottle of red wine. When he returned he (2.) ____________ her a glass and then sat down in his armchair and gave his guest an encouraging (3.) ____________.

"So, you are –?"

"My Name is Cornelia Thomas," she began in a matter-of-fact (4.) ____________.

"Is that your (5.) ____________ name?"

"It will do. I am, as you should have guessed by now, a thief. The house you were in earlier today belongs to a successful dentist and his wife; they are currently on holiday, skiing in Switzerland. I robbed it early this morning. (6.) ____________ is my favourite time for a break-in.

Have you ever seen gold glinting in the soft light of a sunrise? It's unbelievably romantic. Anyway, I deactivated the alarm, took what I wanted and then prepared the house for you. After that, I came here.
As it was Saturday morning, I was quite certain that as usual you would be fast asleep, sleeping off the beer from last night. I *spread out* my *trinkets*. Then you gave me quite a shock by coming home much later than I had expected. That's not your usual style – to stay out until 7 a.m. Did something happen?"
"Oh, nothing important," Carmody said. "The discotheque closed a little earlier than usual. A *funeral* in the family somewhere in the north of England, I believe. So, some friends and I went to another club that doesn't believe in closing at all."
The young woman looked thoughtful.
"Bad luck. I should have been prepared for a late arrival. How careless of me. It's the details that always *trip* one *up*." She sipped at her glass. "Anyway, I was fortunate. You went straight off to bed and fell asleep, so I had all the time in the world to complete my arrangements. Did you like them?"

"Like them?" Carmody *chuckled*. "I've never been more *baffled* in my life. I applaud you."

ÜBUNG 16

Übung 16: Welche Gegenteile gehören zusammen?

1. important	☐ likeness
2. favourite	☐ easy
3. encourage	☐ calm
4. contrast	☐ stout
5. hard	☐ prickly
6. nervous	☐ detested
7. comfortable	☐ minor
8. slender	☐ deter

Cinderella nodded, pleased.

"I wanted you in on the game, and I knew that you wouldn't be able to *resist* a mystery as piquant as this. I'm a fan, Mr Carmody. I've read your books. I've been watching you, too. I was positive you'd rise to the challenge."

"And may I ask why you led me straight into a trap? I take it that you were the one who set off the alarm?"

"Naturally. Let us say, your little *treasure* hunt, *apart from* giving you an appetite, ensured me both your full attention and a good *bargaining* position, for I require your cooperation as well."

"My cooperation? I don't understand."

"You remember that glittering thing on the pillow under the safe?" she asked with a smile. "The brooch you saw this morning. You examined it carefully, didn't you? The police now have in their possession a piece of the *swag* which the burglar must have dropped in his haste. It has your fingerprints all over it."

Übung 17: Welches Wort ist das „schwarze Schaf"?

1. alarm, sound, siren, bell
2. treasure, trophy, booty, swag
3. consumption, notice, consideration, attention
4. thief, swindler, politician, shark
5. normal, usual, natural, sensual
6. nightspot, club, pub, discotheque

Carmody turned white. He started to speak but then said nothing.
"Of course, as you are a moral and upstanding citizen, despite your behaviour in discotheques, the police do not have the matching prints in their computer. Not yet. But a single phone call could take care of all that. You should also remember that the police believe the burglary took place this afternoon, at a time for which I, unlike you, have an alibi. All very neat, wouldn't you say?"
Against his will, Carmody was impressed.
"But why?" he asked, with a mixture of anger and admiration. "Don't tell me you went to all that trouble just to get my autograph."
Now it was Cinderella's turn to *chuckle*.
"Not quite. You see, I'm a successful business-woman, and my business is flourishing. Now, I'm looking to expand. I enjoy the practical aspects of burglary: entering a locked building or climbing through windows and balconies, deactivating various types of alarm systems, locating and opening safes, escaping unobserved and leaving behind no traces. I have sometimes even reactivated alarm systems. I'm very thorough. My weakness, on the other hand, is planning – I don't see the weaknesses in my plans, *hence* I had no back-up plan in case of your early return. I simply lack imagination, I'm afraid. I need someone to work out unusual plans,

someone with a *grasp of* human psychology, someone who understands people and who can predict their unpredictable behaviour. Who better for that job than a writer of crime fiction?"

ÜBUNG 18 !

Übung 18: Lesen Sie weiter und unterstreichen Sie im folgenden Absatz die zehn überflüssigen Wörter!

Carmody's *jaw* dropped.
"You're telling to me that you want me to be your partner in crime?" he *groaned*. He couldn't believe in his ears.
"You could call it that", answered the Cinderella, completely *unperturbed* by Carmody's slow reaction. "It would be a 50/50 partnership, of course, beginning with today's percentage profits, since you are now at the very the least an *accomplice*. And I want to stress that it is burglaries not only: no violence, no weapons, no robbing helpless old women of their life savings. There are to some *windfall* profits, though: the burglary pays better than your publisher, the government won't take its *share* in taxes and its for entertainment value is considerable. It might also be a career move for you: it would give you more experience with the real world of crime, which you could then use in your novels."

Carmody was speechless. Suddenly, images of prison, the French Riviera, a sports car, bobbies with *handcuffs*, a beautiful woman, this beautiful woman at his side began to pass through his head. To his *astonishment*, Carmody found that, as outrageous as Cinderella's proposition certainly was, he could not honestly say he was not tempted. This afternoon had been fun; there was no denying it. He reflected on the alternatives, seeing himself getting old alone behind a computer, escaping the boredom with increasing amounts of alcohol. All things considered, he thought, Cinderella does seem to have a point.

Übung 19: Lesen Sie weiter und füllen Sie die Lücken mit den passenden Wörtern!
(like, deliberation, along, postpone, call, stick)

ÜBUNG 19 !

"May I (1.) ____________ you Geoff?" she asked.

"I think we should (2.) ________________ with Mr Carmody and Cinderella."

"Cinderella? As you (3.) ________________," she said with a smile. "But we are going to be partners."

Carmody rose.

"This *deserves* a bit more (4.) ____________", he said, "and I've had enough for one day. I suggest we (5.) ____________ discussing details until my head is clearer. If I go (6.) ____________ with it, however, there will be at least one condition," he said, looking at her seriously.

"What is it?" Cinderella asked.
"Next time you remove your clothes in my house, I insist on being present."
Cinderella smiled and rose, too. She walked out of the door, and without looking back walked a short distance to a shiny green sports car, got in and drove away.

"No alibi?" he said after watching Cinderella's car disappear from view. "I called Hudson this afternoon and tried to tell him that something strange had happened to me."
He walked into the living room, picked up Cinderella's nearly empty glass – and emptied it himself. Then he took his glass and hers into the kitchen. Suddenly he felt as if he had just stepped off the Tower of London. I called Hudson on my mobile phone, he said to himself. Out of pure laziness I called him on my mobile phone. I can't prove I was at home when I called him.

ÜBUNG 20

Übung 20: Beantworten Sie die Fragen zum Text!

1. What is Cinderella's real name?

2. Did Cinderella set a trap for Carmody?

3. Did Carmody enjoy the "game" Cinderella played with him?

4. Is Carmody in good physical condition?

5. How old is Cinderella?

6. When is Cinderella's favourite time to rob a house?

The following morning, Carmody walked immediately to the closest newsagent and picked up copies of two London newspapers. Back home, he leafed through them, looking for mention of the robbery. Both papers carried short articles on it in the local section. One reported that the break-in took place around 2.30 p.m. The other said that someone had seen a man around the house early in the afternoon, but the description did not fit Carmody – as he had worn a green coat, not a black one – so he was *relieved*.

Übung 21: Wie lauten die Sätze in der richtigen Reihenfolge?

1. read the he newspapers always.

2. to dawn preferred houses she at rob.

3. Carmody Cinderella sent postcard a.

4. people older about getting worry.

5. thief you catch do a how?

Chapter 2: The Perfect Plan

Two days later there was a ringing at the door. Carmody opened it and was surprised.

"So, shall we stay here or do you want to go somewhere to talk about the future?"

Cinderella or Cornelia Thomas was standing in Carmody's doorway, speaking before he even had a chance to invite her in. He had thought of the young woman non-stop for the past forty-eight hours and was *relieved* to see her at last.

"Come in," he said, quickly, "I don't want anyone to see you."

"I'm not a wanted woman," she responded *casually*, and then entered.

"I wouldn't be too sure about that," he said, closing the door.

"Are you paying me a compliment?" she asked, a smile on her face.

Ignoring her question, he said,

"We could go for a pint or go to a café, whichever suits you best, Cinderella. We should go somewhere where we're both anonymous."

"Well, Mr Carmody, to be quite frank, I don't like to mix alcohol with planning – alcohol and business make for a bad mixture."

"A pint of bitter helps my thinking," he said and put on his green coat.

"Not if your last book is anything to judge by."

"I nearly got an award for 'Faces in the Crowd'."

"Writers always get awards for their worst books. Prize committees just try to make up for not noticing the best works when they first came out."

"You think 'Faces in the Crowd' was my worst – ?"

"Yes, but don't take it so hard. Let's go somewhere for a coffee and maybe I'll treat you to dinner afterwards."

Übung 22: Lesen Sie weiter und unterstreichen Sie das passende Wort der zwei Varianten!

On the way to the underground station, they began to (1.) discuss/disturb the situation.
"(2.) So/For, you are looking to change your *approach*, shall we say?"
"In the past I've always robbed people who are not quite rich but (3.) already/almost. The risks are lower but so are the *rewards*."
"And now you want to go after the super-rich?"
"No, they're out of my (4.) list/league. I'm good at what I do, but the super-rich would be too much of a (5.) challenge/change." She led the way down to the trains. "They have better alarm systems and they usually have servants and maids – that sort of thing. The risk is simply too high for me."
"It's good to know your limits. So which group is to be your next (6.) seal/target?"
"The rich. People one step above those I've been targeting so far. *Senior executives*, board members, those will be the target."
"How long have you been in this 'business'?" he asked as the train pulled (7.) onto/into the station.
"Long enough," she answered, walking onto the train.
"That's not very specific."
"That's as specific as it gets."
The train was (8.) somehow/somewhat full.
"I'm trying to decide if I'm going to join you or not and – "
"The decision has already been made. Remember," she changed to a (9.) whisper/yell, "all I have to do is place one phone call and Geoffrey Auberon Carmody, best-selling crime writer, is sitting in police *custody*."
"You wouldn't."

"Trust me," she *flashed* a charming smile, "I would."
"Then I'd just tell the police everything I know," he whispered in her ear.
"Which is what, exactly?" she answered, raising her voice a little.
Carmody was silent for a moment.
"If you have such problems with planning, there's likely to be something to connect you to the job at the dentist's house."
"I have an alibi, remember? And there's enough to connect you to the house."
"It can't be any more real than anything I could come up with."
"But it can be. You see, my alibi has the virtue of being true."
Carmody said nothing further. He stood up straight and looked over her head at all the people around him. University students, mothers with children, a few businessmen and women. She pulled on the sleeve of his coat and he leaned down.
"I have no desire to see you in prison. I want to work with you."

ÜBUNG 23 !

Übung 23: Welche Synonyme gehören zusammen?

1. help	☐ talk about
2. exact	☐ precise
3. charming	☐ delightful
4. limit	☐ boundary
5. discuss	☐ most recent
6. last	☐ aid

Carmody looked into her eyes and noticed that they were bright green. He felt himself *swallowed* up in them. It had been so long since he had been in a relationship with a woman that he was almost *defenceless* against those summer-grass-green eyes.

“We’ll get off here,” she said, and followed many other Londoners off the train. She led Carmody to a café on a side street that he had never noticed before. It was large and dark and targeted at a tourist clientele, which would ensure anonymity.

Übung 24: Lesen Sie weiter und unterstreichen Sie die acht Wörter, die falsch geschrieben sind! Geben Sie die richtige Schreibweise an!

! ÜBUNG 24

She walked to a table in the back of the café and sat on a banch against the wall. Carmody tried to sit next to her but she painted towards the chair on the other side of the small bistro table. Through Carmody enjoyed his view, he usually prefered to sit where Cinderella was sitting. I’ll have to make do, he thought, but I have to find a way to get the uper hand in this little game we’re playing.
“So, are you making any plans at the moment?” Carmody asked carlessly.
“I’m always making plans,” she responded. “You want to leave as little as possible to chance.”
“Bringing in a parterre increases the risk.”
“Naturally,” she answered, “but I’m willing to take that risiko.”

1.________ 2.________ 3.________ 4.________
5.________ 6.________ 7.________ 8.________

The waiter came over and took their order. Carmody wanted to order a pint of bitter but took a tea instead. They sat silently until the waiter came back with their order. She sipped at her café au lait and watched the waiter walk away, watched him rather closely, Carmody thought.

ÜBUNG 25 !

Übung 25: Welche Wörter gehören in die Lücken? Setzen Sie ein!
(challenge, throat, life, jealous, modern, partnership)

"I see he is more to your taste," he said bitterly.

"You mustn't be (1.) ____________, my dear Geoff – "

" – Mr Carmody," he corrected.

"As you like. So, what do you wish to discuss? Our (2.) ____________?"

"You seem to have me by the, er, by the (3.) ________________," Carmody said, not quite believing what he said.

"That won't do at all," she countered. "You should see this as a (4.) ___________, as a *distraction* from every-day (5.) ____________."

"So, we're to be the (6.) ____________ British Bonnie and Clyde, wanted all over England."

"Remember, I said 'No guns.' I have no wish to end up the way they did. And, secondly, I don't want to be 'wanted.' To be 'wanted' is no sign of success: it's a sign of failure."
"So, what is my role?"
"As I said, I want help in planning. I want to move into new territory, and I want some creative input from you."
"I have no real experience."
"Your novels seem to say otherwise. But that's of no importance. I want your creativity, your ideas. Even in your weakest works, like 'Faces in the Crowd', there are *ingenious* crimes."

Carmody turned red. He did not really believe "Faces" to be such a weak work, and to be criticized by someone whose admiration he longed for was also rather painful.

Übung 26: Unterstreichen Sie die englische Entsprechung der folgenden Substantive im Text!
(1. Vorschlag, 2. Firmen, 3. Zahnarzt, 4. Schweiz, 5. Zäune, 6. Diener, 7. Lösung, 8. Forschung)

"So, you simply want me to make a suggestion? You want me to say, for instance, that we should target CEOs of small companies? We should try to get lists of flight passengers in business class where husbands and wives are seated together? We should sit outside nightclubs with the young and beautiful clientele?"
"You're losing your touch, Geoff. How do you think I found out about our dentist, for example? I got a passenger list for a flight to Switzerland. I expect you to come up with something different."
"Okay." Carmody sat there a moment, staring over Cinderella's head, at a wall with roses and fences. "Perhaps you should consider watching who goes to play polo. Find out who some of the single men are and visit their homes when they're playing polo."
"Not bad," she said, but without much interest.
"You would have to follow them home to find out where they live and if they have girlfriends or servants. That might take some time, so perhaps that's not the best solution."
"That's called 'research,' Geoff. If you want something to work *flawlessly*, then you have to prepare well, prepare even for the things you cannot predict. A polo player might fall and break a leg, for instance."

"But that's an opportunity," said Carmody. "If a player falls, he doesn't go home; he goes into hospital. Then you have all the time you need."
"Now that's a good idea. But," she said, looking towards the door leading outside,- "this isn't exactly the time of year for such a plan. It's cold, wet – in a few weeks it will be Christmas."
"Cinderella, my dear, the horses are there all-the-year-round, so there has to be a place where the players can practise even in the autumn and winter. The real difficulty is getting the player into hospital. It isn't every day that they fall off horses while playing, though it's always a possibility. It's what you might call an *occupational hazard*. Someone will have to make sure there's an accident – and then escape without arousing any suspicions."
"I will take care of that," she said coldly.

ÜBUNG 27 !

Übung 27: Wie heißt der Plural der folgenden Substantive? Setzen Sie ein!

1. thief ____________________
2. journey ____________________
3. wife ____________________
4. child ____________________
5. body ____________________
6. novel ____________________
7. leaf ____________________
8. foot ____________________

Suddenly Carmody saw another side to the beautiful, young woman sitting opposite him. Her face was hard and though there was no gun in her hand, the look in her eyes made him *glance* at her hands to see what they were doing. As quickly as this moment came, it was gone.
"You've proven you still have what it takes," she said.
She paid for the coffee and the two got up to leave.
"I'm glad to hear you say that, Cinderella."
"But don't get overconfident," she warned as they stepped outside. The smile left Carmody's face and he walked next to her, somehow smaller than her, though her head only reached up to his shoulders. He followed her to a restaurant where they ate Indian food. The mood was quiet and the conversation pleasant but *superficial*. When they left the restaurant, she offered him her hand and said she would *be* back *in touch* with him soon. Before he knew it, she was gone. He *made* his *way* to one of his usual pubs and stayed until closing time.

Übung 28: Welche Bedeutung haben folgende Redewendungen? Kreuzen Sie die richtige Lösung an!

ÜBUNG 28 !

1. to hit it off with someone
   a) ☐ to get in a fight with someone
   b) ☐ to start a project with someone
   c) ☐ to have a good relationship with someone

2. to have a word with someone
   a) ☐ to speak to someone
   b) ☐ to disagree with someone
   c) ☐ to go into a meeting with someone

3. to lend someone a hand
   a) ☐ to give someone some money
   b) ☐ to give someone a place to stay for the night
   c) ☐ to help someone

4. to rise to the challenge
   a) ☐ to get up with the alarm clock
   b) ☐ to perform well because you have to
   c) ☐ to try and be successful

5. to stick around
   a) ☐ to stay around
   b) ☐ to be in the way
   c) ☐ to enjoy doing something

6. to have someone by the throat
   a) ☐ to be ready to kill someone
   b) ☐ to help someone out with a problem
   c) ☐ someone is defenceless against you

The following morning, he lay in bed, feeling sorry for himself. You're getting yourself in trouble with her. For her. She's not Cinderella; she's my *nemesis*.

ÜBUNG 29 !

Übung 29: Geben Sie die zwei Steigerungsformen an!

1. rich ____________ ____________

2. good ____________ ____________

3. bad ____________ ____________

4. expensive ____________ ____________

5. many ____________ ____________

6. pretty ____________ ____________

Well, he thought, I haven't done anything illegal. I walked into that house thinking it was part of a practical joke and found out that it was something much more serious – but I didn't really do anything. And last night, I only outlined a possibility. If anyone *overheard* us, I could say that I was working on a new story. Then, he continued, I had better start working on that story. He got up, made a pot of tea, sat down at his computer and began to write. For two days he worked on the story, developing strategies for deciding who should be the target. He imagined scenarios at the polo stadium – someone shot at the player and that landed him in hospital; someone shot at the horse with the same result; someone ran onto the pitch and *startled* the horse, which threw its rider. Carmody was not pleased with any of these possibilities, but he was not worried either. It was all in fun, all theoretical; none of it had anything to do with the real world. It was pure amusement. At the end of the second day, he sat back after turning off his computer and crossed his arms, quite pleased with himself. What will I call this story? he wondered. Much of it was based on his own experiences of the past week but slightly modified.

Übung 30: Markieren Sie mit richtig ✔ oder falsch – !

1. Geoffrey Carmody trusts Cinderella completely. ☐
2. Cinderella wants to rob the richest people in the world. ☐
3. Carmody's ideas were not as good as Cinderella had hoped. ☐

ÜBUNG 30 !

4. Carmody believes he has done nothing wrong. ☐
5. Cinderella loved "Faces in the Crowd". ☐
6. Carmody has begun a new novel. ☐

The following morning, the phone rang just as Carmody was preparing to sit down at the computer. The coffee was hot, the sun was shining in and he was congratulating himself that he had hardly thought of Cinderella, or Cornelia Thomas, as she called herself, the last two days. The story had taken off on its own. A third person joined the two *conspirators* and forced an accident on the pitch. Writing always took him away from the real world.

ÜBUNG 31

Übung 31: Welches Wort ist das „schwarze Schaf"?

1. pleased, happy, content, satisfactory
2. illegal, probation, prohibited, unlawful
3. startled, surprised, upset, shocked
4. time, mood, atmosphere, tone
5. congratulate, praise, preserve, applaud
6. run into, meet, chance on, run onto

"Carmody."
"Hello, Geoff," said a familiar voice.
Her voice is silky smooth, he thought.
"Cinderella."
"Cornelia. Cornelia Thomas."
"What can I do for you?"
"I want you to meet me at Marylebone *tube* station."
"When should I meet you?"
"In an hour."

"And why exactly are we meeting?"
"Do you need a reason?"
"You are reason enough, Cinderella."
"I thought you might see it that way."

Übung 32: Setzen Sie die richtigen Präpositionen ein!
(on, in, of, for, by, with)

1. The store closes in five minutes. Can you get there ______ time?
2. I am ______ charge ______ five employees and a large budget.
3. I'm going to New York ______ business next week.
4. The Mayor is responsible ______ running the city government.
5. He went to work ______ spite ______ his cold.
6. The meeting starts at 9 a.m. Please be ______ time.

I'm not doing anything wrong, he told himself, on the *tube* taking him to Marylebone station. This is just for fun. The problem was that he was not sure if he was having fun anymore. Outside the station, the green sports car turned the corner off Harewood Avenue and came to a loud *halt*. Even before he opened the car door, he stopped wondering if he was having fun – it simply was. That luminous smile, the excitement of the car engine waiting to be set free, that body beneath the burgundy dress – so young, so beautiful, so powerful. Her smile as she offered him her *cheek* was enough to make him want to offer her his soul. He wanted to make it a long kiss, but she turned her face away to make sure no cars were coming up behind her, put the car in first gear and they shot into the street and onto Marylebone before he could even fasten his seatbelt.

ÜBUNG 33 !

Übung 33: Unterstreichen Sie die Wörter/Wendungen mit denselben Bedeutungen! ***(cosy, leisure, hurry, demanding, fancy, slight)***

"We seem to be in a bit of a rush," Carmody said, once comfortable and safely in his seat.
"We have a lot to do this morning, Geoff. This isn't about pleasure; we're going on business."
"I prefer a bit of pleasure with my business."
"You prefer a bit too much pleasure with your business," she corrected.
"You're rather hard, Neely."
"Can't you just call me by my first name?"
"I don't know your first name."

Cinderella pulled off the motorway and drove through a village. Just outside the village, they came upon a large, modern building with *Corinthian columns* that gave it a classical look but *revealed* little about its purpose.
"This is an indoor polo stadium. Guard's Crossing, it's called."
"About 45 minutes from central London, I believe," Carmody said.
"But between central London and here there are several areas where the young and not-so-young men have their homes."
"So, what exactly are we doing here, Cinderella? Surely we didn't drive all this way just to look at a building?"
"Very good, Geoff. No, we didn't just drive here to turn around and go back into the city. And I didn't bring you here just because I wanted to spend some time with you. We're going to go inside and find out about membership."
"And we're going to go in as husband and wife?"
"Unless you have a better suggestion."
"I couldn't think of anything better in the world, darling."

Übung 34: Setzen Sie das passende Fragewort ein!

1. ______________ old is Geoffrey Carmody?
2. ______________ is the polo club located?
3. ______________ is the polo club called?
4. ______________ does Cinderella want to work with Carmody?
5. ______________ underground station did they meet at?
6. ______________ does Cinderella prefer to rob houses?

At that moment, Carmody knew that the past two days had been for nothing. He hadn't thought of Cinderella in that time, but as soon as he was in her presence she meant everything to him. She was a woman who knew what she wanted. Unfortunately, she didn't seem to want Carmody. But, he thought, there's always a chance. I'll show her how clever I am and then we can stop these silly games.
The manager, a Mr Thomas Doran, was unavailable but his assistant, an important young woman who did not provide her name, gave them a brief tour and overview of the stadium and the club's members. Cinderella and the assistant manager disliked each other immediately but neither expressed it openly. Less than 200 metres away were the horses' stables, the assistant said, concluding the tour. When Cinderella asked about membership fees, the assistant manager mentioned a sum that was well-beyond what Carmody could have paid, but his "partner" did not lose her smile for a second.
As cool as a cucumber, she asked,
"Is that the quarterly or yearly sum?"
"The yearly sum," answered the assistant with a *venomous* smile.
"Thank you, dear," Cinderella said, "I won't take up any more of your time."

ÜBUNG 35 !

Übung 35: Lesen Sie weiter und übersetzen Sie die vorgegebenen Wörter!

Carmody followed her outside. He'd remained (1. still) __________ for most of the tour, speaking only to answer Cinderella's (2. Fragen) __________.

"You're not thinking of joining, are you?" Carmody asked once they were a short (3. Entfernung) __________ away. Cinderella led him towards the stables, to check out their (4. Lage) __________, just in case the assistant manager took it upon herself to (5. beobachten) __________ their departure.

"It's nice that you're here to make sure I do nothing foolish, Geoff, but (6. echt) __________, I didn't make it this far because I'm *thick*." She turned around and started (7. in Richtung, zu) __________ the car.

"I don't think you're stupid, Cinderella. I just wasn't sure how much of a game this was for you. Investors will tell you that you have to spend money to make money."

"Hmmph," Cinderella answered. "This is no game."

"What did you think of the *facility*?"

"I think their members are right at the level we want. Some of these clubs are more expensive, more exclusive, but the people who play there have servants and staff and I've already told you I don't want to have to *deal with* all that."

Übung 36: Welche Wörter passen zusammen?

1. membership	☐	belt
2. club	☐	down
3. seat	☐	fees
4. tube	☐	members
5. sit	☐	joke
6. practical	☐	station

Changing the topic, Carmody asked:
"When was your last robbery, Cinderella?"
"A week ago."
"I mean – before that, when was the last one?"
"I'm only going to say that it was more than a year ago. Might have been two years; might have been five. The less you know about me, the better for you and for me if anything ever goes wrong. Got the idea?"
"A lot of preparation goes into these 'jobs,'" Carmody continued, ignoring the last sentence from Cinderella. "*Impressive*."
"Yes, there's a lot of preparation. If you don't want to get caught, then you find out as much as possible before you make your move. This time, however, the process is going to be a bit quicker."
"Why?"
"Because it is, Carmody, now stop asking all these questions."
"That's my job: to ask questions. That's what writers do."
"Your job is to stay out of my way. If I want your input, then I'll ask you for it. Trust me."
"Never." They got in the car and drove away. After a few minutes of silence, he asked,
"So why did you invite me along this morning?"

"Are you *thick*? It's a club for men only. Didn't you notice that? Women may work there, but they cannot be members." Carmody was silent. "That's just my luck," she added. "I get an alcoholic writer who doesn't notice anything. It's no wonder your sales are going down. The ideas may be better, but their *implementation*, their *execution*, is not nearly what it was ten years ago."
"And you're the expert?"
"In what I do, I am. If you see any areas that need improvement, please tell me."
"Your relations with others …"
"What do you know about that?" she asked, raising her voice. "You know nothing about me." They drove in silence for a while, and then she rested her hand on his knee and said,
"Let's go and get something to eat. How about a pub not far from here where you can get a pint and I can get a cup of tea?"

ÜBUNG 37 !

Übung 37: Lesen Sie weiter und füllen Sie die Lücken mit den passenden Wörtern!
(reckon, explosion, step x 2, leave, friendly, right, suitable, open)

In the pub, she became a bit more (1.) ____________ and Carmody became a bit more (2.) ____________ too. By the time they left, two pints later, Carmody had already forgotten her earlier (3.) ____________.

"When can I see you again?" he asked once they were both back in her car.

"When everything is ready for the next (4.) ____________."

"What is the next (5.) __________?"

"What do you think it is?"

"I (6.) __________ you have to decide upon a (7.) __________ target."

"Exactly, my dear Carmody. You are so (8.) __________. And how do we go about doing that?"

"First, you have to get a membership list for the club. But how will you do that?"

"(9.) __________ it to me, I'll get the list."

"I want to help you, Cinderella", Carmody said. He knew it was the beer, but he could not stop himself. She was silent for a moment. "Please, Neely." She *frowned* at him. "Please, Cornelia," he corrected himself.
She smiled at him and he looked down at his feet, warm from the heat of the engine. The alcohol from the night before and the beer from lunch had relaxed him *sufficiently* that he was willing to risk something, anything – if only to impress her.
"If I were to ask you to get the list, how would you go about doing it?"
"Well, I might first try the direct *approach*. Just ask them."
"Why would they give you such a list, a list of people who are moderately wealthy?"
"I'm interested in joining the club. I'm a famous writer."
"Number one – how would being a famous writer help you? Number two and more importantly – shouldn't you do this anonymously?"
"Perhaps."

ÜBUNG 38

Übung 38: Welches Wort bedeutet das Gegenteil? Kreuzen Sie an!

1. important
   a) ☐ insolvent, b) ☐ intuition, c) ☐ inconsequential

2. willing
   a) ☐ responsible, b) ☐ reluctant, c) ☐ reliable

3. appease
   a) ☐ proscribe, b) ☐ provoke, c) ☐ promote

4. luck
   a) ☐ misfortune, b) ☐ mislead, c) ☐ mistake

5. expensive
   a) ☐ ecological, b) ☐ ecosystem, c) ☐ economical

After a moment of silence, he continued.
"Perhaps if I went there as a sales representative."
"That's a better suggestion. There are companies that provide sporting equipment to the players. If you came from one of the more established companies, you just might be able to get a membership list."
"Naturally."
"Of course, you would have to do a bit of acting. You'd have to change your appearance, since the assistant manager might recognize you, and you would have to act as if you knew the person you were talking to. The manager isn't simply going to hand over a list of members to you, but if you go there acting as if you and he are friends, have done business together in the past, then maybe you might convince him to give you a list."
"It couldn't *hurt* to try," he said.

Übung 39: Wie lauten die Sätze in der richtigen Reihenfolge?

1. get point point how you A from B to do?

____

2. sport a green she bright drives car.

____

3. 9 a.m. Thursday leave we at on

____

4. I the were would you I if accept job.

____

5. do anonymously you this should.

____

6. visit you London often do how?

____

Cinderella drove to Marylebone station and stopped the car.
"I'll *be in touch*," she said, indirectly inviting him to get out of the car.
"There is another option, Cinderella." He made no move to get out of the car. "I may not be as rich as the people you want to rob, but you could move in with me and you wouldn't need to commit any more robberies. We would be comfortable, and we would have enough money that we could go on holiday occasionally. You wouldn't have to take these risks anymore."
"That's an *enticing* offer," she smiled at him. "I'll have to think about it."

"Please do, because I mean it. Neely, I –"
"Out, Carmody. Get out at once." There was a sudden change in her tone and her look. He slowly got out of the car and then leaned down to look in. She *flashed* him her best smile. He closed the car door and watched her drive off. Her car *recklessly* turned a corner and was out of sight. Carmody walked to the underground station slowly.

ÜBUNG 40 !

Übung 40: Markieren Sie mit richtig ✔ oder falsch – !

1. The polo club allows female membership. ☐
2. Carmody and Cinderella agree to meet at a petrol station. ☐
3. Cinderella does not drink alcohol when she is working. ☐
4. Carmody immediately dislikes the assistant manager. ☐
5. During the tour of the polo club facilities, Carmody was chatty. ☐
6. Cinderella does not demand more active participation from Carmody. ☐

Though he woke with a hangover, Carmody set himself to work at the computer immediately. In the story, he began drawing up plans for the interview with the manager. First he looked up the names of companies that supplied uniforms, helmets, *mallets* and other equipment used in polo – Berenger & Bros. *appeared* to be one of the oldest in existence. Next he researched the polo stadium, Guard's Crossing. Then he selected a *wig* from a costume shop – a *wig* with curly brown hair that would *cover* his thinning, greying hair. The following day, he put on a suit and then *made* his *way* to the manager's office. Once there, he laughed and bluffed his way into the manager's trust. Though it was not immediately certain he would get the list, in the end he did. A triumph. Carmody sat back

and looked at the story. He was proud of himself, though he knew that it was not his best work, that the story was not even finished and that it was perhaps a bit too easy.
I can work on it again later, he said to himself. The important thing is to have the ideas written out. I can always re-work them later.

Übung 41: Lesen Sie weiter und unterstreichen Sie das passende Wort der beiden Varianten!

Using his ideas as a (1.) guard/guide, in the afternoon Carmody went to a shop (2.) specialised/speciality in costumes and was fitted for a *wig*. He (3.) chose/choose one with short curly hair that *hinted* at (4.) youngness/youth and a bit of liveliness. The fitting did not take long, but he had to return the following day to pick (5.) out/up the *wig* and to be shown how to put it on (6.) correctly/accurately. Next, he went to a men's clothing store and purchased a smart black suit with a burgundy tie. It was in the classical style, too, a bit conservative but just the thing that might be worn by a salesman from an (7.) *ancient*/old and established company. Finally, he bought a pair of shoes, Oxfords. The last few years, he had spent little money on anything but the (8.) basic/ground necessities of life and doing a bit of travelling. He loved suits but his suits had lost their sparkle – and like (9.) stares/stars, he needed to *sparkle*, if his plan were to work.

The phone rang.
"Carmody."
"Hello, Geoff. How are things?"
"Fine. I've just been looking in the newspaper to see if there are any reports about the robbery."

"Don't worry, Geoff, the police have no useful *clues* and your secret's safe with me."
"Hmm," Carmody said doubtfully. "Well, I'm just about prepared to go and meet the manager tomorrow. I've got a new suit and shoes. I'll look different too – I've got a *wig* that makes me look ten years younger."
"What company do you work for?"
"Um…"
"Geoff, you have to be able to answer that question immediately. It can't come as a surprise. You need to get your story straight quickly and practise it."
"Are you going to come over and help me?" he sounded happy at the *prospect*.
"I've got too much going on at the moment."
"I'll let you know how it goes," he said.
"How?"
"Why don't you give me your phone number and I'll call you as soon as I'm finished?"
"I don't like people to call me."
"I reckon you'll have to call me, then."

ÜBUNG 42 !

Übung 42: Lesen Sie weiter und unterstreichen Sie im folgenden Absatz die zehn falsch geschriebenen Wörter! Geben Sie danach die richtige Schreibweise an!

Carmody imediatly got on the computer and began to reserch companies that prodused polo equipment. He found one, called "Three Kings", that *claimed* – no surprise – to have served three kings, many more princes and thousands of royally. Had they changed their name twice already? he wandered. Now, so they *claimed* on their homepage, “We are *affordable* to you.” Looking at their prices, Carmody didn’t feel he was the “you” they were referring to, but he read through the company history, printed up a copy of their order forms and product lists and looked through the little bit of information pravided about the company struktur. One of the sales representatatives was called Michael Stewart, and Carmody thought the name suited him. When he had finished researching “Three Kings”, he did a bit of background investigation on the Guard’s Crossing polo club. There was *precious* little information on the club, nothing about how long it had excited – the only real information was that they completed around the UK rather successfully.

1. ______________ 6. ______________
2. ______________ 7. ______________
3. ______________ 8. ______________
4. ______________ 9. ______________
5. ______________ 10. ______________

Although it was unusual for him, Carmody stayed at home, allowed himself only one Martini and then studied the information he had collected. He knew he needed to demonstrate familiarity with the various products, and he had to be able to repeat his boss’ name. It would also be good to know some of the company history and to occasionally include such information in anything he said.

Übung 43: Formulieren Sie die Sätze im Passiv!

1. Cinderella drove the car.

____

2. Cinderella made all the decisions.

3. Someone stole the painting.

4. Workers in China made this product.

5. An anonymous group took responsibility for the crime.

Carmody did have second thoughts, at one point. Maybe I'm getting a bit more involved in this than I should, he thought. Nothing I've done so far could really be called aiding in a criminal act, but maybe this crosses the line. Still, even if I give Cinderella the list, what she does with it is up to her. I can't control that. But Carmody was left with the uncomfortable feeling that he was not quite telling himself the truth.

ÜBUNG 44 !

Übung 44: Welche Gegenteile gehören zusammen?

1. impeccably	☐ latter
2. natural	☐ ignorance
3. familiarity	☐ previous
4. royalty	☐ badly
5. following	☐ artificial
6. former	☐ peasants

Chapter 3: Who's the Target?

The following morning, *impeccably* dressed in his new clothes and looking quite natural in the new *wig*, he drove to the indoor polo stadium. Since his car was light blue and not the colour he thought appropriate for his current role, he parked it where it was not immediately visible from the front door. He walked confidently into the building. Once in the dark cool of the building, he walked directly to Mr Doran's office.

Carmody was sweating. The assistant, he and Cinderella had very briefly spoken to only three days earlier, asked him what she could do for him.

"I'm here to see Mr Doran," he said confidently.

"Do you have an appointment?"

"An appointment?" he said. "Well, of course not. Mr Doran and I know each other far too well to require appointments."

The assistant looked as if she did not quite believe Carmody, but asked his name as she picked up a telephone.

"Michael Stewart."

"Mr Doran, there's a Michael Stewart here for you." There was a pause. "He says he knows you." Another pause. "As I said, he says he knows you and he's standing right here." Another pause. "Right, I'll send him in."

Übung 45: Unterstreichen Sie die Wörter oder Wendungen im Text mit denselben Bedeutungen!
(1. pounded, 2. organizer, 3. moment, 4. alongside, 5. newest, 6. looked, 7. begin, 8. short, 9. advantages, 10. grudgingly)

ÜBUNG 45 !

She put the phone down.

"Right this way," she said, leading Carmody past computers and filing cabinets to a short hallway that took them to Mr Doran's office. She knocked, opened the door and said, "Mr Michael Stewart."
Carmody entered. Mr Doran was standing next to his desk in a suit that looked much like Carmody's. His black hair was perfectly in place. Carmody's short, curly hair was also perfectly in place, but *appeared* almost radical in comparison with Doran's hair.
"Thank you, Ms Hartley. What can I do for you, Mr Stewart?"
"Mr Stewart?" Carmody tried to laugh. "Hello, Thomas. How are things?"
"Things are fine," Doran answered, rather unwillingly.
"Am I catching you at a bad time?" Carmody asked.
"Not really. What company are you with?"
"What company am I with? That's a good one, Doran. "Three Kings". I believe you've heard of us and of me. I was just stopping by to see you about something we've discussed in the past." Carmody went into a brief description of the latest products available from "Three Kings" and was about to *launch into* a discussion of the benefits for members of Guard's Crossing when Mr Doran interrupted him.

"I'm sorry, but what's your name again?"
"You're on a roll today. Michael Stewart." There was a pause and the two men looked at each other. "You don't honestly mean to say you don't remember me, do you?"
"Well, maybe I do. A little."
"Doran, Thomas, Tom –" Carmody was almost ready to try "Tommy", but something (an angel perhaps) told him that the fellow standing a short distance away from him had not been called Tommy since his youth – if he ever had been young.
"It has been several months since we last met, but I don't think people usually forget me so quickly."

"It does happen, though," Mr Doran responded. "Well, what can I do for you, Mr Stewart?"
"It's about something that we discussed back at the end of summer. You suggested I come back just before Christmas and here I am. I wanted to get the members of Guard's Crossing better acquainted with our products. We are the premier company in the world –"
"One of the premier companies," Doran interrupted.
"The premier company," Carmody insisted, "for polo equipment and we want to convince your players of that. We want to make our equipment available to them at a low cost, at below cost actually, so that this club might become known for our products in the future. This is something we've already discussed in some detail, Doran."
"And what is it you want from me? Please remind me, Mr Stewart."

Übung 46: Lesen Sie weiter und ordnen Sie die Buchstaben zu einem sinnvollen Wort!

! ÜBUNG 46

Carmody smiled – or tried to smile – he wasn't sure if he had made any (1. ssegrorp) ____________ in gaining Doran's trust and was beginning to feel a bit insecure.

"Mr Stewart," he (2. edughla) ____________.

"Okay, I'll go along with your little (3. keoj) ____________. All I want from you, Mr Doran, is a list of (4. mmeebrs) ____________ so that I can forward them a copy of our (5. grspin) ____________ catalogue with these extra special (6. setar) ____________ just for them. No other person, no other club in the UK will receive such low prices as these, Mr Doran, I assure you."

"That's out of the question," Mr Doran said *firmly*.
"What is out of the question?"
"Giving you a list of our members."
"What do you mean that's out of the question?" Carmody answered. "We already talked about it. You've already agreed to it. It was settled months ago."
"Just the same, I cannot provide you a list of members."
"*Why the blazes not*? Three months ago, you could and today you cannot?"
"It is strictly against our policy to release such information to the general public."
"I am hardly the general public, Doran. I'm the person who makes sure your members are properly dressed and *equipped* to participate in the sport that gives your institution its business. Guard's Crossing is nothing without the sport that has historically relied upon us for the most modern and yet most classic equipment. When your players practise here or participate in *tournaments* elsewhere, it is "Three Kings" that makes sure they have the classic look required." Carmody stopped speaking and looked at his counterpart.

ÜBUNG 47 !

Übung 47: Was bedeuten die Wörter auf Deutsch?

1. participate	☐ Gipfel
2. confident	☐ streng
3. progress	☐ teilnehmen

4. strict ☐ selbstsicher
5. peak ☐ Nachteil
6. disadvantage ☐ Fortschritt

Mr Doran walked around behind his desk and sat down. He looked at his hands, opened the top drawer of his desk and then smiled briefly at Carmody. He looked around his desk again, quite slowly, and then picked up the telephone.
"Ms Hartley, will you please escort Mr Stewart outside." He hung up the phone.
"I am *insulted*, Mr Doran, and your members will be most disagreeably surprised when they learn of the opportunity you have so disgracefully *deprived* them of." The young woman walked into the room, and Mr Carmody walked towards her.
"Good day, Mr Doran," he said as coldly and as proudly as possible.

Übung 48: Welches Wort ist das „schwarze Schaf"?

ÜBUNG 48 !

1. cheek, courage, nerve, impertinence
2. chance, brake, opportunity, possibility
3. cabinet, desk, table, counter
4. mobile, telephone, handy, cellular
5. record, list, directory, file
6. do, accompany, escort, conduct

They walked together out of Doran's office, back down the short hallway and to the spot where she had first met "Michael Stewart."
"You needn't come with me any further. I can find my way out without any difficulty. I've been here often enough, but I won't be coming back, I can tell you that."

Carmody walked to the doors that led between the *Corinthian columns*. His legs were so weak that the walk to his car seemed a marathon. Once inside, he sat a moment, then started his car. Nothing crossed his mind, at first. He did not think of Mr Doran or what had just taken place; he did not think of Cinderella; he did not think of the *wig* he was wearing, which was now *itchy*, or the suit. He backed his car out without looking and drove away. He got onto the motorway and started back to London. After ten minutes, though, he exited and found a quiet park set on the border of an affluent neighbourhood. He looked around a moment, then turned off the car and started to cry. He did not really think about why he was crying – he just cried. Long and passionately he cried. He *ripped* the *wig* off his head and threw it into the back of the car *with all his might* and then rubbed his hands back and forth across his damp scalp.

ÜBUNG 49 !

Übung 49: Korrigieren Sie die Fehler!

1. Geoffrey Carmody writes always on his computer.

....

2. He drives every day to work.

....

3. She is working as a thief full-time.

....

4. We have been to Manchester last month.

....

5. Carmody won many awards.

6. They are immediately needing new uniforms.

Finally, Carmody began to drive again. He was totally *humiliated*. No negative review, no destructive criticism of one of his books or short stories had ever affected him the way this twenty-five minute ordeal had. How can I tell Cinderella I *failed*? he wondered. He knew he would hide the humiliating aspects as much as possible, but at forty-one he felt himself to be such a leaky ship that he knew she would hear the humiliation in his words.

Übung 50: Beantworten Sie die Fragen zum Text!

ÜBUNG 50 !

1. Why does Carmody get a wig?

2. What company does Carmody say he works for?

3. Does Cinderella ask Carmody to get the list for her?

4. What name does Carmody almost use on Mr Doran?

5. Is Carmody upset after his attempt to get the list fails?

6. How is Carmody supposed to contact Cinderella?

____

Back home, he fixed himself a strong drink. I might just as well have finished off a fifth of gin last night, he thought, for all the good it did to stay *sober*. After a second drink, his nerves were calmer and he had slowly begun to sink into a warm pool of self-pity. By the time Cinderella phoned around 4 pm, his mood was somewhat lighter and he was able to report the news of his failure without *appearing* wounded by it.

ÜBUNG 51 !

Übung 51: Lesen Sie weiter und füllen Sie die passenden Wörter in die Lücken! ***(whole, tell, concluded, events, worry, sound)***

"You don't (1.) __________ surprised at my failure," Carmody said.

"You can never (2.) __________ when charm will work and when it won't," she responded.

"He looked more like a surgeon than a club manager, Cinderella. It's hard to believe he works with (3.) __________, living people. He looked more like the kind of person who *deals* only *with* parts of people – internal organs, bones, tumours, psychoses and the like. So", he (4.) __________, "what do we do now? How are we going to get the list?"

“Don’t (5.) ______________ about it”, Cinderella said, “we’ve already got the list.”

“We – you already have the list?!”

“Well of course, darling. I have the list of members as well as a schedule of (6.) ______________. We shall need both.”

“Then what was the point in sending me all the way out there to meet with Doran?”
“You wanted to do your part, so I let you. What’s the *harm* in that?”
“I wanted to do something necessary,” Carmody answered.
“Carmody, I’ve always got a plan B – I’m not going to sit at home and wait for you to deliver. And, besides, you never know who you can depend on.”
“You know you can depend on me,” Carmody said.
“Did you get me the list, Geoff?” Her voice was suddenly *harsh*.
“Can you get it to me in the next couple of hours?”
“Well, no,” Carmody answered quietly.
“Time is everything, Carmody. I can’t wait forever.”
“What is the hurry?”
“There is no hurry, Geoff. I just want this project to go off as planned.”
“Do you have a timeline for this next ‘project’ of yours?” he asked quietly.
“This project of ours, you mean. Yes, I do.”
“Will you tell me what it is?”
“Not right now.”
Once off the phone, Carmody *proceeded* to finish off the bottle of gin, which was already less than half full, and he then went out to the pub.

ÜBUNG 52 !

Übung 52: Lesen Sie weiter und unterstreichen Sie die englische Übersetzung der folgenden Wörter!
(1. aushalten, 2. verschönern, 3. genau, 4. einschließlich, 5. Kätzchen, 6. widmen, 7. entfernen)

The following morning was brutal, but it was not as bad as some mornings Carmody had endured in the past. He got up and made himself a pot of tea, forced down a bowl of salty porridge and then sat down at the computer. He typed in everything that had happened the previous day in connection with Cinderella. He did not *embellish* anything. He recorded events exactly as he remembered them, including the *wig* that had *failed* and was now a particular focus for his shame. He could see it lying there like a dead kitten in the back of his car. If only someone else would take on the job of retrieving the kitten. He would dedicate his next story – this story! – to who-ever would remove it from his car.

ÜBUNG 53 !

Übung 53: Haben die Wörter eine ähnliche Bedeutung? Markieren Sie mit richtig ✔ oder falsch – !

1. proceeds/profit ☐
2. projected/targeted ☐
3. queue/snake ☐
4. rash/hurry ☐
5. harsh/mean ☐
6. peoples/tribes ☐
7. lighter/gentler ☐

Once he had finished with the story for the day, he began to wonder how Cinderella had got the list – as well as a schedule of events.

Surely she had not driven out there herself and charmed the list and the schedule from Mr Doran or his assistant. Even she could not have broken through, certainly not when Carmody had been there first. There were only two possibilities. Either she had got the material from a member or she had got it with the computer and was, apparently, an *accomplished* hacker. It must be one of the two, he thought. He could easily imagine her following a young club member home and seducing him and thus gaining access to the necessary information. Just as easily, he could see her at her computer working away. He did not have a clear idea of what "hacking" involved, but he had no doubt that if at some time in the past Cinderella had wanted to become an expert at it then she was an expert at it. Though he thought the second possibility the more likely one, the first possibility made him sweat. He wanted Cinderella for himself. How angry he was now that he had no way to contact her. I'm just a fox with my paw caught in a trap, he thought. To break free from her, he knew he would have to chew off an arm or a leg and perhaps both. In the meantime, he would have to wait for her to call, wait for her to breathe the perfume of her life into his lungs and make him whole once again.

Übung 54: Lesen Sie weiter und unterstreichen Sie die fünf inhaltlich nicht dazugehörigen Sätze!

The following day, she phoned late in the morning. It was now about 3.15 p.m.

"Hello, Geoff. Have you recovered from your encounter with Mr Doran?"

"What do you mean, have I recovered? I was searching for sunken *treasure*."

"Every time –" she yelled suddenly and then went silent.

"What do you mean, 'every time'?" Carmody asked. He could hear that she was still on the line but knew nothing more.
"Nothing, darling, nothing," she said at last. "I know that you bought a new suit and shoes and then you were not successful. And you bought a swim-suit and a swimming pool as a Christmas present. I just hope that you are not still thinking about it."
"I've quite recovered in that respect."
"In what respect have you not recovered?"
"I would like very much to see you, Cinderella."
"That can be arranged. Later." She hung up and Carmody was left with silence and then the hum of the phone line. Maybe I'll tape my Christmas cards up on the walls, he thought.
She's going to push me too far one of these days, he thought. But he knew that she would have to push much harder, and do much more damage, in order to drive him away. I should take a walk, down on the beach at the Prince of Wales' castle.

"Some *bubbly*?" Cinderella asked from the shadows.
"How did you get in?" Carmody asked, sitting up in bed.
"That's a trade secret," she answered. "It stinks in here. You drank like a fish last night. Oh, it smells horrible." She waved her hand in front of her face. "It may be cold outside, but I have to open a window before I *suffocate*."
Cinderella walked over to the bedroom window, pushed the curtains aside, and opened a window. The bright light and the cold air quickly invaded the room.
"Please close the curtains," he said weakly. "I can't take that light."
"If I close the curtains," she answered, "then we won't get any more fresh air and I'll *choke*. Besides," she continued, "you need to get up. It's ten in the morning and time for you to be up and about. I'll meet you in the kitchen in five minutes."

Übung 55: Lesen Sie weiter und fügen Sie die richtigen Präpositionen ein! ***(to, to, for, for, in, of, of, of, onto)***

ÜBUNG 55 !

Cinderella left the room and went down (1.) ______ the kitchen. She put the bottle (2.) ______ champagne into the fridge and looked round (3.) ______ some food for breakfast but found nothing that she could cook. After 15 minutes and still no sign (4.) ______ Carmody, she filled a big glass with water and went back up the stairs (5.) ______ his bedroom. Carmody lay (6.) ______ bed still, fast asleep again. She watched him (7.) ______ twenty or thirty seconds, the rise and fall (8.) ______ his chest, his open mouth, then she threw the water directly (9.) ______ his face.

"What the –" he yelled.
"Get out of bed, Geoff. I said 'Get up,' and I meant it."
"You don't give me orders," he *snarled*.
"Yes, I do. We're partners, and I want you up now. Remember, all I have to do is make one little phone call and you'll no longer be my partner and you'll no longer be a free man either." Softening her voice, she added, "You need to cut back on alcohol, Geoff. You're no good to anyone as you are now, and it's a shame if you don't know that."

ÜBUNG 56 !

Übung 56: Welche englischen Wörter sind gemeint?

1. something you know that you do not tell others

______

2. means that something smells terrible

---

3. people who work together are this (not colleagues)

---

4. when you cannot breathe

---

5. an army crosses the border and enters another country

---

6. bubbly

---

7. the material that hangs in front of windows to keep a room dark

---

Carmody threw his legs over the side of the bed and sat up. He reached under the pillow for his pyjamas and *wiped* his face. Suddenly, he became conscious of just how bad he looked. The hair on his chest was long and turning grey, and his belly was resting on his lap. Usually he hid inside suits and jackets and loose-fitting shirts, but Cinderella's visit had caught him by surprise. This is just the sort of body, he thought, that a beautiful, young woman like Cinderella will find attractive. He stood up and quickly walked to the bedroom door to retrieve his bathrobe.

"If you're going to *quaff* alcohol and beer while we're working together, you'll have to get used to the idea of getting over your hangovers somewhere other than your bed. You can't just sleep it off."

Übung 57: Für das englische Wort gibt es verschiedene Übersetzungsmöglichkeiten. Setzen Sie ein!

ÜBUNG 57 !

1. to turn ______ ______
2. to rest ______ ______
3. to call ______ ______
4. little ______ ______
5. chest ______ ______
6. to reach ______ ______

Carmody grumbled but did not say anything. He led the way down to the kitchen.
"Where's the *bubbly*?" he asked.
"I put it away. You don't need anything with alcohol in it."
"That would be the best thing for me", he responded, "something to help me over the –"
"Find something else," she interrupted.
"Would you like some tea?" he offered.
"I'd love some." Her voice became kinder.

Übung 58: Welche der beiden Varianten ist die richtige? Unterstreichen Sie!

ÜBUNG 58 !

Carmody put the kettle on to (1.) cook/boil and Cinderella went about cleaning out the tea (2.) pot/cooker. She opened several cupboards before she found the tea. Carmody watched her at work. He looked at her frail shoulders as she opened (3.) cupboards/shoehorns here and there, looking for things he could have directed her to. It was

hard (4.) of/for him to believe that she was such a (5.) though/tough woman, when at that moment she looked physically weak.
She turned (6.) around/up suddenly and faced him.
"What are you looking at?" she asked (7.) harshly/gently. "Haven't you got something else to do? You need food; you need something in your stomach (8.) for/after last night."

Without a word, Carmody went about putting together something to eat. He opened a can of baked beans, pinto beans in tomato sauce, and poured it into a pan to warm. Then, he got some bread out and toasted it.
"Here," Cinderella said, reaching a cup of tea towards him.
"Excellent."
"I can make a cup of tea, can't I?" she smiled.
"And I can cook."
"If opening a tin and toasting bread is your idea of cooking," Cinderella said, shaking her head, "then I hope you eat out at restaurants a lot."
He finished his first cup of tea, sat down and ate his toast and beans with a second cup of tea.

ÜBUNG 59 !

*Übung 59: Setzen Sie jeweils **for** oder **since** in die Lücke ein!*

1. He has lived in London _____ twenty years.

2. She has been a thief ______ childhood.

3. They have know each other ______ nearly four weeks.

4. He has worked on the story ______ August.

5. We had been at the beach ______ the sun rose that morning.

6. The computer has been working on the problem ____ most of the morning.

When he was finished, he asked, "So what's the plan for the day?"
"We're going to go to Guard's Crossing and watch who drives up. There's a practice this afternoon at 3 p.m. We'll sit there a while and then follow someone home."
"You're not going to rob someone today, are you?"
"We're not going to rob anyone today. We're just doing research."
"I have to go to the loo before we leave," he said.
"Me too."
"Shall I drive?" Carmody asked at the door.
"After everything you drank last night, I think it's best if I drive."
She smiled at Carmody and led him to her car, parked a short distance away on another street.

Übung 60: Beantworten Sie die Fragen zum Text!

1. Why is Carmody's visit with Mr Doran unsuccessful?

____

2. How does Carmody find out that Cinderella has the list?

____

3. How does Carmody recover from the stress of his meeting with Doran?

____

4. What does Cinderella throw at Carmody to wake him up?

____

5. For breakfast, Carmody opens a can of what?

6. Does Cinderella admire Carmody's cooking abilities?

They were on the motorway heading north.
"How are you going to decide who to follow home?" Carmody asked. "Are you just going to base it on good looks, for example?"
"Is that what you really think, Carmody? If I were interested in good looks, I probably wouldn't be in a car with you, now would I?"
"Fair enough," he admitted.
"What would one of your detectives or one of your criminals look for?"
"I imagine," he answered, "one would look at the make of car, for instance. Is it an expensive sports car or foreign import or a luxury car? Perhaps the clothing, too. The walk – an arrogant walk, an I'm-king-of-the-forest walk. Something of that sort. But how are you going to see all this from the car?"

ÜBUNG 61 !

Übung 61: Wie heißt das Simple Past und das Past Participle der folgenden Verben? Setzen Sie ein!

1. shake
2. bleed
3. fight
4. grip
5. hurt

6. drink

Cinderella looked at Carmody with expectation, her eyebrows raised.
"No ideas?" Cinderella asked, and Carmody shook his head "No."
"Really? I don't know how you got where you are, Geoff," she said, sounding truly amazed. "You're lucky your books are as good as they are. For your information, I have binoculars – with night vision, the kind the British army use. One thing I also plan to look for is whether he's wearing a wedding ring or not."
"That might not tell you anything, Cinderella," Carmody warned. "It may be that he's simply not wearing it for polo practice."
"Quite possibly. That's why we're going to follow him home."
"This will be quite a slow process," Carmody said, "if we have to wait for each night of polo practice."
"That would be inefficient, don't you think?" Cinderella said with a bit of sarcasm in her voice. "Naturally, I don't work that way at all. You'll also be taking down the number plates of several of the cars which we decide on and we'll get addresses for them and visit those houses too. We'll look for detached and semi-detached houses as well as cottages and bungalows. We'll just have to see what we come up with."
"How are you going to get addresses for the number plates?"
"Leave that up to me," she answered quickly.
"But I would like to know how," he insisted.
"Leave that up to me," she repeated.
"I'd prefer not to," he replied.
"What you prefer *is of no consequence* at the moment." Her voice was *harsh* and there was clearly no room for compromise.
They sat silently in the car.

ÜBUNG 62 !

Übung 62: Welches Wort ist das „schwarze Schaf"?

1. care, mind, nurse, worry
2. judgement, account, decision, choice
3. pollution, inefficient, incompetent, wasteful
4. big-headed, arrogant, big-hearted, conceited
5. prosperous, affluent, fluent, wealthy
6. cry, weep, sob, hiccough
7. calmly, silently, wordlessly, mutely
8. motorway, highway, freeway, driveway

"I expected a bit more professionalism from you," she added, "a bit more brain-power. I need people with their *wits about them*."
"People?"
"A person," she countered.
"And you don't think I *have* my *wits about me*?"
"I think you're still in a fog of alcohol."
"I am not," he answered, more like a child than a best-selling author.
"I'm disappointed to hear that," she *frowned*.
"The last thing I want to do is disappoint you," Carmody said.
"Then pull yourself together, man."
"What time is the practice?"
"As I said, it begins at 3 o'clock and ends at 5.30."
"We'll be getting there quite early."
"I wasn't sure how quickly I'd be able to get you on your feet. In any case, they'll probably arrive at least half an hour before practice in order to get changed and to have everything, including the horse, prepared. They have to saddle the horse, for example."
"They'll have people to help them."
"No doubt."

Übung 63: Lesen Sie weiter und ersetzen Sie die unterstrichenen Wörter durch das Gegenteil!

Cinderella parked the car (1.) <u>near</u> ____________ from the entrance to the car park. Just (2.) <u>after</u> ____________ entering the car park, she had *covered* up the number plates with white paper.

"So, now we (3.) <u>leave</u> ____________," she said, as she reached for the binoculars. She looked through them, to the (4.) <u>exit</u> ____________ to the clubhouse, and then put them on the handbrake between the two (5.) <u>back</u> ____________ seats.

"How many men should we expect?"

"Certainly not (6.) <u>none</u> ____________ of the members will show up. There are about 40 regular members and then many (7.) <u>fewer</u> ____________ who no longer play but come for the polo matches and the social functions."

They sat in silence but did not have long to wait. Cars began to arrive every few minutes. There were top-of-the-line German and Japanese imports as well as luxury automobiles made in England. Several men drove up in sports cars as well. Some of the men were *accompanied* by wives or girlfriends, but most turned up alone. All carried *duffle bags* inside. Cinderella observed them through the binoculars. They all seemed confident, but she was looking for something more, something she couldn't put into words – something she knew she would recognize if or when she saw it.

In the end, several men did arrive for the polo practice session who were just what Cinderella was looking for – and Carmody wrote down the number plate of each car. These men almost danced out of their cars; they were little bundles of energy – none of them was much over a metre and a half. One young man lit a cigarette and leaned against his car carelessly. Cinderella observed him closely with the binoculars.

ÜBUNG 64 !

Übung 64: Setzen Sie die Wörter in die richtige Reihenfolge und bilden Sie sinnvolle Sätze!

1. fast Cinderella drives always.

____

2. wet southern often weather in is England the.

____

3. you your certain plan must be starting before of

____

4. the men their they get watched out of cars

____

5. a person a lot says about the drives who car it

____

6. telephone recognized her he the voice on

____

"A top of the line Mercedes-Benz," she said. "Not exactly *subtle*

but it's a classic." The car was dark blue, the darkness of the morning sky before the sun has risen. Though by no means small, it was one of the smaller automobiles in the car park.
"Now, he's your type," said Carmody.
"So much for your skills as an observer," Cinderella responded, coolly. "He's not the type for anyone. You may see angel wings, but I see a man who thinks he is the modern Adam. Mummy and Daddy gave him everything – and he was lucky enough to inherit good looks as well. He expects women to look at him – and they do."
"He's probably the kind who laughs loudest at his own jokes."

Übung 65: Welche Gegenteile gehören zusammen?

ÜBUNG 65 !

1. possibly	☐ inattentive
2. classic	☐ commonplace
3. observant	☐ cautiously
4. carelessly	☐ modern
5. confident	☐ certainly
6. luxury	☐ timid

Carmody studied Cinderella observing this young man. Although she was a bit turned off by him, she was also clearly attracted to him. She kept the binoculars steadily focused on him.
"He might be a good candidate," she said. "I can't see that he's wearing a wedding ring."
"He isn't the kind who would wear a ring, even if he were married," Carmody *asserted*.
Cinderella lowered the binoculars for a moment and looked at Carmody. "Now that's the sort of thing I'm looking to hear from you.

Do you think it's your own feeling of insecurity or is it really something you sense?"
"Let me have the binoculars." Close up, Carmody saw a man probably in his late twenties or early thirties with hair just long enough to get in his eyes. He *radiated* self-confidence. "He's posing even though he doesn't know he's being observed."

ÜBUNG 66 !

Übung 66: Lesen Sie weiter und unterstreichen Sie die richtige Variante!

Cinderella (1.) suddenly/immediately turned around and looked out of the (2.) windscreen/back window. Then she looked in the mirrors on the car door. Each movement (3.) moved/rocked the car. Noticing her (4.) panic/upset, Carmody asked,
"What's wrong?"
"Nothing. You just gave me a (5.) fright/*nightmare*."
"How?"
"I thought (6.) of/for a moment that maybe he was just posing (7.) for/by us. What if he were there to *distract* us?"
"Even so, being here isn't (8.) unlegal/illegal."

She rolled her eyes and opened the window briefly to let in some warm air.
"We don't have to be doing anything illegal in order to find ourselves on the wrong side. We are not from the right class, my dear Carmody. You at least are a best-selling writer. I'm nobody."
"A little insecure, are we?"
"Not at all," she answered, *rock-hard*. "You know Carmody, I'm beginning to think you really *are* only *capable of* making one stupid comment after another. I was really excited to meet you, after

reading most of your books, but as a person you're turning out to be a real disappointment."
Carmody sat in *stunned* silence a moment.
"You are a first-class thief, Cinderella," he nearly whispered, then put his hand on Cinderella's leg, just above the knee. He gently rubbed his thumb back and forth, almost massaging her knee. To his surprise, she said and did nothing, so he left his hand where it was.

Übung 67: Markieren Sie mit richtig ✔ oder falsch – !

ÜBUNG 67 !

1. Geoffrey Carmody writes novels about lawyers. ☐
2. Carmody saw Cinderella for the first time in a café. ☐
3. Cinderella made a proposal he dared not refuse. ☐
4. Carmody does not know Cinderella's telephone number. ☐
5. Inspector Hudson and Carmody are best of friends. ☐
6. Cinderella has read most of Carmody's books. ☐

Chapter 4: Little Booty

No other cars came up for more than half an hour. The two sat silently, Carmody with a heart beating to break all records.
"You're making my leg hot," she said at last, and Carmody removed his hand.
He lay back in his seat and closed his eyes. When he opened them again, it had become noticeably darker outside.
"I needed a *kip*, I reckon." When no one answered, he looked to his right, but the driver's seat was empty. "How did she manage to get out of the car without waking me?" he asked aloud.

ÜBUNG 68

Übung 68: Lesen Sie weiter und fügen Sie jeweils die passenden Begriffe in die entsprechenden Lücken ein!
(visible, slipped, ready, escape, managed, spotted, nervous, flicked)

Carmody picked up the binoculars, (1.) __________ the night vision *switch*, and turned towards the parked cars. At first he could not find her, but after a few minutes he saw her looking into one of the cars. It was pure luck that he had even (2.) __________ her, because only the very top part of her head was (3.) __________. She was right outside the car the young man had been leaning against while smoking. Carmody saw the passenger door open ever so slightly, and she must have (4.) __________ into the car like smoke. He was wide awake now. With Cinderella in the car, he now kept (5.) __________ guard over the entrance. He reached for the keys, to be (6.) __________ to start the car immediately should anything go wrong, but discovered that Cinderella had taken the keys with her. Well, he thought, I'll just have to (7.) __________ on foot if anything happens. Get out and run into the forest as quickly as possible. Several minutes later, however, he saw her moving back towards the car and keeping close to the ground. She (8.) __________ to get back in the car almost without opening the door. Immediately she saw that Carmody was awake.

"I'm glad to see you're not sleeping anymore," she said, pulling the door shut so quietly that Carmody almost did not hear it. "Here, take this," she said. He felt a roll of paper in his hand.
"What is it?"
"What is it?" They looked at each other. "Hold it up. There's enough light to see what you've got in your hand."
Carmody did as he was told and saw he was holding a roll of £100 notes in his hand.
Cinderella put the keys in the *ignition*, started the car and they drove away slowly. She did not turn on the headlights until they were out of the car park.
"I thought we were going to wait and follow one of them home."
"There's been a small change of plan. We're going to wait somewhere else, just in case the police get a phone call."

Übung 69: Welche Wörter passen zusammen?

1. look for	☐ read
2. look after	☐ explore
3. look into	☐ care for
4. look over	☐ investigate
5. look about	☐ search for
6. look on	☐ observe

ÜBUNG 69 !

A little over a kilometre away she found what she was looking for and stopped the car.
"Get out and see if you can help me back the car into the bushes."
"What?"
"Just do it, Carmody. Get out!" Carmody got out and lifted the branch of a tree so that Cinderella could back the car into a *hiding place*.

"Take the paper off the back number plate," she added. "Perfect," she said, once they were settled. "I can see the road clearly from here."
It was nearly 6 o'clock and getting dark. Carmody expected to hear the sound of police cars racing towards the club at any moment.

ÜBUNG 70

Übung 70: Beantworten Sie die Fragen zum Text!

1. What emotion does Cinderella attach to Carmody?

____

2. What words best describe the men who get out of the cars at the polo stadium?

____

3. What piece of jewellery does Carmody suggest looking for on the men?

____

4. Is Carmody jealous of the men they are observing?

____

5. What was Carmody doing while Cinderella robbed the car?

____

6. What piece of equipment is quite useful for them?

____

"Count the money," Cinderella said.
Carmody counted it twice, silently, and then said, "£3200."

"Take your half," she said.
"No, I did nothing to get this money. All I did was take a *nap*. It's all yours. You, er, earned it."
"We're partners, Carmody, now take your £1600 and be done with it."
He opened the glove compartment and put the *entire* roll of money inside.
It was almost 7 o'clock when they saw the first cars leaving the polo club coming down the road. Quite a few cars went by before they spotted the one they were looking for.
"Get out," Cinderella said, as she saw it *approaching*.

Übung 71: Wie heißt das Wort auf Deutsch?

ÜBUNG 71

1. binoculars	☐ Schläfchen
2. spot	☐ Ast
3. branch	☐ Abfall
4. nap	☐ Fernglas
5. rubbish	☐ sehen
6. whisper	☐ flüstern

This time Carmody jumped out immediately, and as soon as the car went past he lifted up the tree *limb* and Cinderella drove out onto the road. Once Carmody was back in, Cinderella drove off at top speed to catch up with the other car. *In no time* they were behind their target. They followed him onto the motorway and joined the traffic. The driver immediately got into the passing lane and went far over the speed limit. Cinderella did the same but kept a short distance behind. Occasionally other cars pulled between Cinderella's car and the Mercedes, but Cinderella never lost sight of the car in front.

ÜBUNG 72 !

Übung 72: Setzen Sie das Verb in der korrekten Form ein!

1. Carmody and Cinderella (follow) ________________ a young man from the polo club at the moment.
2. They (work) ________________ together since the beginning of December.
3. Cinderella (believe) ________________ she can control Carmody.
4. The two (have) ________________ a difficult relationship from the beginning.
5. Carmody (never break) ________________ the law before he met Cinderella.
6. Carmody (live) ________________ quietly when Cinderella (come) ________________ into his life.

"It would be amusing if we both got a speeding ticket," Carmody said, "if the police pulled us both to the side of the road, considering we have £3200 of his money sitting in the car."
"Bloody *hilarious*," said Cinderella, sarcastically.
"We could even pay the *fine* with some of his money."
"Maybe you could shut up and keep your eye on the car we're following?"
As traffic got heavier, the Mercedes driver was forced to slow down. They finally exited the motorway together and followed him several kilometres away from the motorway into an exclusive neighbourhood.

Übung 73: Haben die Wörter dieselbe Bedeutung? Markieren Sie richtig ✔ oder falsch –!

ÜBUNG 73 !

1. difficult/heavy ☐
2. sight/view ☐
3. chef/boss ☐
4. humorous/amusing ☐
5. dual carriageway/motorway ☐
6. entertainment/hilarious ☐

"Now this is what I was hoping for," Cinderella said, her voice warming up. "Is he going to turn there? No, he's going further, past some very nice places. Now when he stops, Carmody, if he stops on your side of the street, we need the house number and you have to examine the place as best you can and tell me what kind of place it is, how big it is *and so forth*. If he stops on my side, I need you to try and help me."
At last the Mercedes did turn off and up a curving, U-shaped drive. A detached house set back from the street. It looked as if it had been built in the 1920s. It's *boxy shape* had perhaps been influenced by the American architect Frank Lloyd Wright.
"House number?" Cinderella asked.
"I'm looking – I'm looking," Carmody answered.
"Did you get it?" she asked impatiently.
"Yes. I'm writing it down."

Übung 74: Lesen Sie weiter und fügen Sie die richtigen Präpositionen ein!

ÜBUNG 74 !

Cinderella drove slowly past, turned (1.) ______ the next street and parked the car (2.) ______ the side (3.) ______ the road.

"What are we stopping (4.) ______?"

"I'm going back (5.) ______ a closer look (6.) ______ the house.

On foot. You stay here with the car."
"This time, leave the keys, please."
"Out of the question," she said, turning the car off and putting the keys in a pocket.
"Then I'm coming with you."
"As you like. But if for any reason we should have to run, you'd better be able to keep up with me."
"Don't you worry about that," Carmody laughed. "Your little trick at the house you robbed forced me to run off, so I know what I can do."
The street was empty, and most of the houses were brightly lit. Some had Christmas decorations in the windows, but most were set too far back from the street for the decorations to be seen very well at night.
"Were you a pretty girl at school?"
"Why would you ask such a question?"
"I'm just trying to imagine what you looked like when you were a girl."
"Do you like little girls?"
"Cinderella – can you be nice to me just once today?"
"No. Now keep quiet."

ÜBUNG 75 !

Übung 75: Lesen Sie weiter und unterstreichen Sie die neun falsch geschriebenen Wörter! Geben Sie die richtige Schreibweise an!

They walked up to the horse openly, as if they were invated guests, and then, after a quick glance aroun, slipped into the shadows and begin to walk around the house. A sign warned that the house had a securaty system. Though they had seen the man dive up to his house, there were very few lights on inside. On the ground floor there was only one light on – perhaps in the kitchen. Because she was too shot to see in the windows, Cinderella told Carmody to put her on his shoulders, so he neeled in front of her. Standing up with her on his shoulders was quite dificult at first.

1. ______________________ 6. ______________________

2. ______________________ 7. ______________________

3. ______________________ 8. ______________________

4. ______________________ 9. ______________________

5. ______________________

Though Cinderella was neither big nor heavy, he was not very strong. He managed to hold her steady after a moment and then walked up to a window. At that moment they must have *triggered* a motion sensor, for a light shone on them in the garden. Carmody ran as well as he could into the darkness. Cinderella held herself up on a tree, taking some of her weight off Carmody's shoulders. Nobody came to the window and eventually the light went off. Carmody then walked over to another window as directed by Cinderella. A little ray of light from another room partially lit the room she was looking in.

"What can you see?" Carmody whispered.

"It's not important," she answered, "I just want to get a feel for the place."

ÜBUNG 76 !

Übung 76: Lesen Sie weiter und unterstreichen Sie die englische Übersetzung der folgenden Wörter!
(1. heulen, 2. endlich, 3. einsam, 4. zustimmen, 5. schweigsam, 6. Gegend, 7. ängstlich)

Finally she got down from Carmody's shoulders and then said, "Okay, there's one last thing that I always do. I always check for dogs."
"How are you going to do that?"
Without waiting to answer, Cinderella began to *wail* like a lonesome dog. Other dogs in the area began to answer, but it was silent in the big house next to them.
Carmody, waiting nervously at her side, said, "We should go."
"Okay, let's go," she agreed at last.

Back in the car, Cinderella drove away slowly, as if she were trying to remember everything she could about the location. Then she got back on the motorway and turned the car towards Carmody's far more modest house.
"How are you going to handle the security system?"
"Don't worry, I know what to do."
"I believe that, but I want to know how you are going to disarm it."
"That's a trade secret, Geoff. You never have to *deal with* that in your books since your stories are always set in the 1920s."
Cinderella parked the car a short distance from Carmody's house, and he invited her in for a drink.
"I'm not interested in seeing you drunk," she warned. "I don't find that a *turn-on* at all."
"Don't worry, Cinderella. I'll be on my best behaviour, or almost," Carmody answered.

Übung 77: Formulieren Sie die Sätze im Passiv!

1. Cinderella stole the money.

2. The victim did not call the police.

3. Carmody did not drive the car.

4. The author worked on the novel during the day.

5. She was driving the car in the rain.

6. The police have warned him.

She reached over to the glove compartment and retrieved the money. “Here,” she said, counting out £1600.
“I’ve no right to it,” Carmody answered. “I didn’t help you get it.”
“We’re partners, remember?”
“I’d prefer not to,” Carmody continued.
“Do I need to remind you, Geoff, that one little phone call is all it would take?”
“You just stole £3200 and then *threaten* me?”
“You sat in the car, Geoff, while I did it. And you sat there with me and observed our potential victims, too.”

ÜBUNG 78 !

Übung 78: Übersetzen Sie die Begriffe und enträtseln Sie das Lösungswort!

1. Leber _ _ ☐ _ _
2. Zunge _ ☐ _ _ _ _
3. Magen _ _ _ ☐ _ _ _
4. Nieren _ ☐ _ _ _ _ _
5. Hals _ _ _ _ _ ☐

Lösung: (If you drink too much alcohol you may) _ _ _ _ _

Carmody let her into his house. She walked immediately into the living room and put "his *share*" of the money on the bar. A couple of minutes later, he joined her in the living room with a bottle of red wine.
"You have a well-stocked wine cellar."
"Why didn't you rob me?" he asked her, while reaching into a china cupboard for some red wine *goblets*.
"I thought about it, especially after reading your last novel, but then I decided it would be more interesting to work with you."
Carmody *handed* her a glass of wine, lifted his and said,
"A toast to your beauty."
"To our teamwork," she corrected. Their glasses touched and made a quiet ringing sound.

ÜBUNG 79 !

Übung 79: Welches Wort ist das „schwarze Schaf"?

1. stake, share, steak, portion
2. think, mean, consider, believe
3. contrastingly, additionally, moreover, furthermore
4. intimate, threaten, warn, intimidate

5. dusk, sunset, dawn, evening
6. quaff, drink, guzzle, fizzle

They talked quietly about the evening, especially about the other men who they would investigate. After one glass of wine, however, Cinderella got up to leave.
"Have another glass of wine," Carmody begged.
"I can't. I have to go now."
"You can't leave now, Cinderella. Stay here for a bit longer."
"The name is Cornelia, and I have to leave."
"Neely, stay with me – stay with me tonight." He wanted to make it a sexy appeal, but it sounded pathetic instead.
"Maybe some other time," she answered.
"There's another man waiting for you, isn't there?"
"No, I simply have some things to do."
"Stay with me tonight. You will – "
"I can't. I have my reasons. I'll *be in touch.*"

Übung 80: Markieren Sie mit richtig ✔ oder falsch – !

ÜBUNG 80 !

1. Cinderella gives Carmody £1200. ☐
2. Carmody is happy to have the money and begins planning just how he is going to spend it. ☐
3. Cinderella discourages Carmody from flirting – unsuccessfully. ☐
4. Running alongside Cinderella is no problem for Carmody – or so he thinks. ☐
5. Cinderella always keeps the car keys with her. ☐
6. Outside a potential victim's house, Carmody meows. ☐

She walked towards the door, and Carmody followed her. As she was reaching her hand towards the doorknob, he put his hand on her shoulder and stopped her. He squeezed her shoulder gently but said nothing. Cinderella turned around and looked at him with a quick smile. Carmody leaned forward to kiss her and she turned her lips to him and then quickly pulled away. Suddenly the door was open and she was gone. In the distance he saw Cinderella, walking quickly towards her car parked just around the corner. Carmody suddenly realised the neighbours could see him, so he closed the door and walked back into the living room. He drank up his glass of wine and poured himself another.

ÜBUNG 81

*Übung 81: Setzen Sie **much** oder **some, many** oder **few** ein!*

1. He does not have ____________ friends.
2. Would you like ____________ wine?
3. I don't have ____________ money with me at the moment.
4. I would like ____________ dressing on my salad.
5. I have a ____________ pounds in the bank.
6. Take ____________ cake home with you, dear.

The following three days, Carmody and Cinderella investigated the other three potential candidates for their robbery. Each day, they arrived at the house before dawn. They sat in Cinderella's car and observed the house. There were long silences, times when Carmody kipped a little, times when Cinderella closed her eyes too. They also talked a bit, but the conversation never got really person-

al. Most of the time Carmody answered Cinderella's questions while his questions went unanswered.
Though Carmody asked several times, Cinderella refused to explain how she had got the addresses for the houses. All she had had were the number plates and from that she had somehow *obtained* addresses. Carmody asked the question many different ways, suggested numerous ways in which she might logically have got hold of the addresses, but Cinderella *revealed* nothing. She finally became annoyed with the questioning and told Carmody that if he didn't stop trying to get information from her he would be walking home.

Übung 82: Welche Wörter sind Synonyme?

ÜBUNG 82 !

1. different	☐ tenderly
2. chat	☐ respond
3. answer	☐ diverse
4. potential	☐ banter
5. pathetic	☐ wretched
6. gently	☐ prospective

The first house had white *marble* columns outside and dated back to the 1880s or 1890s. It was a lovely house with many valuables inside, no doubt. The member of the polo club left around 9 a.m. Just before noon, they watched a woman park her minivan in front of the house and let herself in. A few minutes later, she walked out leading a small army of small dogs of various *breeds*. About 45 minutes later, she returned and soon afterwards the minivan was gone. Later in the afternoon, a lorry stopped in front of the house, and it looked as if fresh vegetables were being delivered.
The second house was further outside London and the area was

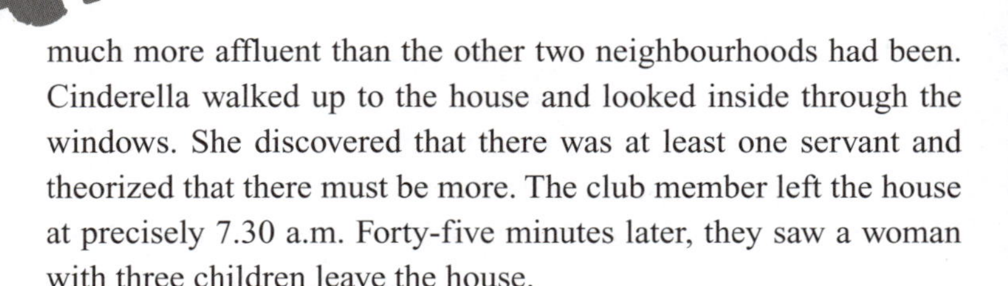

much more affluent than the other two neighbourhoods had been. Cinderella walked up to the house and looked inside through the windows. She discovered that there was at least one servant and theorized that there must be more. The club member left the house at precisely 7.30 a.m. Forty-five minutes later, they saw a woman with three children leave the house.

ÜBUNG 83

Übung 83: Setzen Sie ein sinnvolles Synonym ein!

"Have you seen anything in the newspapers about your (1. theft) r__________?"

"No. I looked for a few days, but then I stopped. I left behind no (2. signs) t__________ – or only yours. Nobody will track the robbery back to you, unless I do something – which is (3. doubtful) u__________." She smiled quickly.

Half an hour later, the woman returned and remained at the house until the middle of the afternoon. "I don't like it," Cinderella said, as they drove away. "No doubt they have plenty of money, but it's too (4. complex) c__________, too many factors –"

"Too many people?"

"Exactly."

The (5. last) f__________ house they observed was more like the first one. The (6. proprietor) o__________ was moderately rich. A maid came at around 8.30 a.m. and soon afterwards was left alone.

Early in the afternoon, the maid left and was replaced, shortly thereafter, by someone who entered with two bags of (7. provisions) f________.

"Very soon, our hero will be home and we can leave, right?"

Cinderella gave Carmody a *weary* smile.
"Perhaps."
"Look, Cinderella, a joke is a joke. There's not going to be any robbery. Let's go home, drink a bottle of wine and get nice and comfortable. I've got a silk robe that will look lovely on you."
Her eyes got big for a moment. "This is no joke, and I'm rather surprised to hear you say it is." She spoke in such a way that he knew it was best to say nothing further.
"Okay," Cinderella said, "as they drove away from the third house, "we need to look a little closer at our friend in the blue Mercedes Benz."
"I knew you were going to say that. We've just been wasting our time the last three days."
"You have had me all to yourself the whole time," Cinderella smiled. "Doesn't that count for anything?"
"A lot of good it has done me," he snapped.
"What more do you want?" Carmody said nothing. "Besides, as you're now learning, if you want to be a good thief you have to do your homework. Sometimes opportunity knocks, as it did that night at the polo club – and we got a nice sum. Usually, though, you have to prepare yourself and plan every step. Now, we're going to look a little closer at our friend's place. By the way, his name is Foster Wellingborough."
"What?" Carmody asked, *astonished*. "How do you know his name?"

ÜBUNG 84 !

Übung 84: Setzen Sie die Sätze in indirekte Rede!

1. I am having a good time.

She/he said (s)he was having a good time.

2. I love good ice cream.

3. I had that for lunch yesterday.

4. I was worried about that yesterday, but I am not anymore.

5. I have been there several times.

Chapter 5: A Writer in Love

He looked at her but saw an expression cross her face he had already seen many times. "I know, I know – it's a trade secret."
"Exactly. As I was saying, if our friend leaves over £3000 just sitting around in his car, we should be able to make sure that no one comes into his house on Thursday afternoons; so that while he's having his arm or leg broken we have plenty of time to search his house for his *ready money* and safe."
"Why Thursday afternoons?"
"Their next practice is not tomorrow but a week from tomorrow. So, we're going to make sure that everything is as I *suspect* it to be."
"I don't believe you really need my help for that."

"You're right. But I enjoy your company, Geoff. You're such a pleasant person to have around."

Übung 85: Unterstreichen Sie die richtige Variante!

Carmody wasn't (1.) certain/curtain just how ironic she was being, but he wanted to (2.) hope/believe that there was some truth to the (3.) state/statement.
"So, we'll (4.) meet us/meet in the afternoon? Around 2 o'clock or (5.) perhaps/so?"
"My dear, Geoff, I'm nothing if not (6.) thorough/through. I'll meet you at 5.30 tomorrow morning."
"You're not (7.) serious/earnest. We've got up at 5 o'clock for the past three mornings. Isn't that enough?"
"We're not finished," she insisted.
"I was hoping to sleep (8.) in/on, finally. You're a *nightmare*, Cinderella."
"I'm far worse than that, Geoff," she said – and then smiled (9.) for/at him.

At 5.30 the next morning, she was waiting in her car and Carmody *staggered* out to the car.
"I can't take these hours, Cinderella."
"You just need a bit of training," she said, pulling into the street. "Have some coffee." She held a silver thermos in her hand.
"I've already had two cups of coffee."
"It doesn't smell as if you were out drinking last night."
"I didn't go out and I didn't drink at home – nothing but healthy London water, straight out of the Thames."
"That explains quite a lot, actually," Cinderella said with a brief laugh.

By 6 o'clock, they were sitting outside Wellingborough's house. It was dark inside. A few lights were on in neighbouring houses, but they were the exception, not the rule."
"Everyone's asleep," Carmody *yawned*, "even in old Wellingborough's house."
"Exactly. We want to see just how many people are asleep in Foster Wellingborough's house."
"What sort of a name is Foster anyway? Why not name him James or Charles or Nigel or Rodney or Richard or something *dignified?* Foster. What does his girlfriend call him when they're *snogging*, 'Fossil'?"
"Actually, it's his mother's *maiden name*," Cinderella said matter-of-factly.
Carmody lifted his head off the headrest of the seat and said, "You're really unbelievable."

! ÜBUNG 86

Übung 86: Lesen Sie weiter und unterstreichen Sie die englische Übersetzung der folgenden Wörter!
(Hausangestellte, oben, murrte, Angebot, unwahrscheinlich, Überredungskunst, Selbstmitleid, höhnische Bemerkung)

Just after seven in the morning, they saw a maid walk up to the house. She let herself in and a light went on in the kitchen. Soon afterwards a light went on upstairs as well.
"I expect Wellingborough's getting his breakfast in bed," Carmody grumbled.
"No one has ever brought you breakfast in bed, Geoff?"
"No."
"You have to give something in order to get something."
"Cinderella, you would always have breakfast in bed if you stayed with me."

"That's an attractive offer," she said.
"An offer you're unlikely to take up, I'm afraid."
"Your powers of *persuasion* are not at their best at the moment," she admitted. "Self-pity works with fourteen-year-old girls but not with a woman nearing thirty."
"Nearing thirty? I thought you were already thirty or even thirty-one."
Cinderella gave Carmody a look that let him know that his *gibe* had *missed its mark.*

Übung 87: Setzen Sie die Wörter in die richtige Reihenfolge und bilden Sie sinnvolle Sätze!

! ÜBUNG 87

1. day I work every drive to. ______
2. Paris has twice to once or she been. ______
3. do tell do him to what not. ______
4. mean so why you are? ______
5. got you something have do to? ______
6. darling look you marvellous. ______

Half an hour later, Cinderella suggested that Carmody go up and look to see what was going on inside the house. "And look to see if you can tell how expensive the furniture is."
"I doubt he has flea market furniture," Carmody responded.
"Why not? You can come across some *valuable* antiques if you know where to look and know what you're looking for."
Carmody got out of the car feeling that he knew nothing at all about

the world he had spent the last twenty years writing about so successfully. The success of my books, he said to himself as he walked up to the house, is based on my readers' ignorance of the world described in them. He passed the midnight blue Mercedes and continued walking up to the house, his mind on his failures. As Cinderella had suggested, he went around the side of the house and looked in the window. It was a living room, about thirty metres long and twenty metres wide. Whether the furniture was modern or not, he could not really tell. Well, he thought, it isn't antique. It may be high quality, but I know this isn't from the 19th century or before. None of this is furniture from the 1920s either. He saw nobody at all, no dogs or cats, so he began walking back around the front of the house and was walking half-way down the drive when he heard a male voice call.

ÜBUNG 88

Übung 88: Fügen Sie die richtigen Präpositionen ein!

1. I'm tired. I'm going to turn ______.

2. Let's turn ______ the television and watch a football game.

3. She turned ______ her neighbour and asked a question.

4. People who wear clothes too young for them turn me ______.

5. When he is stressed he turns ______ a monster.

6. Take your turn ______ the roulette wheel.

"Can I help you?"
Ripped from the *interior* dialogue he had been having with himself, Carmody stopped and turned around.

"Did you ring?"
"No, I didn't."
"What do you want then?" Wellingborough began to walk towards him. He stopped and looked inside his car for a moment before continuing towards Carmody.
"Nothing," Carmody said, holding his ground. "I was just walking and noticed that I'd walked up your drive. I was somewhat surprised, as you can imagine. I must have been thinking about something else and didn't notice that I'd walked off the pavement. I'm rather absent-minded sometimes."

Übung 89: Lesen Sie weiter und bilden Sie sinnvolle Wörter aus dem Buchstabenchaos!

Wellingborough was now 1. (thwini) __________ five metres of Carmody. He turned 2. (dorun) __________ to look back at his house, as if to see what might have been of interest to the man and, at the same time, to check that nothing was 3. (oobvisuyl) __________ out of place. When he turned back around, Carmody was still standing *motionless* on the 4. (rdvei) __________.
It looked as if Wellingborough were going to say something, so Carmody turned around and 5. (geban) __________ walking towards the street again. "I'm sorry I disturbed you," he said over his 6. (redluohs) __________. Wellingborough said nothing, just watched the stranger walk away. Back on the 7. (ntvmpaee) __________, Carmody walked past Cinderella's car and kept

walking until the house was out of sight. He held his 8. (threab) ____________ and counted until 60 – though he had to breathe again by 36. He quickly walked back down the street, looked up at Wellingborough's house, and was *relieved* to see the empty 9. (nalw) ____________. He got inside Cinderella's car and *slumped* in the seat.

"He saw me," Carmody said after a minute.
"This may come as a surprise, Geoff, but I saw everything." The two sat silently for a while. "Did he recognize you?"
"I don't think so. It's not as if I'm a famous pop star or football player or something of that nature."
"No, but there's a picture of you on the back of some of your novels – a picture that should be updated, by the way."
Carmody looked at Cinderella and shook his head. "*I'm out of my depth* here."
"You are so right," she said, and gave his hand a squeeze.
"What exactly is it you want me to do? What is my role in all this? Am I just here to help with the planning?"
"That – and you'll do the driving. You'll drive the getaway car."
"I'm not the kind of person who would do well on prison food."
"Then you'd better be a good driver."
They watched Wellingborough get in his car, back it down the drive and onto the street. Carmody sank deep into his seat as Wellingborough began driving towards Cinderella's car.
"You can sit up now," Cinderella said. "He's turned the corner and gone."
"I wonder what he does," Carmody said. He saw that Cinderella was about to speak so he added, "No, I don't really want to know."

Up to that point, he had done nothing illegal. He'd been in the car when Cinderella had stolen the money, but that was the closest he had come to being an *accomplice*. Everything else, from walking into the house that had been robbed to sitting outside houses in the affluent London suburbs, had involved no intentionally illegal action. It might not have looked good, but he had broken no law himself. The £1600 was sitting in a glass in his bar, untouched. He could hear Cinderella's repeated threat going through his head: one phone call, Carmody, that's all it would take. He looked over at her. She was so dark and beautiful and young and lively and all the things that he wished he was and all the things he wanted in a woman. She's the perfect woman for me, he thought, if only she were not a thief.

"I'll give you a ring tomorrow," she said as she stopped the car near Carmody's house. "I reckon you're going to go out and have a few pints tonight?"

"That would be a safe bet, Cinderella."

"You might also think about making sure you're in better shape for next Thursday."

"All I have to do is drive."

"You should always be prepared to do a bit of running." With these words, she pulled the door shut and drove away quickly.

Übung 90: Übersetzen Sie ins Deutsche!

1. on horseback ______________________
2. to ride a horse ______________________
3. horse-shoe ______________________
4. horse-hair ______________________

5. stirrup ______________________

6. saddle ______________________

Cinderella called Carmody a couple of times over the next few days. She always called late in the morning when she could be relatively certain he would be awake and out of bed. The conversation never focused on the project that had brought them together. In fact, they tended to flirt over the phone, though Carmody was the more active player, making suggestions and promises.
Carmody spent most of the days working through the text he had written about his joint venture with Cinderella: updating and expanding it, adding details, giving the material he had a finishing touch. If Cinderella thought my last book was weak, he said to himself, she should be pleased with this one. Maybe so pleased that she'll be a bit more open to me. Of course, she may not like the character based on her. She may think I've been a bit hard on her. But she is a hard woman at times.

ÜBUNG 91 !

Übung 91: Lesen Sie weiter und setzen Sie die Verben in der richtigen Zeitform ein!

Each morning he (1. wake) ____________ hoping she would call. If she (2. not call) ____________ by noon, he (3. know) ____________ that she was probably not going to call, so he focused his energy on writing. For many people, these love pains (4. be) ____________ an unpleasant *distraction*; they (5. can) ____________ think of nothing and speak of nothing other than these pains. Carmody, however,

(6. be) ______________ used to working in such circumstances. He (7. often be) ______________ very productive just before or just after a woman left him. This time, it was even easier, because when Cinderella was not around, she (8. become) ______________ a bit unreal, like someone you have met in a dream several times but who (9. do) ______________ not exist in the waking world. She was shadowy and hard to hold onto.

On Tuesday morning, she called him earlier than normal. He answered the phone on the third ring.
"What do you say to seeing me today?" she said.
"Just what you would expect me to say: when? Where?"
"But not: why?"
"Perhaps for you there must be a 'why' but not for me. I'm ready to meet you at the drop of a hat."
"Let's meet for dinner, an early dinner."
"Great idea. Afterwards we'll come back to my place."
"That wasn't exactly my plan."
"What was your plan?"
"You go back to your place and I return to mine."
"That's hardly new or romantic. It's not even fun."
"You know that my work has different hours and is not all fun and games. Have you ever heard of the Bearded Lady?"
"Yes, it's an *awful* restaurant. The food is terrible, the waiting staff is lazy and unprofessional and the building itself lacks anything *remotely* interesting. Otherwise it's a *top-notch* restaurant."
"It should be empty then. Meet me there this afternoon at 5.30."
Without waiting for Carmody's reaction, Cinderella hung up.

Übung 92: Welche ist die richtige Bedeutung der Idiome? Kreuzen Sie die richtige Lösung an!

1. to do something at the drop of a hat
   a) ☐ to do something immediately
   b) ☐ to do something because something else happened
   c) ☐ to do something quickly

2. to have your wits about you
   a) ☐ to have money in your purse
   b) ☐ to be thinking quickly
   c) ☐ to have a group of humourous friends

3. to get back on your feet
   a) ☐ to recover from a serious illness
   b) ☐ to look after yourself
   c) ☐ to stand up for yourself

4. to be absent-minded
   a) ☐ to be ignorant
   b) ☐ to be reading
   c) ☐ to be a daydreamer

5. to snog
   a) ☐ to sneeze
   b) ☐ to kiss someone a lot
   c) ☐ to walk through mud and rain

Precisely at twenty minutes to six, Cinderella entered the restaurant. Carmody was already standing at the bar drinking a pint and chatting with the bartender. As soon as he saw Cinderella, he began

walking over to her. The head waiter began guiding her towards a table and disappeared once he had *handed* the two of them their menus. A moment later, a waitress came up to them and asked if they wanted to order drinks. Carmody ordered another lager and hastily emptied the pint he had. Cinderella ordered a cup of tea.
As the waitress went up to the bar, Cinderella watched her appreciatively.
"If I were a man, instead of talking to the waiter I would have been *chatting* her *up*."
"That's bad taste when you're meeting another woman for dinner. But maybe after you leave tonight, I'll take your advice."
"It wasn't advice, Geoff, only an observation. So tell me: what have you been doing with yourself since we last saw each other?"
"State secret. For Queen and country and all that, you know? And you, my dear? What have you been doing?"
"Trade secret."
"I believe we're going to be rather short on conversation tonight. I'd like to think that after spending four days with me, you called because you were beginning to miss me, but I know better. Maybe we should get right to the point."
"I thought you said you didn't need a reason to see me."
"I don't. You're a *feast for the eyes* in that black dress. It brings out the green in your eyes and the light brown of your skin."
"Thank you. Have you been writing?" she asked and then lifted her tea-cup to her mouth.
Carmody watched the cup reach her lips. Her lower lip was fuller than her upper lip, he noticed. "I never talk about what I'm working on, so I'm simply not going to answer your question."
"So," said Cinderella, changing the topic, "are you ready for Thursday?"
"I reckon the question is whether you are ready for Thursday. All I

have to do is drive. You're responsible for seeing that Foster Wellingborough takes a bad fall and then breaking into his house, while I sit in a car. My car or yours?"
"My car. It's faster than yours. You're not thinking of backing out, are you?"
"Not at all. I know, you have only to make one phone call and I'm behind bars. I'm really not the kind of guy who would enjoy such a life. But as far as I'm concerned, we're going to visit a friend of yours on Thursday. Or I'll say I thought it was a friend of yours until you robbed the place."
"There won't be any police to explain that to, Geoff. I've never had any contact with police in connection with a robbery."
"Only parking and speeding violations?"
"Just so. We're going to go in once darkness falls. We'll be parking on another street and entering the house from behind. I have walkie-talkies that we'll use to communicate if and when necessary. Since baby-phones sometimes pick up walkie-talkie transmissions, we'll have to keep communication to a minimum. In short, we'll only communicate in case of an emergency."
"Some of the neighbours have babies?"
"I don't know, but I don't want to risk it."

! ÜBUNG 93

Übung 93: Lesen Sie weiter und finden Sie die Synonyme für die Wörter in Klammern!

The waitress brought their food, (1. disturbing) i__________ their conversation.

"You (2. to *be unaware of*) d______k______ if any of them have babies." Carmody said, once the waitress had disappeared. "You

(3. *astonish*) s_________ me, Cinderella."

"Okay, Geoff. You can stop the (4. cynicism) s_________."

"How long do you plan on being inside?"

"Naturally, I want to be in and out of there as (5. rapidly) q_________ as possible. But it may take as long as an hour. I hope that Wellingborough will at least have to be x-rayed, which should take at least an hour. I 6. (think) i_________ he won't be home until late, perhaps ten or eleven or possibly even midnight, but I want to be out of there by 7 o'clock. I should be able to (7. defuse) d_________ the security system and find my way around in that time."

"I know what you'll probably say, but I'll ask just the same. Who's going to take care of Wellingborough?"
"I'll let you in on a secret. Someone I have worked with in the past is going to be taking the place of a member who's away on holiday. With a little make-up and a bit of distance and a rough sport like polo, the players won't notice that he's not their team-*mate*."
"Am I going to meet him?"
"I hadn't thought about that. Why? Would you like to?"
"Naturally. I'd like to know everyone I'm working with."
"You don't trust me?"
"I *trust* you *implicitly*."
"We'll meet early on Thursday."
"Not at 5.30, I hope."
"No, around midday. I have lots to do tomorrow and then I want to

relax on Thursday morning before we have our rather stressful but profitable afternoon and evening."

"Does it ever bother you? Do you ever feel guilty about stealing from other people?"

"If I did, Geoff, I wouldn't do it, now would I? Besides, I'm not stealing from poor people. If you steal from the poor, you can ruin them. The rich always get their money back."

"Just not from you."

"I'm beginning to really like you, Geoff. You have a way of cutting right through to the facts."

"So, you're – " Carmody began.

"Still not going home with you," she finished. After she had paid, they stood and left the restaurant.

"As bad as ever," Carmody said, standing outside on the street.

"I'll see you on Thursday, at noon. Meet me where I usually park my car. Just look as though you're going for a walk."

"Will do."

Carmody went home and wrote until he fell over, exhausted.

ÜBUNG 94 !

Übung 94: Unterstreichen Sie die richtige Variante!

He was waiting, as (1.) ordered/requested, when Cinderella drove (2.) on/up.

"Cornelia Thomas," Carmody said, opening the door. "I'm Geoffrey Carmody, (3.) novelist/journalist." He sat down next to her and looked (4.) foreword/forward.

"Pleased to meet you, Mr Carmody," she said, driving (5.) away/on.

"I want to make one thing (6.) transparent/clear," he said. "I am not sitting (7.) in/within this car, while you are inside Wellingborough's house, unless I have the keys."

Cinderella rolled her eyes. “As you like, Geoff.”
“Well, I think I’m rather a fool if I sit in a car without keys.”
“You can’t leave without me.”
“I can but I won’t. So, where are we going first?”
“We’re going to relax and eat a little something.”
“You’re not going to take me back to the Bearded Lady, I hope.”
Cinderella drove to a *crowded* pub restaurant in the city centre where no one would remember them. She led Carmody to a table where another young man was already sitting, a half-pint glass of beer in front of him.
“Martin Evers, I’d like you to meet Geoffrey Carmody, crime novelist. You said you wanted to meet our partner, Geoff. Here he is: Martin.”
Evers stood and offered his hand to Carmody who shook it warmly, examining the younger man.
“You’re to be the horseman?” Carmody asked once they were seated.
“He is,” Cinderella answered quickly. “I know it’s noisy here, but let’s keep our voices down. I hope that’s your first one,” she said to Evers, nodding towards his beer.
“It is.”
“I hope you’re good on a horse,” Carmody said.
“Not to worry,” Evers answered.
“He’s amazing on a horse,” Cinderella explained. “He’s been on horses and playing polo all his life.”
“I’ve only been playing polo seriously for the last week,” Evers corrected, “but I’m a quick learner.”
Carmody and Cinderella each ordered a *shandy* and food. While waiting, Carmody looked back and forth between the two younger people, trying to decide if they were a couple or not. He decided not to ask directly, as the truth – if they were a couple – would have been too much for him at that moment.

"How long have you two been working together?" he asked at last.
"Trade secret," Cinderella answered, without looking at him.
"I should have known better than to ask."
"Yes, you should have," she said.
"We know each other well enough to work together well," Evers answered.
"So what are we going to do after lunch?" Carmody asked very curiously.
"Martin's going to go and get ready to do his part, and we're going to a hardware store."

As they were leaving their table, a tall man briefly exchanged a smile with Cinderella and walked ahead of the three of them. Outside, Cinderella and Carmody said goodbye to Evers and wished him luck. Carmody, meanwhile, looked all around for the other man, but he had disappeared. Where have I seen him before? he wondered.
Cinderella and Carmody walked towards her car. Cinderella held out the keys to Carmody. "You might as well start driving so you get used to it," she said. "It's got a lot more power than your family car."
"Is it my imagination, or is the number plate different?"
"As I said, Carmody, I'm thorough."
They got in the car and Carmody adjusted the seat and the mirrors and then started the car. "Can you drive with winter gloves on? I mean by that, can you really drive, should it become necessary to escape the police, for instance?"
"Of course," Carmody answered, but he removed the gloves just the same. He pulled smoothly into the traffic and drove away. "So, where to?" he asked.
"We're just going to drive around for a while. Martin's going to call

me on my mobile phone when Wellingborough arrives at the club. Once he calls we'll drive to Wellingborough's house and sit there to make sure nobody is there."

"We could go there now to really be sure no one is there."

"But I don't want the car sitting near his house for too long. People will remember a green sports car. We've already spent one day there and a second might be *suspicious*. Besides, I need to pop into a hardware store."

"What do you need at a hardware store?"

"Geoff, you ask so many questions."

"That's my nature."

Cinderella saw a hardware store.

"Turn here," she said. When he had parked the car, she told him to wait. "I won't be a minute."

She was gone nearly half an hour. That was to be expected, Carmody said to himself. Whenever anyone says, "I'll be back immediately," they usually mean you'll have to wait. After fifteen minutes, Carmody couldn't decide whether he should simply get out of the car and walk away or walk inside the hardware store. He spent nearly ten minutes trying to decide which step would be the best, so Cinderella was back before he had finally made up his mind.

"That was a damned long minute," he complained.

Cinderella *patted* him on the hand.

"I had to make sure I got what I wanted."

"And what would that be?"

"A little tool that changes magnetism."

"And how is that helpful?"

"It works wonderfully well with security systems, if you know what you're doing."

"I can hardly wait!" Carmody said ironical.

Übung 95: Welches Wort ist das „schwarze Schaf"?

1. suspicious, dubious, crafty, dodgy
2. obligatory, necessary, vital, charitably
3. for instance, for example, a case in point, for once
4. splash, vanish, disappear, dissolve
5. dive into, nip into, pop into, dash into

Chapter 6: Trapped

I'm only the driver, Carmody said to himself.

"You know, Cinderella, we could still stop all this and just go to my place. You could move in and we could live together quite happily. You wouldn't have to rob me because everything that's mine would be yours. One of my books is under consideration by a film studio – I could be very rich or we could be very rich very soon, even without robbing a house tonight. Call up your friend Martin and tell him it's all off."

"That's *tempting*, but I like the challenge of what I do."

"But what about the risks? It would be a shame for a beautiful woman like you to spend some of the best years of your life, the most beautiful years of your life, in prison."

"But I'm not going to go to prison. It's sweet of you to worry about me, though." They drove around, put more petrol in the car and then drove around some more until finally Martin called. They then turned the car towards Wellingborough's house. They parked, facing the wrong direction on the street, a short distance away and sat.

"It looks rather empty," Carmody observed, as it began to get dark. "No lights on."

They sat a little longer. Cinderella leaned over and began to kiss

Carmody deeply. She kissed him and *moaned*, "Geoff," and kissed him some more. Suddenly, an old woman knocked on the window. Carmody, *startled*, broke off the kiss and rolled his window down, while Cinderella leaned back.
"Can't you do that somewhere else, young man?"

Übung 96: Unterstreichen Sie im nächsten Absatz die englische Übersetzung der Wörter in Klammern!
(1. wohin jetzt, 2. Schal/Kopftuch, 3. Fenster, 4. klopfen, 5. Stirn)

ÜBUNG 96 !

Carmody looked from the old woman, a scarf stretched over her head, to Cinderella and back again. The woman turned around and walked back up to her house and went inside. Carmody, still not thinking clearly after the double shock of Cinderella's kiss and the old woman's knock on the window, started the car and drove away. He looked at Cinderella and wanted to ask what had come over her. Instead, he simply asked, "Where to now?" the cold sweat burning on his forehead, her kiss still on his lips.
"Turn here – and here." They went around the corner. "Behind this house is Wellingborough's, if you can believe it. There's a small patch of forest between the two. Soon, it'll be dark enough to go through and enter Wellingborough's house from behind."
"I thought dawn was your favourite time for this sort of activity."
"It is, but sometimes you have to *bow* to necessity."
"I suppose your targets have usually been single men, like myself, who were out far too late in the night." Cinderella did not reply. "I should consider myself lucky, if I weren't a bit worried about – "
Cinderella's mobile phone rang.
"Yes. Yes. What? Did you really? Good job. Get out of there as quickly as you can. See you tonight." She turned her phone off.

"See you tonight?"
"Yes," she said seriously, "after we're finished here, we're going to meet and divide the *swag*."
"So, he has taken care of Wellingborough?"
"I should think so. It looks like a broken arm and a separated shoulder. The fall took care of the shoulder and a horse took care of the break."
"I'd prefer not to think about it."
"They're waiting for an ambulance as we speak." Cinderella reached into the *storage area* behind the seats. "Here's the walkie-talkie. All you have to do is leave it on and the channel open. Do not speak to me on it unless you absolutely have to, you understand? If there's an emergency, then I'll let you know – I'll probably just tell you to drive away."
"I couldn't just leave you there."
"Well, you can't go to prison with me, either. They have separate prisons for men and women, so don't play the hero."
Cinderella pulled a black bag out of the *storage area*, put on a black knitted hat and smeared *thick* black cream on her face.
"What's in the bag?"
She dropped the walkie-talkie in the bag. "Torches. Two large, one small." She dropped the new tool in it. "Here we go," she said, getting out of the car. "Don't leave without me, unless I tell you to."

ÜBUNG 97 !

Übung 97: Fügen Sie die richtigen Präpositionen ein!

1. We are going to have to move ______ another city.

2. It's time to move ______. This project is a dead end.

3. Our new neighbours are moving ______ tomorrow.

4. My partner moved ______ after five years of living together.

5. You are so slow. Get a move ______!

Carmody watched her disappear into the night, reflecting on the fact that she had answered two questions thoroughly in the last few hours. He reached for the car keys and touched them with relief. He had expected them to be gone. How can you love someone you don't even trust? he asked himself. He pressed a button on his watch and noticed the time: 5.34 p.m. She wants to be out by 7 o'clock, he said to himself. He was nervous, naturally, but suddenly found himself *gloomy* as well. There in the darkness, all he could do was wait. If I had a character in a book in this situation, I'd be yelling at him to get out of there as fast as he could. Nothing could go right in such a situation. But I can't leave Cinderella. I'll have to leave her tomorrow, tell her tomorrow that I can't live like this, that this isn't the life for me. I can't leave her tonight, though; I can't risk that I would be the one to send her to prison by *abandoning* her. He also knew that if she were to *set her sights on* revenge, then she would have her revenge – and no doubt he would be an easy target. Suddenly, Carmody remembered where he had seen the young man at the pub who had smiled at Cinderella. He had been the waiter at the café where he and Cinderella had first gone together.

He looked at his watch. 6.02 p.m. She should be inside and *gathering* the *swag*.

What does it mean? he asked himself. Is this person important? What does it mean? Is he her lover? Or her partner? Then who was Martin? How many partners does she have?

It's 6.21 p.m.

"Carmody," the walkie-talkie crackled, "Carmody, I need your help. I've *hurt* myself. Come in the back door, on the left side. You should be able to just push it open. Quick. I'm *hurt*."

"Where are you, Cinderella?" Carmody asked. "Where are you?"

ÜBUNG 98 !

Übung 98: Beantworten Sie die Fragen zum Text!

1. What does Carmody compare his love for Cinderella to?

2. Cinderella worries that Evers has had too much to drink. What is Carmody worried about?

3. Who is to drive the get-away-car?

4. Is Martin Evers their only partner?

5. What injuries does Wellingborough receive?

6. Does Cinderella take the car keys with her into the house?

When he received no answer, Carmody got out of the car, locked it and ran towards Wellingborough's house. He was quickly in the wooded area. He stopped for a moment as a doubt crossed his mind. What if this is a trick? he asked himself. What if it's a trick?

She's done it before – at that first house. But if it isn't a trick, I can't just leave her there. She kissed me. He stood where the trees stopped and looked at Wellingborough's house. The back of the house was clearly a modern addition. All glass, a sun-room to warm and add natural light. No lights were on in the house. He saw the door. It looked closed. The houses to the left and right were lit up. Carmody thought of the waiter again, saw him smile at Cinderella, and then he ran towards the house, bounding up the steps to the door into the sun-room. He gently pushed the door open and walked inside. He *glanced* around the sun-room and then quickly went into each room on the ground floor. There were four large rooms, including the sun-room – a formal dining and living room, a kitchen large enough for a restaurant, and a large foyer. Old paintings hung on all the walls, except in the foyer, where more modern paintings were hung. There was no sign of Cinderella, so Carmody ran to the stairs and went up to the first floor.

"Cinderella," he called softly. "Cornelia. Neely."

He heard no answer – or else the darkness *swallowed* the answer. Here on the first floor there were four, five or six doors. One was open and he ran towards it. It was a bedroom and lying on the bed was a bag, but as Carmody ran towards the bed he saw no sign of Cinderella anywhere in the room.

This is a trick, he thought, picking up the thin nylon bag. "If this is a trick," he said out loud, "I'm going to take you down with me." Inside the bag were jewels and a couple of *syringes* in their original packaging. He ran into hallway with the bag and opened the door to another room – meant to be a library but with only a few books on the shelves. The next room was a sort of office with a large wooden desk and a computer sitting on it. He entered each room and looked around quickly, *glanced* in all directions, then walked back into the hallway. The next room was another bedroom. One of the

windows was open in this room, but not far enough for Cinderella to have crawled through. The window looked out onto the house next door. Carmody lifted the window up and leaned out. Cinderella was not on the ground and it was too steep here for her to have crawled out and *made* her *way* down. He pulled his head back inside and turned around. As he walked back to the door, he saw a walkie-talkie lying on the floor. I have got to get out of here, he said to himself. "Cinderella, you ...!" he screamed.
He ran down the stairs. Just over the front doorway, he saw a red light *flashing*. The alarm must be going off, he thought as he ran towards the back door. He began to hear the sounds of sirens coming closer. He ran to the sunroom, threw open the door, jumped to the bottom of the outdoor steps and ran to the wooded area, then through it and back to the car.

ÜBUNG 99 !

Übung 99: Setzen Sie die Sätze in indirekte Rede!

1. You can drive.

____

2. I fell down and hurt myself.

____

3. Wait for me in the car!

____

4. I'll be back in a moment.

____

5. I have worked with Martin Evers for three years.

____

6. Where do you go at Christmas time?

"It's gone," he said, suddenly feeling *dizzy*. Cinderella's green sports car was gone. "She left me here." The bag dropped from his hand. The sirens were coming ever closer. What do I do now? Walk away. Walk away quickly but not too quickly. Absent-mindedly, he picked the bag up and began to walk. A first and then a second police car went past at high speed, the sirens screaming. After the second one passed, he realised what he was carrying in his hand and threw the bag into some shrubberies. A third car drove by with its lights on but much slower. The officer in the passenger seat observed Carmody quite closely. The car continued past and Carmody breathed a *sigh of relief.* He kept walking and didn't notice that the police car had stopped. There was a sound of *squealing* tyres and suddenly the police car was driving backwards down the road. It stopped and the officers got out and walked towards Carmody.

"There's been a robbery not far from here," one of the police officers said. Carmody could not see either of them very well in the darkness. "May we see some identification?"

"I don't have anything with me," he said, though in fact he did. "I just came out for a walk."

"Do you live around here?"

"Yes," he answered.

"May we take you home?"

"But I'm out for a walk. I don't want to go home yet."

"May we see your keys?" the other officer asked.

Carmody held out his own house keys.

"Someone meeting your description was seen carrying a small bag. What happened to it?"

"As I said, I came out for a walk. I didn't bring anything with me."
"What's your address?"
When Carmody did not answer immediately, one of the officers said, "Okay, let's walk back the way you came," and pulled out a torch and began sweeping the ground with it.

ÜBUNG 100 !

Übung 100: Welche Wörter haben dieselbe Bedeutung?

1. description	☐ bush
2. shrubbery	☐ siren
3. identification	☐ instantly
4. warning	☐ portrayal
5. theft	☐ credentials
6. immediately	☐ burglary

They began to walk, Carmody helplessly sandwiched between the two men. They walked for about two hundred metres when the nylon bag was lit up in the *shrubbery*. One of the officers leaned over and picked up the bag. He opened it and pulled out a *syringe*.
"Now that's a *nasty* habit," he said.
"That's not my bag. I've never seen it before in my life. Besides, I don't even like *syringes*. I'm scared of them."
"That's a good one," one of the officers answered sarcastically.
"Now, do I look like a drug user?" Carmody asked.
Neither officer answered the question. "There's some jewellery in here as well, but not very much. Where's the rest?" he asked Carmody.
"How should I know? I've never seen the bag before in my life."
"I think you'd better come with us."
"I'd rather just go home."

"Can you tell us your street address?"
Carmody stood there silently. He did not know the address of the house he had spent nearly an hour in front of. "I can direct you there."
"You want me to believe that you just forgot your address?"
"You make me nervous, the two of you, accusing me of being a drug addict and a thief."
"Come with us, please." They led him to the police car and sat him in the back seat.

Übung 101: Welche Antwort passt zur Frage? Kreuzen Sie an!

1. What is Carmody doing at the moment?
   a) ☐ He walks with police officers.
   b) ☐ He has walked with police officers.
   c) ☐ He is walking with police officers.

2. How long have Carmody and Cinderella known each other?
   a) ☐ For about four weeks.
   b) ☐ Since about four weeks.
   c) ☐ They knew each other about four weeks.

3. Where do you live?
   a) ☐ I am living not far from here.
   b) ☐ I am live not far from here.
   c) ☐ I live not far from here.

4. Where is the bag you were carrying?
   a) ☐ I carry not a bag.
   b) ☐ I was not carrying a bag.
   c) ☐ I am not carrying a bag.

5. What are you doing out so late at night?

a) ☐ I am taking a walk.

b) ☐ I take a walk.

c) ☐ I have taken a walk.

Once they were both in the front seat, they drove to Wellingborough's house and parked alongside the other two police cars. The two officers then got out of the car and walked up to the other officers. When they came back, the shorter one asked for Carmody's name.

"Geoffrey Thomas," he answered.

"Your profession, Mr Thomas?"

"Why am I being asked these questions? Am I a *suspect?*"

"At the moment, everyone is a *suspect*."

"Even you?"

The officer looked at him and *frowned*. "Don't be *ridiculous*."

"What is *ridiculous*," said Carmody, *gathering* all his courage, "is that a man can't take a walk in his own neighbourhood without being picked up by the police."

"Tell us your address."

"I'm not going to. I don't want to be taken home by the police. That's just the sort of thing to get neighbours talking, if they should see me getting out of a police car. You have no reason to be holding me."

"We have the bag with jewels and your *syringes*."

"I already told you, I never saw that bag before in my life. It isn't mine. And as for the *syringes*, you can check my arms: I have no needle marks at all. I find such a habit as distasteful as you do."

"We're going to take you down to the station and take your fingerprints and then you'll be free to go," said the shorter police officer. "First, however, we will need an address."

Carmody sat quietly while the officers drove to their station. Once there, they *handed* him over to an assistant who took down his information and took his fingerprints. Carmody gave the same name but this time he provided an old address, not as far from the crime scene as where he currently lived. Before he left, he was allowed to make a call to a friend to give him a lift home.
"Yes, I know. Yes. I know. Well find someone who hasn't been drinking then. Just come here and pick me up, will you?" he yelled into the phone.

Übung 102: Lesen Sie weiter und setzen Sie die Verben in der richtigen Zeitform ein!

ÜBUNG 102

Everything (1. go) ________________ wrong in his life in the last few weeks. Ever since he (2. meet) ________________ Cinderella his life (3. simply *spiral*) ________________ out of control. Now, he (4. know) ________________ that she (5. never be) ________________ interested in him. She had *set* him *up*. But, really, he (6. do) ________________ nothing wrong. It (7. not look) ____________ good, but he (8. not do) ________________ anything illegal – except, perhaps, for driving a getaway car.

But he had been left at the house, so he had not even driven the getaway car. Things had turned out quite differently from the way he had planned them. In his story, he and Cinderella were together at the end. He had left it unclear whether she actually committed the robbery or not. He had always hoped that he could talk her out of it.

He had wanted to discover that being a thief was not important for her; it would not be a fundamental change in his eyes. Now it was clear that he had completely underestimated her. Though they had spoken on the phone several times and met a handful of times, he had never really got an insight into the real Cornelia Thomas – or whatever her name was. When he got home, Carmody thoroughly searched his house for jewels and money, looking for anything that was not his. He searched the house but came up empty. Finally, at 3 o'clock in the morning, exhausted, he lay down in his bed and hoped for a *blissful* night of sleep.

Chapter 7: No Way out?

Bump, bump bump!
Carmody rolled out of bed.
He pulled a robe on and went downstairs to the front door.
"Who is it?" he called out.
"The police."

ÜBUNG 103 !

Übung 103: Finden Sie die Synonyme für die Wörter in Klammern!

Carmody opened the door and they walked in. They showed him some (1. documents) p__________, which he did not (2. trouble) b__________ to read, and began to search the house.

"Why didn't you give us your (3. actual) r__________ name and address?" an officer asked. Carmody did not (4. identify) r__________ the officer. When Carmody did not answer, he

(5. went on) c_______________: “That was a big (6. blunder) m__________. And what were you doing so far away from central London on foot?” This officer and another asked several more (7. enquiries) q__________ of a similar sort.

“I was up there with my girlfriend,” Carmody finally answered. “We had an argument, and she got in her car and drove away.”
“What were you doing there? That’s not one of the usual romantic areas for lovers. You ever heard of the white cliffs of Dover or the Pennines?”
“I like architecture.”
“You like architecture.”
“Do you know what happened to Foster Wellingborough?”
“No. Should I?”
“His house was robbed of more than £18,000 cash and several priceless pieces of jewellery and he’s in hospital.”
“I had nothing to do with the robbery, and I certainly didn’t do anything to him.”
“No, he fell from a horse,” the officer said. “Someone posing as a member knocked him off his horse.”
“We found your fingerprints inside the house,” another officer reported. “On the open window on the first floor. And we found them on jewellery at a Dr Zeno’s house. Do you know a Dr Zeno? No? He’s a dentist. His house was robbed about three weeks ago while he and his wife were away on holiday. There’s a brooch and several other pieces of jewellery with your fingerprints on them.”
Carmody turned white and all the spirit of resistance *drained* out of him. He sat down on his sofa and watched the officers taking his place apart bit by bit.

"You gave us the wrong name, but someone recognized your picture. I reckon you're a little too famous now."

"I would like to speak to Inspector Hudson," he said at last.

"A solicitor might be a better choice," the officer recommended.

"I'm afraid I'm beyond the help of any solicitor."

"I would have to agree," one of the officers said.

The police took him to a larger police station and put him in a cell and there he waited. He had no idea whether he was going to be questioned or whether Cornelia Thomas might just somehow turn up and set him free. That afternoon, he was taken out of his cell twice and put into a police *line-up*. As he later learned, he was positively identified twice – by Foster Wellingborough's elderly neighbour and by Wellingborough himself.

"The elderly neighbour saw you *snogging* a 'dark-haired beauty' on the day of the robbery. Is this 'dark-haired beauty' your *accomplice*?"

"I had no *accomplice*," Carmody answered, "because I committed no crime."

"Wellingborough couldn't say exactly what day it was, but he saw you walking up to his house several days before the robbery. He too positively identified you yesterday."

"I would like to speak with Inspector James Hudson of Scotland Yard," Carmody answered.

"Are you one of the Inspector's friends? Do you think he can just set you free? You forget, Mr Carmody, we have fingerprints – your fingerprints – in Dr Zeno's house and in Foster Wellingborough's house. We also have a very interesting story written by the famous Geoffrey Auberon Carmody, wherein a novelist is *led astray* by a young thief, with long, dark brown hair, named Cinderella. Why don't you give us her real name, tell us where she lives and tell us anything and everything else you know about her and these two robberies. Perhaps you were *led astray*."

"I want to speak to Inspector Hudson," Carmody said, his voice going suddenly weak. How could he have forgotten about the story?! He should have sent it to his agent and then deleted it from his computer; if not his agent, he should have sent it to someone else, his sister perhaps, but to have left it on his computer: how stupid can you be? he thought. The answer of course was quite simple: stupid enough to leave it on his computer.

Übung 104: Fügen Sie die richtigen Präpositionen ein!

The following day a solicitor visited him (1.) ______ his cell. He was a heavy-set pink-cheeked man (2.) ______ his mid-40s, who was familiar (3.) ______ two (4.) ______ Carmody's books. Carmody signed the books placed (5.) ______ the table (6.) ______ front (7.) ______ him; however, he refused to speak to him (8.) ______ the case, beyond saying that he had already told the police everything he knew.

"You're on the express train to jail, you know? I mean," he said loudly, "this is a high-speed train to jail you're on. They have fingerprints inside two different houses and on jewellery that was recovered from both houses. Moreover, you may not know this, but the green sports car the neighbour saw you sitting in with 'Cinderella' – or whatever you wish to call her – turned up *abandoned* yesterday. It was stolen five weeks ago. Whoever drove it was careful – your fingerprints were still on the steering wheel. They can prove you were driving a stolen vehicle. You clearly had accomplices, but if you *cover for* them then the only person who is going to suffer is you."

"The only person who can help me," Carmody said emphatically, "is Inspector James Hudson of Scotland Yard."

"I don't think that even he can help you," the solicitor said, shaking his head.

"Thank you for coming, Inspector."

"I don't know what I can do for you, Mr Carmody."

They stood in a large, dark room, with a massive wooden table in the centre. In this room, Carmody had been questioned several times already and as he was being led to the room he was fully expecting yet another round of questions. He had been quite pleased therefore to see Inspector Hudson standing quietly in a corner of the room, his hands in his trouser pockets. Dressed in a dark suit with a bright burgundy shirt, Hudson did not smile as he saw Carmody brought into the room. Carmody on the other hand smiled broadly at the inspector.

"I read your story," Hudson said, once the two men were alone. "It made for some very interesting reading. It should help get you in jail – and then on another best-seller list, if your publisher is smart enough to bring it out. Your description of Dr Zeno's house and the jewellery that you *claim* you found in your house, or that you took from Dr Zeno's house, was quite accurate. Naturally, the police think that the story is a fictionalised version of your life the last few weeks put on your computer especially for them – as your alibi."

"That story is the truth," Carmody said. "I've never written anything truer."

"In the story, she says she prefers to rob houses at dawn. Why rob Wellingborough at 5.30 at night?"

"Pure necessity."

"And the plan came from you?"
"Yes, but I never meant for it to really happen. The details were all planned and carried out by her."
"I've never really seen you as pathetic, Carmody. And this young woman played a game with you and had you wrapped around her finger, so that you would do anything for her? You want me to believe that? You're usually the aggressive type, aren't you, when it comes to women? At least that's how I remember you."

Übung 105: Unterstreichen Sie die richtige Variante!

Ignoring (1.) that/this last statement, Carmody declared, "I didn't rob (2.) anyone/no-one and you can search my house and my bank accounts and you won't find (3.) nothing/anything (4.) a/n bookholder/accountant can't explain."
"So you've hidden the (5.) treasure/swag somewhere," Hudson suggested. "Simply because they can't (6.) find/found it, does not mean you don't have it."
"You must (7.) remind/remember that I called you about three or four weeks ago and you (8.) lay down/hung up on me. That was the day I found the jewellery in my (9.) building/house."
"You should have called the police (10.) straight on/immediately."

"I called you instead. And soon after that I stopped thinking straight, as you know from the story: I met Cinderella."
"What's her real name?"
"Cornelia Thomas." Carmody watched Hudson pull out a little black notebook, open it and write the name inside.
"I'll look her up immediately," he said, putting his pen and notebook back in his inside pocket.

"There's no point, Inspector. It isn't her real name."
"How do you know?"
"I know."
"But you don't know her real name?"
"No. I don't know much about her at all. I never got a phone number or an address for her. She always made the contact, and I was so happy to talk to her or see her that I didn't *dare* push for more from her. I think at least one or two men may have worked with her but I don't know for certain." Carmody described his visit to the pub the day of the robbery.
"I admit that I was with her the night of the robbery. I sat in the car that was to help her escape with the *swag*. I told her she didn't need to steal from people, that she could live with me, but she said 'No.' She said that such a life was not interesting to her. She called me on the walkie-talkie, while I was waiting for her in the car, and said she had been injured. I didn't know what had happened, and even then I *suspected* it was a trick. Be that as it may, I went in Wellingborough's house and looked for her everywhere. I saw a window open on the first floor, found the bag and then heard the sirens."
"A walkie-talkie was found in Wellingborough's house, but it had no fingerprints on it."
"She *set* me *up*. I don't know why, but she did. She got me in the house, got some jewels in my hands and made sure the police were on their way. And the *syringes* were simply *the icing on the cake* – to make it look particularly bad."
"You're moving a little fast, Carmody. I'm not sure I believe you were *set up*." Hudson looked at Carmody with the grim face he reserved for hardened criminals. "And I have to tell you that in any case it doesn't look good. Nobody believes your story. The district attorney thinks your *trial* should be a rather brief one. He feels there's no need to waste time on a long *trial*. Even your solicitor

told me the best he could do for you was to get a reduced prison term. It doesn't matter whether you were *seduced* or not. You're still responsible for your own actions."

"But I didn't do anything," Carmody said, sinking into his chair. "I was led into the Zenos' house as part of a trap. I went into Wellingborough's house only to save Cinderella. I did not rob either house, and I didn't intend to rob either house. I'm innocent of everything – except being foolish."

"Most of the people in prison could say the same thing," Hudson answered.

"I suppose you're right," Carmody responded, shaking his head. "But she *set* me *up*. She said she was not a good planner, but she is a master planner. If anyone can capture her, you can."

"I'll see what I can do," Hudson said, relaxing, "but I'm certain you will be behind bars before I find anything out."

"I can wait," Carmody said.

"I don't see that you have any other choice." Hudson was silent a moment. "But, if there is some truth to your story, you won't be behind bars for long, I can assure you of that. If there is a Cinderella, then it's nearly midnight for her."

Carmody did not look at Hudson very happily.

THE END

Abschlusstest

Übung 1: Welches Wort ist das „schwarze Schaf"?

1. think, pond, reflect, consider
2. natural, normal, sensual, usual
3. upset, shocked, surprised, startled
4. directory, list, file, record
5. threaten, intimate, warn, intimidate
6. vanish, dissolve, splash, disappear

Übung 2: Setzen Sie die Verben in die richtige Zeitform!

1. They (know) ____________ each other for a long time.

2. We (work) ____________ on a report at the moment.

3. She always (drive) ____________ like a maniac.

4. Last summer, I (fly) ____________ to Paris.

5. He (live) ___________ in Oxfordshire since 1999.

6. They (talk) ____________ in the kitchen, when the phone (ring) ____________.

Übung 3: Finden Sie das passende Gegenteil!

1. amateur	☐ reluctant
2. strange	☐ important
3. calm	☐ expert

4. willing ☐ nervous
5. inconsequential ☐ artifical
6. natural ☐ ordinary

Übung 4: Fügen Sie die richtigen Präpositionen ein!

1. Will you look ______ this report for me?

2. Punctuality means being _____ time.

3. The mayor is ______ charge ______ running the city.

4. There was no sign ______ our dog anywhere.

5. He turned ______ his wife and asked her the same question.

6. They moved ______ after only two years.

Übung 5: Welche Synonyme gehören zusammen?

1. shattered ☐ proprietor
2. excited ☐ trace
3. limit ☐ wretched
4. exact ☐ exhausted
5. pathetic ☐ papers
6. potential ☐ think
7. sign ☐ real
8. owner ☐ wound up
9. documents ☐ boundary
10. imagine ☐ prospective
11. actual ☐ precise

Übung 6: Wie lauten die Sätze in der richtigen Reihenfolge?

1. one late home morning got he

---

2. day do have something you to every

---

3. weekend swimming often go we the at

---

4. work do how get you to?

---

5. try will you you hard succeed if

---

6. Finland been I never to have

Übung 7: Bilden Sie sinnvolle Wörter aus dem Buchstabenchaos!

1. rusesirp ______________________
2. fertfo ______________________
3. vopelene ______________________
4. nithiw ______________________
5. tacavnio ______________________
6. haedeorf ______________________

Gemeinsamer Abschlusstest

Übung 1: Setzen Sie die Sätze in indirekte Rede!

1. You are wonderful.

....

2. Your English has improved quite a bit.

....

3. You can always stay with me.

....

4. If you call me, I'll tell you.

....

5. I was there yesterday.

....

6. She should always do what she is told.

....

Übung 2: Welche ist die richtige Bedeutung der Idiome? Kreuzen Sie die richtige Lösung an!

1. to hit it off with someone
   a) ☐ to look for something in a field
   b) ☐ to start a venture with someone
   c) ☐ to have a good relationship with someone

2. to have your wits about you
   a) ☐ to have money in your purse (not just the bank)
   b) ☐ to have a group of entertaining friends (not just funny)
   c) ☐ to be intelligent (not just book knowledge though)

3. to lend someone a hand
   a) ☐ to help someone
   b) ☐ to give someone a place to stay for the night
   c) ☐ to give someone some food

4. to be absent-minded
   a) ☐ to be a daydreamer
   b) ☐ to be reading
   c) ☐ to be unintelligent

5. to rise to the challenge
   a) ☐ to get up with the alarm clock
   b) ☐ to perform well because you have to
   c) ☐ to try and be successful

6. to have a word with someone
   a) ☐ to speak with someone
   b) ☐ to go into a meeting with someone
   c) ☐ to disagree with someone

Übung 3: Markieren Sie mit richtig ✔ oder falsch – !

1. Geoffrey Carmody and Inspector Hudson are the best of friends. ☐
2. Cinderella is about 19 years old. ☐

3. A dentist is robbed as the story begins. ☐
4. The other partner is called Martin Springer. ☐
5. Carmody is a writer whose novels deal with crimes. ☐
6. A green sports car was stolen. ☐
7. Cinderella drives off to a store, leaving Carmody behind. ☐
8. Carmody is arrested. ☐
9. Inspector Hudson believes Carmody's story. ☐

Übung 4: Simple Present oder Verlaufsform? Unterstreichen Sie die richtige Form des Präsens!

1. Mrs Drum plays/is playing cards at the moment.
2. It snows/is snowing outside.
3. David Bucket never knows/is knowing what to do.
4. Miss Elliot usually travels/is travelling by car.
5. Inspector Hudson goes/is going home now.
6. Where does/do Marc Drum stay?

Übung 5: Welche Synonyme gehören zusammen!

1. boat	☐	force
2. enquiry	☐	proceed
3. huge	☐	innocent
4. funeral	☐	investigation
5. blameless	☐	ship
6. advance	☐	enormous
7. might	☐	memorial service

Übung 6: Setzen Sie das passende Adjektiv bzw. Adverb ein.
(well, helpful, safe, abruptly, ancient, high, harmless)

1. Inspector Hudson did very ______________.

2. The tower was very ______________.

3. Sergeant Wood was a ______________ man.

4. The Tower of London is not old, it is ______________.

5. The thief dressed in black was anything but ______________.

6. Miss Elliot braked ______________.

7. Buckingham Palace is a ______________ place.

Übung 7: Was gehört zusammen? Bilden Sie sinnvolle Paare!

1. well	☐ thing
2. bed	☐ time
3. agree	☐ bonnet
4. real	☐ done
5. Tudor	☐ Warder
6. foot	☐ fully
7. Yeoman	☐ guard

Übung 8: Übersetzen Sie!

1. Die Baronin McKee schien schwer über etwas nachzudenken.

....

2. Philip Havisham wurde mit einer Pistole erschossen.

3. Er schüttelte den Kopf und schaute sehr besorgt.

4. Detective Carlyle nahm ein Blatt Papier aus seiner Tasche und entfaltete es.

5. Seine Augen funkelten, als er das sagte.

6. Das würde bedeuten, dass etwas im Haus war oder immer noch ist, das in irgendeiner Weise mit dem Mord zusammenhängt.

7. Es sind einige Dinge, die nicht ganz ins Bild passen.

Übung 9: Ordnen Sie die Buchstaben zu einem sinnvollen Wort!

1. tpsuayo ____________
2. sosucipius ____________
3. onicnten ____________
4. relaruq ____________
5. itwsnes ____________

6. rgblayru ______________________

7. rupcrot ______________________

Übung 10: Welche Gegenteile gehören zusammen?

1. innocent	☐ hate
2. friend	☐ guilty
3. love	☐ enemy
4. question	☐ dishonest
5. superior	☐ false
6. honest	☐ inferior
7. true	☐ answer

Übung 11: Setzen Sie die passende Präposition ein!

1. The waiter came ________ and took their order.
2. You need to get ________ now or you'll be late.
3. I'll meet you ________ the kitchen ________ five minutes.
4. Her voice was harsh and there was no room ________ compromise.
5. How did she manage to get ________ the car ________ waking me?
6. She walked immediately ________ the living room.
7. It would be more interesting to work ________ you.
8. He looked ________ his watch.

Übung 12: Wie lauten die Sätze in der richtigen Reihenfolge?

1. thoughtful woman the looked young

2. that remember glittering you the under safe the pillow on thing?

3. her to he a followed restaurant food ate Indian they where

4. got Carmody and up made of tea pot a himself

5. lowered for binoculars Cinderella the a looked moment and Carmody at

6. sirens coming the were of police the car closer

7. came from plan you the?

Übung 13: Geben Sie die Pluralform an!

1. box ____________________

2. policeman ____________________

3. breath ____________________

4. class ________________

5. lady ________________

6. foot ________________

7. mouse ________________

8. echo ________________

9. handkerchief ________________

10. life ________________

Übung 14: Ordnen Sie die Buchstaben in Klammern zu einem sinnvollen Wort!

Inspector Hudson still looked (1. csetpacil) ________________. They walked out of the (2. hcrhcu) ________________ into the evening air. The inspector stopped and (3. olkdeo) ________________ straight at Elvira Elliot.

"Okay, let's say he does have a (4. tomevi) ________________ and he stole the (5. omdaidn) ________________. First question is: Did the (6. cpinre) ________________ pay Marc Drum and David Bucket to help him (7. esatl) ________________ the diamond? Second question is: Did he (8. likl) ________________ Marc Drum after the (9. byrbore) ________________? If he did, he wasn't very (10. rcealuf) ________________, was he?"

Übung 15: Wie heißt das Wort auf Deutsch?

1. pile ____________________
2. handcuffs ____________________
3. conspirator ____________________
4. tube ____________________
5. clue ____________________
6. fail ____________________
7. threaten ____________________
8. obtain ____________________
9. suspicious ____________________
10. treasure ____________________

Lösungen

In the Shadow of the Tower

Übung 1: 1. was 2. got 3. went 4. heard 5. fell 6. came 7. did 8. ate 9. let 10. said
Übung 2: 1. along 2. archway 3. think 4. guard 5. direction 6. escort 7. answer
Übung 3: 1. car 2. armed 3. guard 4. lantern 5. money 6. shoot 7. disappointed 8. happy Lösung: ceremony
Übung 4: 1. hurry/slow down 2. shout/whisper 3. cover/uncover 4. nervous/calm 5. strong/weak 6. keep/give 7. pull/push 8. light/heavy 9. friend/enemy 10. reply/ask
Übung 5: 1. helpful 2. exhausted 3. clever 4. strange 5. funny 6. good
Übung 6: 1. removed 2. placed 3. covered 4. propped 5. knocked 6. frowned
Übung 7: 1. Inspector Hudson looked forward to reading his book. 2. Inspector Hudson wore his pyjamas. 3. The thieves stole the Kohinoor diamond. 4. Miss Paddington tried to listen to the telephone conversation. 5. Inspector Hudson forgot to put on his shoes.
Übung 8: 1. nobody 2. his 3. sat 4. bright 5. think 6. far 7. blood 8. ambulance 9. socks 10. later
Übung 9: 1. – 2. The 3. a 4. an 5. – 6. the 7. – 8. the
Übung 10: 1. That is very impressive. 2. They walked towards the glass case. 3. Inspector Hudson admired the jewels. 4. Sir Reginald smiled triumphantly. 5. There were almost no witnesses. 6. Inspector Hudson looked pensively around the room. 7. Sir Reginald shrugged.
Übung 11: 1. Where 2. which 3. What 4. Who 5. Whose 6. Which 7. Why
Übung 12: 1. exited 2. walked 3. diamond 4. special 5. shrugged 6. speeded 7. pleased
Übung 13: 1. on 2. over 3. in 4. on 5. to 6. under 7. onto
Übung 14: 1. danger 2. miserable 3. thorny 4. alert 5. loads 6. argue 7. excess
Übung 15: 1. he isn't 2. they aren't 3. we won't 4. she didn't 5. it can't 6. she wouldn't 7. we haven't 8. they shouldn't
Übung 16: 1. called 2. He 3. I 4. interestedly 5. no 6. say 7. Calm 8. doing
Übung 17: 1. ask/inquire 2. innocent/blameless 3. exclaim/shout 4. close/shut 5. accomplice/assistant 6. pull/heave 7. understand/comprehend 8. force/might 9. proceed/advance 10. rough/violent
Übung 18: 1. much 2. much 3. many 4. many 5. much 6. many
Übung 19: 1. gently 2. thoughtfully 3. uneasily 4. harmlessly 5. safely 6. roughly 7. abruptly 8. mysteriously
Übung 20: 1. falsch 2. falsch 3. richtig 4. richtig 5. falsch 6. richtig 7. richtig
Übung 21: 1. arrived, arrived 2. run, ran 3. hide, hidden 4. made, made 5. keep, kept 6. shine, shone 7. thought, thought 8. wear, wore
Übung 22: 1. bellboy 2. joyride 3. hotel lobby 4. police badge 5. bookshelf 6. old-fashioned 7. typewriter

Übung 23: 1. Uhr, beobachten 2. Uniform, gleich 3. Ring, anrufen/läuten 4. Hand, geben 5. meines, Mine 6. Muse, grübeln
Übung 24: 1. waved 2. approached 3. inquired 4. generous 5. usual 6. point 7. eagerly
Übung 25: 1. Miss Elliot always drives fast. 2. Suddenly she saw the bellboy. 3. Inspector Hudson and Elvira Elliot just walked into the hotel. 4. Prince Vikram had just left. 5. Inspector Hudson should probably have asked the bellboy first.
Übung 26: 1. They walked outside. 2. It was a very modern building. 3. It was a very cheap copy. 4. They could see land in the distance. 5. It was like a rainbow.
Übung 27: 1. me 2. them 3. his 4. mine 5. him 6. your, mine
Übung 28: 1. Inspector Hudson would never let Miss Elliot drive his car. 2. Elvira Elliot would never admit that she drives too fast. 3. Inspector Hudson would never find the Whispering Gallery on his own. 4. Prince Vikram would never leave the house without his turban. 5. Sir Reginald would really like to catch the thief. 6. Miss Elliot would always work together with the inspector.
Übung 29: 1. cathedral 2. pillar 3. Renaissance 4. aisle 5. altar 6. nave 7. caretaker
Übung 30: 1. rang 2. answered 3. is 4. found 5. have checked 6. seems 7. seeing 8. meeting 9. are trying 10. know
Übung 31: 1. herself 2. himself 3. themselves 4. yourself 5. ourselves 6. itself
Übung 32: 1. brakes 2. tyres 3. heart attack 4. people 5. store 6. glimpse 7. gem
Übung 33: 1. street 2. borough 3. car 4. toot 5. square 6. shop 7. residential 8. hotel 9. Tower of London
Übung 34: 1. sparkling 2. talk 3. matter 4. gracefully 5. private 6. accompany
Übung 35: 1. reverse 2. finally/eventually 3. police badge 4. closed 5. unreliable 6. opening hours 7. enter 8. to bow 9. suspect
Übung 36: 1. longer, longest 2. deeper, deepest 3. nicer, nicest 4. more helpful, most helpful 5. narrower, narrowest 6. more exhausted, most exhausted 7. worse, worst 8. more comfortable, most comfortable
Übung 37: 1. ago 2. since 3. ago 4. for 5. since 6. for 7. for
Übung 38: 1. richtig 2. falsch 3. richtig 4. richtig 5. falsch 6. falsch
Übung 39: 1. connection 2. proudly 3. sounds 4. stops 5. hesitated 6. clues 7. solve
Übung 40: 1. standing 2. never 3. (very) small 4. bored 5. loves 6. towards 7. difficult
Übung 41: 1. Go! 2. Stop her/them! 3. Don't tell him! 4. Stop it! 5. Leave me alone! 6. Stay here!
Übung 42: 1. They were staying at a two-star hotel on Piccadilly Circus. 2. Yes, the underground was near the hotel. 3. They think Mr and Mrs Moore can help because Mr Moore filmed during the robbery at the Tower. 4. Yes, it was the same person. 5. A knife fell out of his pocket. 6. No, he didn't manage to steal the tape. 7. The Moores took the Piccadilly Line and the Circle Line.

Übung 43: 1. b 2. a 3. c 4. b 5. a
Übung 44: 1. picked 2. asked 3. thought 4. laughed 5. knew 6. teased 7. tried 8. walked 9. inserted 10. swallowed 11. pulled
Übung 45: 1. disregard 2. three 3. why 4. terrible 5. good 6. day 7. path
Übung 46: 1. real/false 2. hold/let go 3. fast-forward/rewind 4. miss/hit 5. clear/vague 6. whisper/scream 7. record/play
Übung 47: 1. triumphantly 2. exactly 3. calmly 4. hard 5. disapprovingly 6. reproachfully
Übung 48: 1. will 2. are going to 3. is going to 4. will 5. are going to 6. am going to
Übung 49: 1. we are taking 2. we are preferring 3. we are travelling 4. we are lying 5. we are running 6. we are humming
Übung 50: 1. bald 2. towards 3. asked 4. long 5. sure 6. living 7. hope 8. late 9. good
Übung 51: 1. pressure 2. publicity 3. ringing 4. secretary 5. investigation 6. relieved 7. evidence 8. disbelief
Übung 52: 1. during 2. Last 3. ago 4. last 5. ago 6. during
Übung 53: 1. who 2. which 3. who 4. – 5. who 6. whose
Übung 54: 1. half past six 2. ten past ten 3. (a) quarter past three 4. twenty-five to nine 5. (a) quarter to one 6. five to eight 7. five past five
Übung 55: 1. remarcked (remarked) 2. collegue (colleague) 3. stoped (stopped) 4. quite (quiet) 5. here (hear) 6. wispered (whispered)
Übung 56: 1. would he 2. wouldn't she 3. wasn't she 4. isn't he 5. hasn't she 6. can't he 7. didn't he 8. won't they
Übung 57: 1. sneak 2. opposite 3. crashed 4. dashing 5. bumped 6. Near 7. heading
Übung 58: 1. sitting 2. see 3. asked 4. entered 5. going 6. exclaimed 7. believe 8. insisted
Übung 59: 1. groß 2. groß 3. – 4. – 5. groß 6. groß 7. –
Übung 60: 1. he does 2. he is doing 3. he did 4. he was doing 5. he has done 6. he has been doing 7. he is going to do 8. he will do
Übung 61: 1. the 2. – 3. a 4. – 5. the 6. the 7. a 8. –
Übung 62: 1. bodies 2. rivers 3. wives 4. busses 5. sheep 6. days 7. women drivers 8. knives 9. boxes 10. policemen
Übung 63: 1. Where 2. Who 3. Whose 4. Which 5. Why 6. What 7. Whom 8. Where
Übung 64: 1. Inspector Hudson arrived at the crime scene that/which was near the Thames. 2. They fought their way through curious spectators, who were in the way. 3. The Tower, which was close to the bridge, could be seen in the distance. 4. The body was found near the Thames, which was not good news. 5. Inspector Reid, who was working in the distance, could see them coming. 6. They nearly bumped into Sergeant Wood, who was holding a cup of coffee.
Übung 65: 1. stroked away 2. smiled (back) at 3. looked down 4. swollen up 5. looked away 6. pulling together 7. weighed down
Übung 66: 1. by 2. in 3. at 4. from 5. in 6. for 7. after 8. to

Übung 67: 1. nervous 2. murderer 3. colleagues 4. spectator 5. hesitate 6. accomplice 7. stretch Lösung: suspect
Übung 68: 1. falsch 2. falsch 3. falsch 4. richtig 5. richtig 6. falsch 7. falsch
Übung 69: 1. is calling 2. drives 3. believes 4. is having 5. does not help 6. says, leaves
Übung 70: 1. cathedral/church 2. ship/boat 3. large/huge 4. enter/go into 5. understand/comprehend 6. investigation/enquiry 7. inside/within
Übung 71: 1. Inspector Hudson has solved many crimes. 2. The caretaker has seen different kinds of tourists. 3. Prince Vikram has been near St. Paul's Cathedral. 4. Inspector Hudson has caught many criminals. 5. Elvira Elliot has worked a lot with Inspector Hudson. 6. They have been looking for a loose stone.
Übung 72: 1. crouch down 2. mix up 3. run away 4. stand up 5. hide from 6. calm down 7. stare at 8. bump into
Übung 73: 1. some 2. any 3. some 4. any 5. any 6. some 7. some
Übung 74: 1. right 2. Perhaps 3. much 4. row 5. something 6. shrugged 7. India 8. prince 9. diamond
Übung 75: 1. admonish/praise 2. greed/moderation 3. be silent/speak 4. assist/fight 5. always/never 6. pull/push 7. empty/full
Übung 76: 1. difficult 2. wide 3. busy 4. frightened 5. low 6. helpful 7. ancient
Übung 77: 1. will 2. would 3. would have 4. will 5. will 6. would
Übung 78: A miss is as good as a mile. = Knapp daneben ist auch vorbei.
Übung 79: 1. after 2. headed 3. carrying 4. group 5. warmly 6. dressed 7. gigantic
Übung 80: 1. small/great 2. coldly/warmly 3. ugly/beautiful 4. free-time/business 5. downwards/upwards 6. closed/opened 7. loudly/quietly
Übung 81: 1. h 2. e 3. d 4. b 5. c 6. g 7. a 8. f
Übung 82: 1. nothing 2. anything 3. anywhere 4. anybody 5. nobody 6. anything 7. nothing
Übung 83: 1. Prince Vikram is richer than Inspector Hudson. 2. The tower is higher than the bridge. 3. The London Eye is bigger than the Prater Wheel. 4. The Savoy is more expensive than a two-star hotel. 5. Westminster Abbey is older than Madame Tussaud's. 6. The unknown thief is worse than David Bucket. 7. Elvira Elliot drives faster than Inspector Hudson.
Übung 84: 1. we hit 2. we are hitting 3. we hit 4. we were hitting 5. we have hit 6. we have been hitting 7. we are going to hit 8. we will hit
Übung 85: 1. afraid of 2. drive fast 3. fingerprints 4. belong to 5. true story 6. gentleman 7. fed up 8. narrow-shouldered 9. on duty
Übung 86: 1. down 2. out 3. started 4. conclusion 5. wrong 6. thought 7. too 8. impressed 9. plausible 10. nobody
Übung 87: 1. The scandal was caused by Inspector Hudson. 2. Marc Drum was killed by the thieves. 3. Sir Reginald's point is understood by the inspector. 4. The newspaper was slammed on the desk by Sir Reginald. 5. A scandalous article was written by the journalist. 6. The mobile was put into his pocket by the inspector.

Übung 88: 1. knife 2. queen 3. scandal 4. sigh 5. halt 6. headline 7. question 8. tube
Übung 89: 1. No wonder 2. dryly 3. lawyer 4. suddenly 5. try 6. him 7. murderer 8. explain 9. searched
Übung 90: 1. c 2. a 3. b 4. a 5. c
Übung 91: 1. was dressed in 2. funeral 3. distressed 4. sadly 5. went back 6. came across 7. passed
Übung 92: 1. Prince Vikram stayed at the Savoy. 2. His bodyguards were very strong. 3. Inspector Hudson liked Miss Elliot. 4. Miss Elliot likes the way Inspector Hudson dresses. 5. Everybody/Somebody knew who stole the Kohinoor diamond. 6. Mrs Drum has blue eyes. 7. Inspector Hudson found Mrs Drum in the kitchen.
Übung 93: 1. to 2. too 3. to 4. to, too 5. too 6. to 7. to
Übung 94: 1. "I used to do gymnastics." 2. "I am in the middle of organizing my late husband's funeral." 3. "Where is your bathroom, please?" 4. "I like working with Inspector Hudson." 5. "I would like to be an inspector one day." 6. "Put your phone down!"
Übung 95: 1. make 2. make 3. do 4. do 5. make 6. do 7. Do
Übung 96: 1. b 2. b 3. a 4. a 5. b 6. b 7. b
Übung 97: 1. maiden name 2. joke 3. dumbfounded 4. immediately 5. robbery 6. posh 7. assume 8. admonish 9. mobile 10. trigger 11. bow 12. casually
Übung 98: 1. in London 2. in London 3. in London 4. nicht in London 5. nicht in London 6. in London 7. in London
Übung 99: 1. barked 2. was 3. took 4. looked 5. sparkled 6. arrived 7. looked 8. could (not) 9. approached
Übung 100: 1. obey 2. poor 3. under 4. bottom 5. kind 6. knowing 7. shoot

Lösungen Abschlusstest

Übung 1: 1. slow down/hurry 2. weak/strong 3. never/always 4. stand/walk 5. towards/away from 6. scream/whisper 7. grab/let go
Übung 2: 1. b 2. a 3. b 4. b 5. b
Übung 3: 1. heard 2. came 3. did 4. made 5. swam 6. walked 7. laid 8. hid 9. wore 10. dabbed
Übung 4: 1. crouch down 2. call on 3. mix up 4. fill in 5. back off 6. drop by 7. eat out
Übung 5: 1. – 2. a 3. an 4. – 5. the 6. a 7. an
Übung 6: 1. London Eye 2. Big Ben 3. Buckingham Palace 4. Westminster 5. St. Paul's Cathedral 6. Jubilee Gardens 7. Madame Tussaud's 8. Tower Bridge

Death of a Dandy

Übung 1: 1. stairs 2. bright 3. room 4. pour 5. glasses 6. peace
Übung 2: 1. rowing competition 2. Thames 3. river 4. water 5. boats 6. riverbank 7. landing stages 8. watermen
Übung 3: 1. crowded/empty 2. good/evil 3. mild/cold 4. bold/cowardly 5. long/short 6. stop/move 7. win/lose
Übung 4: 1. coach 2. Victorian 3. bright 4. horse 5. it 6. house 7. because 8. father 9. peace 10. cost Lösung = aristocrat
Übung 5: 1. rowing boat 2. horse rider 3. coach driver 4. canoe paddle 5. ice skate 6. fishing net
Übung 6: 1. win/succeed 2. smile/grin 3. shout/cry 4. enter/go in 5. distant/far 6. good/excellent 7. close/near
Übung 7: 1. The restaurant is called Criterion. 2. He studies at the Royal Music Academy in London. 3. He plays the violin. 4. Well-to-do people dine at the Criterion. 5. He likes that it is cosy and private. 6. The waiter takes the coats to the cloak-room. 7. He sees an extremely attractive woman.
Übung 8: 1. waiter 2. musician 3. husband 4. boatman 5. royal 6. charm
Übung 9: 1. The restaurant only had three tables. 2. He heard their cheerful voices. 3. They drank a bottle of wine. 4. They say she used to be very beautiful in her time. 5. He read the menu. 6. Did you have any luck? 7. Mr Havisham lifted his glass.
Übung 10: 1. "Here's to you, Philip!" they shouted. 2. He flew into the evening sky. 3. Then he threw it onto the floor. 4. He was really happy they were leaving. 5. Afterwards his glass was full.
Übung 11: 1. His face was red with anger. 2. He calmly wiped his trousers. 3. He downed his wine in one. 4. This is no place for a quarrel. 5. The man tried to move towards him. 6. Nobody understood why. 7. He felt awkward.
Übung 12: 1. sad 2. grim 3. silly 4. tragic 5. short 6. awkward 7. dull
Übung 13: 1. accent 2. from 3. boss 4. tragedy 5. alongside 6. floor 7. open 8. heart
Übung 14: 1. smile 2. beggar 3. stand 4. leave 5. terrible 6. sad 7. silence 8. careless 9. happy 10. vulnerable
Übung 15: 1. to dine 2. to have lunch 3. to have breakfast 4. dinner 5. lunch 6. breakfast
Übung 16: 1. After 2. Before 3. After 4. before 5. Before 6. after
Übung 17: 1. popular/unpopular 2. important/unimportant 3. fictional/true 4. dangerous/safe 5. bitter/sweet 6. miserable/happy
Übung 18: 1. richtig 2. falsch 3. falsch 4. richtig 5. falsch 6. falsch 7. falsch
Übung 19: 1. Dr Brown wasn't sober. 2. He didn't lose his balance. 3. Detective Carlyle doesn't know who the murderer is. 4. The constables weren't listening. 5. The sergeant's men haven't found a clue.

Übung 20: 1. I can't 2. I'll 3. I don't 4. you're 5. we'll 6. it's 7. couldn't 8. I'm 9. he's 10. doesn't

Übung 21: 1. in front of 2. entered 3. hope 4. surprised 5. last night 6. money problems 7. eye 8. curious

Übung 22: 1. sea (see) 2. scrapps (scraps) 3. evning (evening) 4. new (knew) 5. peace (piece) 6. luke (look) 7. campain (campaign) 8. shoed (showed)

Übung 23: 1. on 2. over 3. in 4. under 5. at 6. near

Übung 24: 1. Lord Spencer received a message. 2. He (always) had visitors. 3. I can. 4. Yes, of course. 5. Yes, please. 6. I will come. 7. I (do) care.

Übung 25: 1. winged demon 2. gravestone 3. churchyard 4. house/home 5. locked door 6. overgrown garden 7. minister/cleric

Übung 26: 1. witnesses 2. doors 3. dresses 4. ladies 5. wives 6. halves 7. sheep 8. scarves 9. days 10. teeth

Übung 27: 1. too 2. to 3. to 4. too 5. too 6. too

Übung 28: 1. c 2. b 3. c 4. a 5. c 6. c

Übung 29: 1. hotel 2. duke 3. cathedral 4. typewriter 5. coincidence 6. sergeant 7. secret passage 8. lamp 9. minute 10. after

Übung 30: 1. Everything was neat. 2. He took a sip of tea. 3. Detective Carlyle closed the secret passage. 4. It suddenly bent down and plucked a flower. 5. The bright sun almost blinded him.

Übung 31: 1. stairs 2. grave 3. charge 4. good 5. arrive 6. collar 7. introduce 8. fast Lösung = sergeant

Übung 32: 1. b 2. b 3. a 4. b 5. b 6. b

Übung 33: 1. hurry/rush 2. honest/truthful 3. mock/scorn 4. assume/suppose 5. murderer/killer 6. conversation/talk 7. quarrel/argue 8. testify/bear witness 9. angry/annoyed 10. idea/suggestion

Übung 34: 1. next 2. called 3. as 4. his 5. about 6. all 7. at

Übung 35: 1. half past six 2. eight o'clock 3. quarter past four 4. ten past seven 5. twenty-five past ten 6. quarter to six 7. twenty-five to eight 8. ten to four 9. five past two 10. twenty past four

Übung 36: 1. hesitate/wait 2. slam/door 3. burn/flame 4. police/detective 5. murder/crime 6. ocean/calm 7. horse/coach

Übung 37: 1. impatiently 2. shouting 3. free 4. overwhelming 5. sooner 6. gun

Übung 38: 1. b 2. b 3. c 4. a 5. b 6. a 7. b

Übung 39: 1. richtig 2. falsch 3. falsch 4. richtig 5. richtig 6. falsch 7. falsch

Übung 40: 1. myself 2. yourself 3. himself 4. herself 5. itself 6. ourselves 7. yourselves 8. themselves

Übung 41: 1. solve the case 2. knock at the door 3. commit a murder 4. conduct an interview 5. eat a steak 6. make a fuss

Übung 42: 1. exclaimed 2. gasped 3. baffled 4. unbelievable

Übung 43: 1. Sir/Mr 2. chap/guy 3. Madame/Mrs 4. drawing-room/living-room 5. lady's man/womanizer 6. ante-room/foyer 7. patter/talk

Übung 44: 1. will 2. will 3. going to 4. going to 5. going to

Übung 45: 1. diary 2. hide-out 3. bedroom 4. constable 5. volunteer 6. murder weapon 7. a mess
Übung 46: 1. a lot of 2. a lot of 3. a lot of 4. much 5. much
Übung 47: 1. good 2. well 3. good 4. good 5. well. 6. good 7. well
Übung 48: 1. mislay 2. dread 3. wish 4. right 5. guilty 6. doubt 7. reveal 8. glad
Übung 49: 1. the 2. – 3. – 4. – 5. the 6. the
Übung 50: 1. c 2. a 3. b 4. b 5. c
Übung 51: 1. e 2. k 3. g 4. i 5. c 6. b 7. a 8. f 9. d 10. h
Übung 52: 1. shameful 2. shocking 3. disgraceful 4. despicable 5. appalling
Übung 53: 1. He had a relationship with a woman called Baroness McKee. 2. They had steaming cups of tea in front of them. 3. This place looks more like a fortress, if you ask me. 4. After he won her heart he left her. 5. Could Baroness McKee really murder a person? 6. Philip Havisham is a devious man. 7. He took a share of the diaries and sat at the corner of the bed. 8. Sergeant Thompson did not want to read the books.
Übung 54: 1. wish 2. investigating 3. observed 4. unnoticeable 5. statue 6. home 7. message 8. contact 9. luck
Übung 55: 1. stil (still) 2. wissdom (wisdom) 3. suden (sudden) 4. amuced (amused) 5. remot (remote) 6. dreem (dream) 7. meen (mean)
Übung 56: 1. a 2. b 3. c 4. b 5. a
Übung 57: 1. down 2. about 3. to 4. under 5. used 6. at 7. down 8. up 9. to 10. behind
Übung 58: 1. Who 2. Where 3. Whose 4. which 5. What 6. Who 7. Whose
Übung 59: 1. The baroness had a secretive aura. 2. They could not see into the room properly. 3. Sergeant Thompson put his hand into his inside pocket. 4. As soon as William Butcher leaves the café we will follow him. 5. The policemen carefully approached the boxes. 6. Detective Carlyle saw the curtain move.
Übung 60: 1. accusing 2. to be indiscreet 3. did you find out about 4. trust him 5. believe
Übung 61: 1. good-natured 2. leave 3. unspoken 4. penniless 5. sign 6. account 7. breakfast 8. age
Übung 62: 1. Baroness 2. Lady 3. Queen 4. Viscountess 5. Duchess 6. Princess
Übung 63: 1. who's 2. whose 3. that 4. who 5. which
Übung 64: 1. as soon as possible 2. chapter 3. senior 4. Great Britain 5. circa 6. before Christ
Übung 65: 1. minute 2. progress 3. pale 4. perplexed 5. understand 6. chuckle 7. jealousy 8. eager 9. victims 10. case Lösung = upper-class
Übung 66: 1. They were walking across Grosvenor Square. 2. He thought he could read his mind. 3. He found Lord Spencer's wallet. 4. He is late for his class at the Royal Music Academy. 5. He stuck it between the door's wooden frames. 6. He found him in the kitchen. 7. He was trying to pull up a wooden plank from the kitchen floor.
Übung 67: 1. say 2. him 3. yours 4. where 5. meet 6. by 7. about

Übung 68: 1. envelope 2. wallet 3. jail 4. reincarnation 5. exist 6. search
Übung 69: 1. Sit down! 2. Go away, will you! 3. Stay here! 4. Do it right! 5. Enough of this! 6. Don't do it! 7. Come here! 8. Don't run! 9. Stop it! 10. Not now!
Übung 70: 1. victim 2. suspect 3. investigation 4. innocent 5. court
Übung 71: 1. sneaked 2. fault 3. want 4. carefully 5. hurt 6. hysterical 7. gradually 8. him 9. approaching
Übung 72: 1. make 2. do 3. do 4. make 5. make 6. do
Übung 73: 1. b 2. a 3. a 4. b 5. b 6. b 7. b
Übung 74: 1. cried out 2. rotted 3. behind 4. certain 5. near 6. more 7. no one
Übung 75: 1. more discreet 2. cleverer 3. funniest 4. more difficult 5. better 6. thinner 7. narrower 8. nicest
Übung 76: 1. his 2. your 3. them 4. mine 5. me 6. him
Übung 77: 1. best 2. again 3. returned 4. handcuffed 5. take 6. dangerous 7. cause
Übung 78: 1. He was upset because some of his hotel interior had been destroyed. 2. He jumped out of the window. 3. He fired into the air once. 4. No, he didn't. 5. He was drinking a cup of tea. 6. No, he had more of a professional interest in him. 7. He lay Lord Spencer's wallet on the desk.
Übung 79: 1. immoral 2. sad 3. dishonest 4. angry 5. unlucky 6. narrow 7. difficult 8. lazy 9. helpful 10. low
Übung 80: 1. blame on 2. sit down 3. eat up 4. involved in 5. escort to 6. black out 7. stay with
Übung 81: 1. worse 2. silly 3. commotion 4. evidence 5. inquire 6. accidental 7. landlord
Übung 82: 1. certainly 2. disgusting 3. discussion 4. maybe 5. replied 6. shocked 7. hot
Übung 83: 1. thought 2. arrested 3. did 4. asked 5. mentioned 6. looked 7. remarked
Übung 84: 1. a 2. an 3. – 4. a 5. an 6. a 7. a 8. a 9. – 10. –
Übung 85: 1. pure coincidence 2. real life 3. reality bites 4. plain bread 5. true love 6. open mind
Übung 86: 1. John Pirrip looked very pale. 2. The three men did not want tea. 3. Simon Manlove has never heard of a woman with the initials SW. 4. He has never been the same since his fiancée died. 5. Stewart Portman thought Detective Carlyle's office was horrible. 6. No, sorry, that does not ring a bell. 7. Detective Carlyle went out of the office and closed the door behind him.
Übung 87: 1. cup of tea 2. plate of chips 3. pile of boxes 4. bunch of flowers 5. glass of wine 6. barrel of beer
Übung 88: 1. c 2. a 3. b 4. b 5. a
Übung 89: 1. Does 2. Does 3. Do 4. Does 5. do/do 6. does 7. does

Übung 90: 1. shouted 2. difficult 3. death 4. earlier 5. unfaithfulness
Übung 91: 1. fooled 2. reason 3. blame 4. into 5. exclaimed 6. violin 7. assume 8. hindsight 9. investigations 10. credit
Übung 92: 1. dinner/dine 2. jacket/pocket 3. waiter/table 4. paper/document 5. Victorian London 6. dark lane 7. matches/cigarette 8. pipe/smoke 9. case/clothes
Übung 93: 1. richtig 2. richtig 3. richtig 4. falsch 5. falsch 6. falsch
Übung 94: 1. entrance 2. beside 3. careful 4. bedroom 5. gun 6. found 7. chair 8. near
Übung 95: 1. pull the trigger 2. press the button 3. push the coach 4. crack the whip 5. throw the ball 6. fire the gun 7. read the menu
Übung 96: 1. drive slowly 2. smile wearily 3. done well 4. recommended highly 5. wink friendly 6. sing deeply
Übung 97: 1. dumb/stupid 2. try/attempt 3. shake/tremble 4. deep/bottomless 5. attack/assault 6. located/positioned 7. favourite/preferred 8. book/novel 9. threaten/warn 10. chance/opportunity
Übung 98: 1. a 2. b 3. c 4. b 5. c
Übung 99: 1. led 2. coach 3. whip 4. relieved 5. tipped 6. case 7. distance 8. nearly
Übung 100: 1. richtig 2. richtig 3. falsch 4. richtig 5. richtig 6. richtig 7. falsch 8. richtig

Lösungen Abschlusstest

Übung 1: 1. win/succeed 2. enter/go in 3. hurry/rush 4. quarrel/argue 5. shake/tremble 6. try/attempt 7. grin/smile
Übung 2: 1. waiter 2. Wife 3. from 4. After 5. coincidence 6. before 7. themselves 8. hide-out 9. a lot of
Übung 3: 1. rowing boat 2. gravestone 3. churchyard 4. slam/door 5. burn/flame 6. solve the case 7. make a fuss 8. chap/guy 9. barrel of beer 10. bunch of flowers
Übung 4: 1. a 2. b 3. a 4. b 5. b
Übung 5: 1. boy 2. wealthy 3. book 4. dine 5. well-to-do 6. blue 7. enter
Übung 6: 1. women 2. wives 3. baronesses 4. policewomen 5. waitresses 6. hostesses 7. actresses
Übung 7: 1. brand new/old 2. more/less 3. empty/crowded 4. cowardly/bold 5. far away/near 6. safe/dangerous 7. cover/reveal
Übung 8: 1. breath 2. pulled 3. nicer 4. meet 5. piece 6. on 7. into
Übung 9: 1. ante-room 2. chap 3. patter 4. sir 5. madame 6. lady's man 7. drawing-room
Übung 10: 1. a 2. an 3. the 4. – 5. a 6. – 7. an

Theft at dawn

Übung 1: 1. awoke 2. was 3. ached/was aching 4. convinced 5. swallowed 6. decided 7. met 8. froze
Übung 2: 1. mind 2. afternoon 3. ferocious 4. exhibitionist 5. open
Übung 3: 1. materialise/disappear 2. expert/amateur 3. ornate/plain 4. common/unusual 5. expected/bewildering 6. previous/next
Übung 4: 1. in 2. of 3. at 4. in 5. of 6. to 7. in
Übung 5: 1. insult 2. impolite 3. unbekannt/nicht identifiziert 4. suit 5. ernstlich 6. reasonable
Übung 6: 1. surprised 2. doorbell 3. letter 4. effort 5. envelope 6. frowned
Übung 7: 1. leaves 2. bough 3. stem 4. tree trunk 5. blossoms 6. thorns, Lösung: autumn
Übung 8: 1. He wrote very simple stories. 2. He got home late one morning. 3. What does that word mean? 4. He was already on the train. 5. A woman took all her clothes off. 6. Cinderella is a beautiful young woman.
Übung 9: 1. silents (silence) 2. chamdelier (chandelier) 3. corridoor (corridor) 4. dout (doubt) 5. intereor (interior) 6. sported (spotted) 7. stomache (stomach) 8. luxurusly (luxuriously) 9. antiq (antique) 10. pilow (pillow)
Übung 10: 1. He writes crime novels. 2. He sees a dress. 3. The dress is black. 4. It is a nature picture – with a branch and blossoms on it. 5. The shoe reminds him of a cat. 6. The shoe reminds him of the character Cinderella.
Übung 11: 1. richtig 2. falsch 3. richtig 4. richtig 5. falsch 6. richtig
Übung 12: 1. Ente 2. Adler 3. Schlange 4. Eule 5. Esel 6. Eichhörnchen 7. Maultier/Maulesel 8. Fledermaus
Übung 13: 1. later/afterwards 2. tired/shattered 3. wound up/excited 4. notice/observe 5. opposite/across from 6. taking a deep breath/plunging in
Übung 14: 1. cut 2. bought 3. sought 4. could 5. wore 6. stood
Übung 15: 1. fetch 2. handed 3. smile 4. tone 5. real 6. dawn
Übung 16: 1. important/minor 2. favourite/detested 3. encourage/deter 4. contrast/likeness 5. hard/easy 6. nervous/calm 7. comfortable/prickly 8. slender/stout
Übung 17: 1. sound 2. trophy 3. consumption 4. politician 5. sensual 6. pub
Übung 18: 1. telling **to** me 2. believe **in** his ears 3. **the** Cinderella 4. **slow** reaction 5. **percentage** profits 6. very **the** least 7. burglaries **not** only 8. are **to** some 9. **the** burglary 10. its **for** entertainment
Übung 19: 1. call 2. stick 3. like 4. deliberation 5. postpone 6. along
Übung 20: 1. It might be Cornelia Thomas. 2. Yes, she did. 3. Yes, he did. 4. No, he is not. (It took him 30 minutes to recover from his run.) 5. She is in her late twenties. 6. Her favourite time to rob a house is at dawn.
Übung 21: 1. He always read the newspapers. 2. She preferred to rob houses at dawn. 3. Cinderella sent Carmody a postcard. 4. People worry about getting older. 5. How do you catch a thief?

Übung 22: 1. discuss 2. So 3. almost 4. league 5. challenge 6. target 7. into 8. somewhat 9. whisper
Übung 23: 1. aid 2. precise 3. delightful 4. boundary 5. talk about 6. most recent
Übung 24: 1. banch (bench) 2. painted (pointed) 3. through (though) 4. prefered (preferred) 5. uper (upper) 6. carlessly (carelessly) 7. parterre (partner) 8. risiko (risk)
Übung 25: 1. jealous 2. partnership 3. throat 4. challenge 5. life 6. modern
Übung 26: 1. Vorschlag/suggestion 2. Firmen/companies 3. Zahnarzt/dentist 4. Schweiz/Switzerland 5. Zäune/fences 6. Diener/servants 7. Lösung/solution 8. Forschung/research
Übung 27: 1. thieves 2. journeys 3. wives 4. children 5. bodies 6. novels 7. leaves 8. feet
Übung 28: 1. c 2. a 3. c 4. b 5. a 6. c
Übung 29: 1. richer/richest 2. better/best 3. worse/worst 4. more expensive/most expensive 5. more/most 6. prettier/prettiest
Übung 30: 1. falsch 2. falsch 3. richtig 4. richtig 5. falsch 6. richtig
Übung 31: 1. satisfactory 2. probation 3. upset 4. time 5. preserve 6. run onto
Übung 32: 1. in 2. in/of 3. on 4. for 5. in/of 6. on
Übung 33: 1. cosy/comfortable 2. leisure/pleasure 3. hurry/rush 4. demanding/hard 5. fancy/prefer 6. slight/bit of a
Übung 34: 1. How 2. Where 3. What 4. Why 5. Which 6. When
Übung 35: 1. silent 2. questions 3. distance 4. location 5. observe 6. really 7. towards
Übung 36: 1. membership fees 2. club members 3. seat belt 4. tube station 5. sit down 6. practical joke
Übung 37: 1. friendly 2. open 3. explosion 4. step 5. step 6. reckon 7. suitable 8. right 9. leave
Übung 38: 1. c 2. b 3. b 4. a 5. c
Übung 39: 1. How do you get from point A to point B? 2. She drives a bright green sports car. 3. We leave on Thursday at 9 a.m. 4. If I were you, I would accept the job/I would accept the job if I were you. 5. You should do this anonymously. 6. How often do you visit London?
Übung 40: 1. falsch 2. falsch 3. richtig 4. falsch 5. falsch 6. richtig
Übung 41: 1. guide 2. specialising 3. chose 4. youth 5. up 6. correctly 7. old 8. basic 9. stars
Übung 42: 1. imediately (immediately) 2. reserch (research) 3. prodused (produced) 4. royally (royalty) 5. wandered (wondered) 6. provided (provided) 7. struktur (structure) 8. representatatives (representatives) 9. excited (existed) 10. completed (competed)
Übung 43: 1. The car was driven by Cinderella. 2. All (the) decisions were made by Cinderella. 3. The painting was stolen (by someone). 4. This product was made (by workers) in China. 5. Responsibility for the crime was taken by an anonymous group.
Übung 44: 1. badly 2. artificial 3. ignorance 4. peasants 5. previous 6. latter

Übung 45: 1. pounded/knocked 2. organizer/filing cabinet 3. moment/time 4. alongside/next to 5. newest/latest 6. looked/appeared 7. begin/launch into 8. short/brief 9. advantages/benefits 10. grudgingly/unwillingly
Übung 46: 1. progress 2. laughed 3. joke 4. members 5. spring 6. rates
Übung 47: 1. teilnehmen 2. selbstsicher 3. Fortschritt 4. streng 5. Gipfel 6. Nachteil
Übung 48: 1. courage 2. brake 3. cabinet 4. handy 5. file 6. do
Übung 49: 1. Geoffrey Carmody always writes on his computer. 2. He drives to work every day. 3. She works full-time as a thief. 4. We were in Manchester last month/We went to Manchester last month. 5. Carmody has won many awards. 6. They need new uniforms immediately.
Übung 50: 1. He does not want the assistant manager to recognize him. 2. He says he works for *Three Kings.* 3. No, she does not. 4. He almost calls him "Tommy." 5. Yes, indeed he is. 6. (A trick question!) He cannot contact Cinderella – he has no phone number or address for her.
Übung 51: 1. sound 2. tell 3. whole 4. concluded 5. worry 6. events
Übung 52: 1. endure 2. embellish 3. exactly 4. including 5. kitten 6. dedicate 7. remove
Übung 53: 1. richtig 2. richtig 3. falsch 4. falsch 5. falsch 6. richtig 7. falsch
Übung 54: 1. It was now about 3.15 p.m. 2. I was searching for sunken treasure. 3. And you bought a swim-suit and a swimming pool as a Christmas present. 4. Maybe I'll tape my Christmas cards up on the walls, he thought. 5. I should take a walk, down on the beach at the Prince of Wales' castle.
Übung 55: 1. to 2. of 3. for 4. of 5. to 6. in 7. for 8. of 9. onto
Übung 56: 1. a secret 2. stinks 3. partners 4. you suffocate 5. invades 6. champagne 7. curtains
Übung 57: 1. abbiegen, werden 2. ausruhen, lehnen 3. anrufen, nennen 4. klein, kurz 5. Kiste, Brustkasten 6. erreichen, ausstrecken
Übung 58: 1. boil 2. pot 3. cupboards 4. for 5. tough 6. around 7. harshly 8. after
Übung 59: 1. for 2. since 3. for 4. since 5. since 6. for
Übung 60: 1. Doran is not allowed to give the list to people outside the company. 2. She tells him on the phone. 3. He drinks a lot of alcohol. 4. A glass of water. 5. He opens a can of baked beans. 6. She certainly does not admire his cooking.
Übung 61: 1. shook, shaken 2. bled, bled 3. fought, fought 4. gripped, gripped 5. hurt, hurt 6. drank, drunk
Übung 62: 1. nurse 2. account 3. pollution 4. big-hearted 5. fluent 6. hiccough 7. calmly 8. driveway
Übung 63: 1. away 2. before 3. wait 4. entrance 5. front 6. all 7. more
Übung 64: 1. Cinderella always drives fast. 2. The weather is often wet in southern England. 3. You must be certain of your plan before starting. 4. They watched the men get out of their cars. 5. A car says a lot about the person who drives it. 6. He recognized her voice on the telephone.
Übung 65: 1. certainly 2. modern 3. inattentive 4. cautiously 5. timid 6. commonplace

Übung 66: 1. suddenly 2. back window 3. rocked 4. panic 5. fright 6. for 7. for 8. illegal
Übung 67: 1. falsch 2. falsch 3. richtig 4. richtig 5. falsch 6. richtig
Übung 68: 1. flicked 2. spotted 3. visible 4. slipped 5. nervous 6. ready 7. escape 8. managed
Übung 69: 1. search for 2. care for 3. investigate 4. read 5. explore 6. observe
Übung 70: 1. disappointment 2. confident, energetic 3. a wedding ring 4. Yes, he is. 5. He was sleeping. 6. binoculars with night vision
Übung 71: 1. Fernglas 2. sehen 3. Ast 4. Schläfchen 5. Abfall 6. flüstern
Übung 72: 1. are following 2. have worked/have been working 3. believes 4. have had 5. had never broken 6. was living/had been living/came
Übung 73: 1. falsch 2. richtig 3. falsch 4. richtig 5. falsch 6. falsch
Übung 74: 1. onto 2. on 3. of 4. for 5. for 6. at
Übung 75: 1. horse (house) 2. invated (invited) 3. aroun (around) 4. begin (began) 5. securaty (security) 6. dive (drive) 7. shot (short) 8. neeled (kneeled) 9. dificult (difficult)
Übung 76: 1. heulen – wail 2. endlich – finally 3. einsam – lonesome 4. zustimmen – agree 5. schweigsam – silent 6. Gegend – area 7. ängstlich – nervously
Übung 77: 1. The money was stolen by Cinderella. 2. The police were not called by the victim. 3. The car was not driven by Carmody. 4. The novel was worked on during the day (by the author). 5. The car was being driven in the rain (by her). 6. He has been warned by the police.
Übung 78: 1. liver 2. tongue 3. stomach 4. kidneys 5. throat, Lösung: vomit
Übung 79: 1. steak 2. mean 3. contrastingly 4. intimate 5. dawn 6. fizzle
Übung 80: 1. falsch 2. falsch 3. richtig 4. richtig 5. richtig 6. falsch
Übung 81: 1. many 2. some 3. much 4. some 5. few 6. some
Übung 82: 1. diverse 2. banter 3. respond 4. prospective 5. wretched 6. tenderly
Übung 83: 1. robbery 2. traces 3. unlikely 4. complicated 5. final 6. owner 7. food
Übung 84: She/he said: (s)he was having a good time. 2. He/she loved good ice cream. 3. She/he had had that for lunch yesterday. 4. He/she had been worried about that yesterday but he/she wasn't anymore. 5. She/he had been there several times.
Übung 85: 1. certain 2. believe 3. statement 4. meet 5. so 6. thorough 7. serious 8. in 9. at
Übung 86: 1. Hausangestellte/maid 2. oben/upstairs 3. murrte/grumbled 4. Angebot/offer 5. unwahrscheinlich/unlikely 6. Überredungskunst/powers of persuasion 7. Selbstmitleid/self-pity 8. höhnische Bemerkung/gibe
Übung 87: 1. I drive to work every day. 2. She has been to Paris once or twice. 3. Do not tell him what to do. 4. Why are you so mean? 5. Have you got something to do? 6. You look marvellous, darling.
Übung 88: 1. in 2. on 3. to 4. off 5. into 6. at
Übung 89: 1. within 2. round 3. obviously 4. drive 5. began 6. shoulder 7. pavement 8. breath 9. lawn

Übung 90: 1. zu Pferde 2. reiten 3. Hufeisen 4. Rosshaar 5. Steigbügel 6. Sattel
Übung 91: 1. woke 2. had not called 3. knew 4. are 5. can 6. was 7. had often been 8. became 9. does
Übung 92: 1. a 2. b 3. a 4. c 5. b
Übung 93: 1. interrupting 2. don't know 3. surprise 4. sarcasm 5. quickly 6. imagine 7. disarm
Übung 94: 1. requested 2. up 3. novelist 4. forward 5. away 6. clear 7. in
Übung 95: 1. crafty 2. charitably 3. for once 4. splash 5. dive into
Übung 96: 1. where to now 2. scarf 3. window 4. knock 5. forehead
Übung 97: 1. to 2. on 3. in 4. out 5. on
Übung 98: 1. He compares it to a disease. 2. He is worried about how well Evers can ride a horse. 3. Carmody is to drive. 4. That's a good question! It is not clear, is it? 5. He has a broken arm and a separated shoulder. 6. No, she doesn't.
Übung 99: 1. She/he said you/I could drive. 2. He/she said that he/she had fallen down and hurt himself/herself. 3. She/he said I should wait for her/him in the car. 4. He/she said he/she would be back in a moment. 5. She/he said she/he had worked with Martin Evers for three years. 6. He/she asked where I went at Christmas time.
Übung 100: 1. portrayal 2. bush 3. credentials 4. siren 5. burglary 6. instantly
Übung 101: 1. c 2. a 3. c 4. b 5. a
Übung 102: 1. had gone wrong 2. had met 3. had simply spiralled 4. knew 5. had never been 6. had done 7. did not look 8. had not done
Übung 103: 1. papers 2. bother 3. real 4. recognize 5. continued 6. mistake 7. questions
Übung 104: 1. in 2. in 3. with 4. of 5. on 6. in 7. of 8. about
Übung 105: 1. this 2. anyone 3. anything 4. an accountant 5. swag 6. find 7. remember 8. hung up 9. house 10. immediately

Lösungen Abschlusstest

Übung 1: 1. pond 2. sensual 3. upset 4. file 5. intimate 6. splash
Übung 2: 1. have known 2. are working 3. drives 4. flew 5. has lived 6. were talking/rang
Übung 3: 1. expert 2. ordinary 3. nervous 4. reluctant 5. important 6. artificial
Übung 4: 1. over 2. on 3. in/of 4. of 5. to 6. away/out
Übung 5: 1. exhausted 2. wound up 3. boundary 4. precise 5. wretched 6. prospective 7. trace 8. proprietor 9. papers 10. think 11. real
Übung 6: 1. He got home late one morning. 2. You have to do something every day. 3. We often go swimming at the weekend. 4. How do you get to work? 5. If you try hard, you will succeed. 6. I have never been to Finland.
Übung 7: 1. surprise 2. effort 3. envelope 4. within 5. vacation 6. forehead

Lösungen gemeinsamer Abschlusstest

Übung 1: 1. She said I was wonderful. 2. He said my English had improved quite a bit. 3. She said I could always stay with her. 4. He said (that) I called him, he would tell me. 5. She said she was/had been there yesterday. 6. He said she should always do what she was told.
Übung 2: 1. c 2. c 3. a 4. a 5. b 6. a
Übung 3: 1. falsch 2. falsch 3. richtig 4. falsch 5. richtig 6. richtig 7. falsch 8. richtig 9. falsch. Er ist noch unentschieden.
Übung 4: 1. is playing 2. is snowing 3. knows 4. travels 5. is going 6. does
Übung 5: 1. boat/ship 2. enquiry/investigation 3. huge/enormous 4. funeral/memorial service 5. blameless/innocent 6. advance/proceed 7. force/might
Übung 6: 1. well 2. high 3. helpful 4. ancient 5. harmless 6. abruptly 7. safe
Übung 7: 1. well done 2. bedtime 3. agree fully 4. real thing 5. Tudor bonnet 6. foot guard 7. Yeoman Warder
Übung 8: 1. Baroness McKee seemed to be thinking hard about something. 2. Philip Havisham was shot dead with a gun. 3. He shook his head and looked very worried. 4. Detective Carlyle took a piece of paper out of his pocket and unfolded it. 5. His eyes sparkled when he said this. 6. That would mean there was or still is something in the house which is connected in some way to the murder. 7. There are a few things which don't quite fit into the picture.
Übung 9: 1. autopsy 2. suspicious 3. innocent 4. quarrel 5. witness 6. burglary 7. corrupt
Übung 10: 1. innocent/guilty 2. friend/enemy 3. love/hate 4. question/answer 5. superior/inferior 6. honest/dishonest 7. true/false
Übung 11: 1. over 2. up 3. in, in 4. for 5. out of, without 6. into 7. with/for 8. at
Übung 12: 1. The young woman looked thoughtful. 2. You remember that glittering thing on the pillow under the safe? 3. He followed her to a restaurant where they ate Indian food. 4. Carmody got up and made himself a pot of tea. 5. Cinderella lowered the binoculars for a moment and looked at Carmody. 6. The sirens of the police car were coming closer. 7. The plan came from you?
Übung 13: 1. boxes 2. policemen 3. breaths 4. classes 5. ladies 6. feet 7. mice 8. echoes 9. handkerchiefs 10. lives
Übung 14: 1. sceptical 2. church 3. looked 4. motive 5. diamond 6. prince 7. steal 8. kill 9. robbery 10. careful
Übung 15: 1. Stapel 2. Handschellen 3. Verschwörer 4. Londoner U-Bahn 5. Hinweis/Indiz 6. scheitern 7. drohen/bedrohen 8. bekommen/erhalten 9. verdächtig 10. Schatz

Glossar

Abkürzungsverzeichnis:

fam	umgangssprachlich
fig	bildlich
pl	Plural
v	Verb

abandon *v*	hier: im Stich lassen; abbrechen
aboard	an Bord
abortion	Abtreibung
abundance	Überfluss
accidentally	versehentlich; zufällig
accompany *v*	begleiten
accomplice	Komplize/Komplizin
accomplished	ausgebildet; versiert
accusation	Anschuldigung
acknowledge *v*	bestätigen, anerkennen
addiction	Sucht
admonish *v*	ermahnen
affectionately	liebevoll
affordable	bezahlbar
aggravated	gereizt, verärgert
agony	großer Schmerz
aim *v* **(at)**	zielen (auf)
air raid	Luftangriff
aisle	Gang (zwischen Sitzbänken etc.)
ajar	angelehnt, halb offen
alleged(ly)	angeblich, vorgeblich
allow sth. free rein	etwas freien Lauf lassen
alter *v*	sich verändern; ändern
A miss is as good as a mile.	Knapp daneben ist auch vorbei.
ancestor	Vorfahr(in), Ahne/Ahnin
ancient	sehr alt; altertümlich
and so forth	und so weiter
ant	Ameise
anteroom	Vorzimmer
anxiously	ängstlich, beunruhigt
apart from	abgesehen von
appear *v*	auftauchen, erscheinen; scheinen
apprehensively	ängstlich
approach	Zugang
approach *v*	nahen, sich annähern

archway	Bogengang, gewölbter Eingang
armed	bewaffnet
arouse *v*	aufwecken
asparagus	Spargel
assault	hier: Körperverletzung; Angriff
assault *v*	gegen jemanden tätlich werden
assert *v*	behaupten, beteuern
assume *v*	vermuten, annehmen
astonish *v*	erstaunen; überraschen
astonishment	Überraschung
astounded	höchst erstaunt
audible	hörbar
avoid *v*	scheuen; (ver)meiden
awful	furchtbar
awkwardly	verlegen; ungeschickt
babbling	plappernd
badge	Dienstmarke, Abzeichen
bad tempered	schlecht gelaunt
baffle *v*	verblüffen
bait *fig*	Köder
banister	(Treppen-)Geländer
bar	hier: Stange, Stab
bargaining	Verhandeln
bark *v*	jdn. anherrschen; bellen
barracks	Kaserne
bat *fam*	alte Schrulle *fam*
be (was, been) *v* **addicted to**	süchtig sein
be (was, been) *v* **all ears** *fig*	ganz Ohr sein *fig*
be (was, been) *v* **(un)aware (of sth.)**	sich etwas (nicht) bewusst sein
be (was, been) *v* **capable of**	im Stande sein zu; können
be (was, been) *v* **charged with murder**	des Mordes beschuldigt werden
be (was, been) *v* **fed up** *fam*	die Nase voll haben *fam*

be (was, been) *v* **in great distress**	sehr leiden
be (was, been) *v* **in touch**	hier: sich melden; mit jemandem in Verbindung sein
be (was, been) *v* **of assistance**	hilfreich sein, behilflich sein
be (was, been) *v* **of no consequence**	keine Rolle spielen
be (was, been) *v* **out of one's depth** *fig*	ins Schwimmen geraten *fig*
be (was, been) *v* **related to**	verwandt sein mit
be (was, been) *v* **startled**	erschrecken
beam	Lichtstrahl
beam *v*	(an)strahlen
Beat it! *fam*	Hau ab! *fam*
bedstead	Bettgestell
Beefeater	Wärter im Tower of London, königlicher Leibgardist
bellboy	Hotelpage
belongings *pl*	Eigentum, Sachen
belt bag	Gürteltasche
bend (bent, bent) *v* **(down)**	beugen; sich bücken
betray *v*	verraten; im Stich lassen
bewildered	verwirrt, durcheinander
bewildering	verwirrend
bigotry	Bigotterie; Borniertheit
blade	Klinge
blazing	lodernd, flammend
bleeding	blutend
blind	hier: Blende, Rollo
blissful	glückselig
blow *fig*	Schlag
blunt	stumpf
boast *v*	prahlen
boldly	dreist, gewagt
bolster *v*	stützen, untermauern

bonnet	Mütze
bough	Ast
bounce *v* **off**	abprallen
boundary	Begrenzung, Grenze
bow *v*	sich verbeugen
boxy shape	kastenartige Form
brass	Messing
bravery	Tapferkeit
breathtaking	atemberaubend
breed	Rasse
briskly	rasch, flott
brush *v* **off**	abstauben, abbürsten
bubbly *fam*	Schampus *fam*
budge *v*	sich bewegen
bump	hier: Unebenheit; Bums *fam*
bump *v* **into**	zusammenstoßen
bunch (of people) *fam*	Haufen, Gruppe (von Menschen)
by (any) chance	zufällig, durch Zufall
cane	(Spazier-)Stock
capsule	hier: Gondel; Kapsel
caretaker	Hausmeister
carry *v* **on**	weitermachen
cast *v fig*	werfen; auswerfen
cast-iron	hier: lückenlos; gusseisern
casually	nebenbei, beiläufig, lässig
cat of prey	Raubkatze
catch (caught, caught) *v* **s.o.'s eye**	jds. Blick/Aufmerksamkeit auf sich ziehen
Ceremony of the Keys	Zeremonie im Tower of London, bei der die Burg jede Nacht gesichert wird.
change *v* **hands**	den Besitzer wechseln
chap *fam*	Kerl, Typ
chat *v* **s.o. up**	anquatschen *fam*; auf jdn. einreden
cheek	Wange; Unverschämtheit

cheer *v* **(s.o.) up**	(jdn.) aufheitern
choke *v*	ersticken
chuckle *v*	leise in sich hinein lachen
claim *v*	behaupten; Anspruch erheben (auf)
clench *v*	ballen
closet	(Wand-)Schrank
clue	Hinweis, Indiz
cobbled	mit Kopfstein gepflastert
coincidence	Zufall
collar	Kragen
collide *v*	zusammenstoßen
commotion	Aufregung, Tumult, Aufruhr
companion	Begleiter(in); Freund(in)
company promoter	Firmengründer; Finanzierungsvermittler
compassionately	mitfühlend
con *v* **s.o. out of sth.** *fam*	jdn. um etwas bringen, hereinlegen
confirm *v*	bestätigen
conspirator	Verschwörer(in)
conspiratorially	verschwörerisch
copper *fam*	Bulle *fam,* Polizist
Corinthian column	korinthische Säule
costly	teuer, kostspielig
cosy	gemütlich
cover *v*	berichten über; bedecken
cover *v* **for**	decken; vertreten
crack *v* **up** *fam*	durchdrehen, zusammenbrechen
craftsmanship	Kunstfertigkeit
creepy	unheimlich
crisp	frisch; knusprig
crouch *v*	sich ducken, niederkauern
crowded	überfüllt
crowds *pl*	Zuschauermenge, Menschenmenge

cry *v* **one's heart out** *fig*	sich die Seele aus dem Leib weinen *fig*
custody	Obhut, Gewahrsam
dab *v*	abtupfen
dare *v*	es wagen, sich trauen
dart *v*	flitzen; (herbei)schießen *fam*
dashboard	Armaturenbrett
deal *v* **with**	sich kümmern um; verhandeln
death penalty	Todesstrafe
death threat	Morddrohung
debut	Debüt
deceit	Betrug, Täuschung
deceive *v*	betrügen, täuschen
decline *v*	hier: ablehnen; weniger werden
defenceless	schutzlos
deliberately	absichtlich
demanding	anspruchsvoll
demote *v*	degradieren; zurückstufen
depict *v*	darstellen
depressed	deprimiert; depressiv
deprive *v*	jdm. etwas vorenthalten
descent	hier: Abstammung; Absteigen
deserve *v*	verdienen
detest *v*	verabscheuen
detrimental	schädlich
devastated	hier: am Boden zerstört; verwüstet
device	Vorrichtung
devious	hinterhältig, verschlagen
devoid	ohne
dignified	würdig
disappear *v* **into thin air** *fig*	sich in Luft auflösen *fig*
disapproving(ly)	missbilligend
discarded	abgelegt, weggeworfen
disgust	Empörung; Ekel
distinctive	charakteristisch, markant

distracted	abgelenkt
distraction	Unaufmerksamkeit; Ablenkung
distressed	bekümmert, verzweifelt
ditch	Graben
diversion	Ablenkung
dizzy	schwindelig
dodge *v*	(schnell) ausweichen
dome	Kuppel
drain *v*	hier: weichen; entwässern
dreadful	furchtbar
drive (drove, driven) *v* **s.o. mad**	jdn. verrückt machen
drown *v*	ertränken; ertrinken
drowsy	schläfrig
drunk	Betrunkene(r)
due	aufgrund, wegen
duffle bag	Matchbeutel, Seesack
dull(y)	dumpf; trüb; matt
dumbfounded	sprachlos, verblüfft
duster	Staublappen
eager(ly)	begierig, eifrig; gespannt
ease *v*	(sich) entspannen
embellish *v*	(aus)schmücken
emblazoned	geschmückt, verziert
empress	Kaiserin
enraged	wütend, aufgebracht
enticing	verlockend
entire	ganz, gesamt
equilibrium	Gleichgewicht
equipped	ausgerüstet
eternal	ewig, immerwährend
evidence	Beweis(e); Anhaltspunkt
evidently	augenscheinlich, offenkundig
execution	Ausführung
extent	Ausmaß

exude *v*	hier: ausstrahlen; absondern
facility	Einrichtung
fade *v*	hier: verschwinden; verblassen
fail *v*	scheitern, misslingen
faint *v*	ohnmächtig werden
faith	Glaube
fake	falsch, nachgemacht
far-fetched	weit hergeholt
fast-forward *v*	vorspulen
fate	Schicksal
fathom *v*	verstehen, ermessen
feast for the eyes *fig*	Augenweide, Augenschmaus *fig*
feature	Gesichtszug; Merkmal
fervently	leidenschaftlich
fiancée, fiancé	Verlobte(r)
fierce(ly)	grimmig; wild
filth *fig*	Sauerei *fig*, Schweinerei *fig*
fine	hier: Bußgeld; Geldstrafe
firm(ly)	bestimmt; fest; sicher
fishy *fam*	verdächtig; faul *fam*
flash	Blitz(licht)
flash *v*	blitzen, blinken
flawlessly	fehlerlos, tadellos
flick *v* **through**	durchblättern
flinch *v*	zurückweichen, (zurück)zucken
flirtatious	kokett, flirtend
float *v*	treiben, schwimmen
floorboard	Diele, Bohle
fodder	Futter
footage	Filmmaterial
foot guard	Wächter zu Fuß
fountain pen	Füllfederhalter
frantically	verzweifelt
frown *v*	die Stirn runzeln; finster schauen
fumble *v*	herumtasten

funeral	Beerdigung
furious	wütend; wild
fuss	Wirbel, Getue
gamble *v*	spielen (um Geld)
gambling	Spielen
gambling debts *pl*	Spielschulden
gap	Lücke; Abstand
gasp *v*	keuchen
gather *v*	sammeln; zusammenpacken
gem	Edelstein
get (got, got) *v* **rid of**	loswerden
get (got, got) *v* **round to sth.**	dazu kommen, etwas zu tun
ghastly	grässlich; scheußlich
gibe	Stichelei
give (gave, given) *v* **way**	nachgeben; ausweichen
glance *v*	blicken, den Blick werfen auf
glimpse	flüchtiger Blick
gloomy/gloomily	düster, finster; bedrückt
go (went, gone) *v* **into hiding**	untertauchen
go (went, gone) *v* **to much bother to do sth.**	sich mit etwas viel Mühe geben
goblet	hier: Kelchglas; Pokal
God-fearing	gottesfürchtig
gossip *v*	klatschen *fam*, tratschen *fam*
grab *v*	(zu)packen, schnappen
gracefully	anmutig
grand entrance *fig*	großer Auftritt *fig*
grasp of *fig*	Verständnis für
graveyard	Friedhof
greed	Gier
grimly	grimmig, streng
grip	Griff; Halt
groan *v*	stöhnen
groomed	gepflegt

growl *v*	(an)knurren
grunt *v*	hier: brummeln; grunzen
gulp *v*	hier: hervorpressen; schlucken
gust	Bö(e)
halt	Stillstand; Halt
hand *v*	geben, reichen
handcuffs *pl*	Handschellen
handkerchief	Taschentuch
harm	Leid, Schaden
harsh(ly)	scharf, hart
have (had, had) *v* **a good grasp of sth**	etwas gut beherrschen
have (had, had) *v* **one's wits about one**	einen klaren Kopf haben
head *v* **back**	umkehren, zurückgehen
head *v* **for**	zusteuern auf
headline	Schlagzeile
headquarters	Hauptquartier
heirloom	Erbstück
hence	also, daher
hiccough *v*	hicksen, Schluckauf haben
hide-out	Versteck
hiding place	Versteck
hilarious	urkomisch
hint *v* **at**	andeuten
hiss *v*	fauchen, zischen
holler *v*	brüllen
hollow	hohl
Home Secretary	Innenminister (UK)
honourable	ehrenwert, ehrenhaft
hoofe, hooves *pl*	Huf, Hufe
howl	Heulen; Pfeifen
humiliate *v*	demütigen, erniedrigen
hurt (hurt, hurt) *v*	verletzen; schaden
the icing on the cake *fig*	die Krönung des Ganzen *fig*

ignition	hier: Zündschloss; Zündung
illuminate *v*	erleuchten, erhellen
impeccable/-bly	tadellos
implementation	Ausführung, Durchführung
impressive	beeindruckend
incense *fig*	hier: Duft; Weihrauch
incredible	unglaublich
incredulously	ungläubig, skeptisch
indeed	wirklich, tatsächlich
ingenious	genial, raffiniert
inhale *v*	einatmen
in no time	im Nu
inquire *v*	nachfragen, sich erkundigen
inquiry	Anfrage; Erkundigung
inquisitive	neugierig
insanity	Irrsinn, Wahnsinn
insert *v*	einfügen
inspect *v*	untersuchen
instantly	sofort, unverzüglich
insult *v*	beleidigen
interior	das Innere; Innen...; Interieur
interrogation	Verhör, Befragung
intervene *v*	einschreiten, eingreifen
in the picture *fig*	im Bilde *fig*
intimidated	eingeschüchtert
intruder	Eindringling
investigator	Ermittler(in)
invisible	unsichtbar
itchy	juckend
It's all right for some.	Manche haben's wirklich gut.
ivory	Elfenbein
jam *v*	hier: blockieren; verklemmen
jaw	Kinnlade, Kiefer
jealousy	Eifersucht
jerk *v*	ruckeln; schleudern

jewel-encrusted	juwelenbesetzt
joyride	Spritztour
jump *v* **out of one's skin** *fig*	aus der Haut fahren *fig*
jump *v* **to conclusions**	voreilige Schlüsse ziehen
keen on	erpicht auf, stark interessiert an
Keep me posted!	Halt mich auf dem Laufenden!
kip	Schläfchen
landing	hier: Flur, Gang; Landung
landing stage	Anlegestelle, Bootssteg
lantern	Laterne
lark	hier: Spaß; Lerche
late	hier: jüngst verstorben
latter	das Letztere
launch *v* **into**	hier: loslegen; angreifen
lead	Spur, Fährte; Führung
lead *v* **astray s.o.** *fig*	jdn. vom rechten Weg abbringen
leak *v*	durchsickern, auslaufen; tropfen
leek	Lauch, Porree
let (let, let) *v* **on**	verraten
limb	hier: Ast; Glied
line-up	Aufstellung; Reihe
lodgings *pl*	möblierte(s) Zimmer
loop-shaped	schlaufenförmig
loot	Beute
lure *v*	(an)locken
lurid	grell
lush	saftig; üppig
maiden name	Mädchenname
make (made, made) *v* **one's way**	sich auf den Weg machen, sich begeben
malfunction	Defekt
malicious	boshaft; bösartig
mallet	hier: Poloschläger; Holzhammer
mankind	Menschheit

mantelpiece	Kaminsims
marble	Marmor
marital	ehelich
marksman	Schütze
martial arts *pl*	Kampfsportarten
marvel *v* **(at)**	staunen (über)
mate *fam*	Kumpel, Kamerad, Gefährte
matter-of-factly	nüchtern, sachlich
merchandise	Ware(n)
mercy	Gnade
minor	gering, geringer
mischievous	schelmisch, verschmitzt
misfortune	Unglück
miss *v* **one's mark**	sein Ziel verfehlen
moan *v*	stöhnen, jammern
moat	Burggraben
mock *v*	verhöhnen, verspotten
mocking	Spott
mockingly	höhnisch, spöttisch
motionless	regungslos, bewegungslos
motion *v* **s.o. to do sth.**	jdm. bedeuten, etwas zu tun
moustache	Schnurrbart
multi-purpose hall	Mehrzweckhalle
mumble *v*	nuscheln, murmeln
musing	Grübelei, Überlegungen
nap	Schläfchen, Nickerchen
narrow-shouldered	mit schmalen Schultern
nasty	scheußlich; böse
nave	Kirchenschiff
neatly	ordentlich; gewandt; treffend
nemesis	Nemesis; die gerechte Strafe
night-cap	hier: Schlaftrunk; Nachtmütze
nightmare	Albtraum
nope *fam*	nö *fam*, nein

not have (had, had) *v* **the foggiest idea** *fam*	keinen Schimmer haben *fam*
nothing (in) particular	nichts Besonderes
notorious	berüchtigt
oak	Eiche
objection	Ablehnung; Einwand
observation wheel	Riesenrad
obtain *v*	bekommen, erhalten
occupational hazard	Berufsrisiko
odd	übrig; ungerade; merkwürdig
on duty	Dienst haben, im Dienst
outrage	Empörung, Entrüstung; Skandal
outshine, outshone, outshone *v, fig*	übertreffen, in den Schatten stellen *fig*
outskirts *pl*	Stadtrand; Außenbezirke
overhear, overheard, overheard *v*	zufällig (mit)hören
overwhelming	überwältigend
owe *v*	schulden; verdanken
palm	Handfläche; Palme
pant *v*	schnaufen, keuchen
paramedic	Sanitäter(in)
participant	Teilnehmer(in); Beteiligte(r)
pat *v*	klapsen, tätscheln
Patience is the companion of whisdom. *fig*	Die Geduld ist die Begleiterin der Weisheit. *fig*
pattern	Muster; Design
peculiar	seltsam
pendant	(Ketten-)Anhänger
pensively	nachdenklich
persuasion	Überredung, Überzeugung
petal	Blütenblatt
philistine	Banause/Banausin
piercing	durchdringend, stechend
pig-sty *fig*	Schweinestall

pile	Stapel
pillar	Säule
plaster	(Ver-)Putz
play *v* **(it) safe**	auf Nummer sicher gehen *fam*
plea	Bitte
plead *v*	flehen, bitten
pop *v*	knallen; stecken *fam*
posh *fam*	vornehm, piekfein *fam*
praise *v*	loben
precious	kostbar
premises *pl*	Gelände, Anwesen
pressure	Druck
pretend *v*	so tun als ob; vorgeben
prevent *v* **s.o. from sth.**	jdn. von etwas abhalten
prick *v* **up one's ears** *fig*	die Ohren spitzen *fig*
pricey	teuer
proceed *v*	weitergehen; fortfahren
prop *v* **up**	aufrichten
property	hier: Besitz; Eigentum
prospect	Aussicht
public parking facility	öffentliche Parkmöglichkeit
puff *v*	pusten
pull *v* **(sth.) off** *fam*	(etwas) durchziehen, abziehen *fam*
punch *v*	boxen
pursue *v*	verfolgen
put (put, put) *v* **the blame on s.o.**	jdm. die Schuld an etwas geben
puzzled	verdutzt, verblüfft
quaff *v*	trinken, zechen
quarrel	Streit, Auseinandersetzung
Queen's Keys	Schlüssel für die Burgtore des Towers of London
quest	Suche
rack *v*	quälen
radiate *v*	ausstrahlen

railing	Geländer
rash	voreilig; unbedacht
ready money	jederzeit verfügbares Geld
rear-view mirror	Rückspiegel
reassuring(ly)	beruhigend, unterstützend
recklessly	hier: rücksichtslos; leichtsinnig
recording	Aufnahme
regretfully	mit Bedauern, bedauernd
reject *v*	zurückweisen; ablehnen
relieved	erleichtert
reluctantly	ungern, widerstrebend
remorseful	reumütig
remote control	Fernbedienung
remotely	entfernt; fern
renowned (for)	berühmt (für), renommiert
repercussion	Auswirkung; Nachspiel
reproachfully	vorwurfsvoll
reputation	Ruf, Ansehen
residential area	Wohngebiet
resist *v*	widerstehen; widersetzen
reveal *v*	zu erkennen geben; zum Vorschein bringen
reverse	hier: Rückwärtsgang; Gegenteil
reward	Belohnung
rewind, rewound, rewound *v*	zurückspulen
riches *pl*	Reichtümer
riddle	hier: Rätsel; Sieb
ridiculous	lächerlich
rifle	Gewehr
rightful	rechtmäßig
rip *v*	reißen
rock-hard	steinhart
rogue	Gauner(in), Schurke/Schurkin
roller-coaster	Achterbahn…, achterbahnmäßig

rotted	morsch; verfault
row *v*	rudern
rower	Ruderer/Ruderin
rueful	reuevoll
rug	Teppich; Läufer
safety regulations *pl*	Sicherheitsbestimmungen
sardonic(ally)	höhnisch, süffisant
SAS (Special Air Service)	Spezialeinheit der britischen Armee
scarcely	kaum
scarlet	scharlachrot
scary	unheimlich
scent	Duft, Geruch
sceptre	Zepter
scoundrel	Schurke
scrap	Stückchen; Fetzen
scratch *v*	kratzen
screw *v* **up one's face**	sein Gesicht verziehen
scrutinize *v*	genau prüfen
sculptress	Bildhauerin
scum *fam*	Abschaum
secluded	abgelegen
secretive	heimlich; verschwiegen; geheimnisvoll
secure *v*	sichern; festmachen
seduce *v*	verführen
seeming(ly)	scheinbar
see-through	durchsichtig
seize *v*	ergreifen, packen
self-centred	ichbezogen, egozentrisch
self-consciously	befangen; bewusst
self-pitying	selbstbemitleidend
senior executive	leitende(r) Angestellte(r)
sensation-craving	sensationslüstern
sentry, sentries *pl*	Wachen

set (set, set) *v* **one's sight on sth.** *fig*	ein Auge auf etwas werfen *fig*
set (set, set) *v* **s.o. up**	jdm. etwas anhängen
set-up *fam*	abgekartetes Spiel *fam*; Falle
shabby	schäbig
shaken	erschüttert, mitgenommen
shaky	zittrig; unsicher
shandy	Bier mit Limonade
share	Anteil
shatter *v*	erschüttern; zerschlagen
shatter-proof	bruchsicher
shed	Stall; Halle
shed (shed, shed) *v* **a good light on sth.**	ein gutes Licht auf etwas werfen *fig*
shiver *v*	schaudern, zittern
shove *v*	schieben; stoßen
shrubbery	Büsche, Sträucher
shrug *v*	mit den Schultern zucken
shudder *v*	(er)schaudern
shutter	Fensterladen
sigh *v*	seufzen
sigh of relief	Seufzer der Erleichterung
sketch	Skizze
slam *v* **the door in the face of s.o.**	jdm. die Tür vor der Nase zuschlagen
slippers *pl*	Hausschuhe
slope *v*	(sich) neigen
slumber	Schlummer, Nickerchen
slump *v* **into**	sich fallen lassen in
slyly	schlau, verschlagen; hinterhältig
smash *v*	zerschmettern
smirk *v*	grinsen (hämisch)
snarl *v*	knurren; anfauchen
snatch *v*	schnappen; erhaschen
sneak *v*	schleichen

sneak *v* **up**	(sich) heranschleichen
sneer	spöttisches Lächeln
snobbishness	Snobismus, Großspurigkeit
snog *v, fam*	rumknutschen *fam*
sob *v*	schluchzen
sober	nüchtern
sole	Seezunge
soothe *v* **(s.o.)**	(jdn.) beruhigen, trösten
sophisticated	elegant, gepflegt; kultiviert
spaceship	Raumschiff
sparkle *v*	funkeln
spear-shaped	speerförmig
species	Lebensform, Spezies
spectator	Zuschauer(in)
speed *v*	rasen, schnell fahren
spellbound	fasziniert, verzaubert
spiral *v*	sich winden
spiritual guidance	geistiger Rat
spiritual justice	himmlische Gerechtigkeit
spit, spat, spat *v*	zischen; spucken
spoil-sport	Spielverderber(in)
spread, spread, spread *v*	(sich) ausbreiten
square metre	Quadratmeter
squeal *v*	kreischen, schreien
squeal of delight	Wonneschrei
stagger *v*	schwanken
stammer *v*	stammeln, stottern
start *v*	hier: zusammenzucken
startl *v*	erschrecken
stately	würdevoll, stattlich
stick (stuck, stuck) *v* **out**	vorstehen
storage area	Ablage; Laderaum
stout	untersetzt, korpulent
straight away	sofort
strain *v*	strapazieren, belasten

strained	angespannt; angestrengt
stray	hier: herrenlos; verirrt
strike (struck, struck) *v* **(s.o.) down**	(jdn.) niederschlagen
striped	gestreift
stroke *v*	streicheln
stroll *v*	schlendern, bummeln
struggle *v*	sich wehren, sich winden
stubborn	stur, störrisch
stuffy	stickig
stun *v*	betäuben; fassungslos machen
subtle	hier: raffiniert; fein
sufficiently	genug, genügend
suffocate *v*	ersticken
sulk *v*	schmollen
sullenly	mürrisch, missmutig
superficial	oberflächlich
superior	Vorgesetzte(r)
superstitious	abergläubisch
supposed	vermutlich, mutmaßlich
surface *v fig*	auftauchen
suspect	Verdächtige(r)
suspect *v*	verdächtigen; vermuten
suspicious(ly)	verdächtig; misstrauisch
swag *fam*	Beute
swallow *v*	(ver)schlucken
swiftly	eilig
switch	Schalter
swollen	geschwollen
sword	Schwert
sympathetically	mitfühlend
syringe	Spritze
take (took, taken) *v* **hold of**	ergreifen
taken aback	erstaunt; betroffen

take (took, taken) *v* **to one's gun**	seine Waffe in Anschlag nehmen
tatty	schmuddelig
teasingly	neckend, scherzend
temporal justice	weltliche Gerechtigkeit
tempting	verlockend, verführerisch
tense(ly)	angespannt, nervös
terrifying	entsetzlich, erschreckend
testify *v*	bezeugen
thanking the fates	dem Himmel sei Dank
thick	hier: dumm
threaten *v*	drohen, bedrohen
thunder *v*	hier: zupreschen auf; donnern, dröhnen
tip *v* **s.o. off**	jdm. einen Tipp geben
tiptoe *v*	auf Zehenspitzen schleichen
tombstone	Grabstein
toot	tuten, hupen
top hat	Zylinder
top-notch *fam*	erstklassig
topple *v* **over**	umkippen, umfallen
tournament	Turnier
tow *v*	(ab)schleppen
Traitor's Gate	„Verrätertor", ein Eingangstor zum Tower of London
tranquillizer	Beruhigungsmittel
treasure	Schatz
tremble *v* **(with)**	beben, zittern (vor)
trespassing	unbefugtes Betreten
trial	Gerichtsverfahren, Prozess
trickle *v*	sickern, rieseln, rinnen
trigger	Abzug (Waffe)
trigger *v*	auslösen
trimming	Dekoration; Besatz
trinket	Schmuckstück

trip *v* **up**	hier: stolpern lassen, zu Fall bringen; stolpern
trophy	Trophäe
truncheon	(Gummi-)Knüppel
trust *v* **s.o. implicitly**	jdm. blind vertrauen
tube *fam*	die Londoner U-Bahn; Röhre
tug *v*	ziehen
turmoil	Aufruhr; Durcheinander
turn *v* **sth upside down** *fig*	etwas auf den Kopf stellen
turn-on *fam*	etwas, das einen anmacht *fam*
tut *v*	sich mokieren
twinge	Zucken
twitch *v*	zucken
typewriter	Schreibmaschine
unconscious	bewusstlos
under one's breath	im Flüsterton, flüsternd
unease	Unbehagen
uneasily	unsicher; unbehaglich
unperturbed	nicht beunruhigt, gelassen
unreliable	unzuverlässig
unsteady	unsicher, wackelig
upmarket	gehoben, vornehm
uproar	Aufruhr, Tumult
upset	bestürzt; mitgenommen *fam*
valuable	wertvoll
vanish *v*	verschwinden
vast	enorm, gewaltig
velvet	Samt
venomous	hier: vernichtend; giftig
Victorian	viktorianisch, aus dem 19ten Jahrhundert
vital	hier: entscheidend; lebenswichtig
voice modifier	Stimmenwandler
volunteer *v*	etwas freiwillig tun; sich anbieten, etwas zu tun

wail *v*	hier: heulen; schreien
waste of time	Zeitverschwendung
waterman	Fährmann
wave *v* **down**	anhalten, stoppen
weary/-ily	müde; resigniert
whilst	solange, während
whip	Peitsche
whiskers *pl*	Schnurrbart; Backenbart
whist	Whist (Kartenspiel)
whistle	Pfeife; Pfiff
whistle *v*	pfeifen
Why the blazes not? *fam*	Warum, zum Teufel, nicht? *fam*
wickedly	boshaft, bösartig
wig	Perücke
wimp *fam*	Schwächling, Weichei *fam*
windfall *fig*	unverhoffter Glücksfall
winged	mit Flügeln
wink *v*	zwinkern
wipe *v*	wischen; trockenreiben
wisely	klugerweise; weise
with all due respect	bei allem Respekt
with all one's might	mit aller Kraft
witness	Zeuge/Zeugin
wobble *v*	wackeln
worked up	aufgeregt
wrongful	unrechtmäßig
yawn *v*	gähnen
Yeoman Warder	Wärter im Tower of London